500 of the
Healthiest
Recipes &
HealthTips
you'll ever need

500 of the

Healthiest Recipes & HealthTips

you'll ever need

to improve your health, boost your energy,
stimulate your brain, and stay young

**Hazel Courteney and
Stephen Langley**

CICO BOOKS
LONDON NEW YORK

acknowledgments

There are several people that I would like to thank for helping to bring this book into being. Firstly, thanks to my publisher Cindy Richards at CICO Books for the original concept for this project, and to Dawn Bates for being such a helpful editor.

A big hug to my wonderful housekeeper Pat Tahayekt for writing up a few of my favorite recipes. Thanks also to nutritionist Carole Brough for sharing her wonderful chocolate cake recipe.

Without doubt, my biggest debt of gratitude goes to my wonderful co-author Stephen Langley, a brilliant naturopath and a great guy to work with—thanks Steve for all your patience, valuable input, and hard work.

Published in 2012 by CICO Books
An imprint of Ryland Peters & Small
519 Broadway, 5th Floor, New York NY 10012
20–21 Jockey's Fields, London WC1R 4BW
www.cicobooks.com

10 9 8 7 6 5 4 3 2 1

Text copyright © Hazel Courteney 2012
Recipes copyright © Vatcharin Bhumichitr, Tamsin Burnett-Hall, Maxine Clark, Lyndel Costain, Hazel Courteney, Ross Dobson, Nicola Graimes, Rachael Anne Hill, Jane Noraika, and Ryland Peters and Small 2012

Design, photography, and illustration copyright © CICO Books and Ryland Peters and Small 2012

A CIP catalog record for this book is available from the Library of Congress and the British Library.

ISBN: 978-1-907563-63-8

Printed in China

Cookery writer: Nicola Graimes

Editor: Jan Cutler
Design: Jerry Goldie Graphic Design
Photography: Stuart West (styling: Luis Peral-Aranda; home economy: Eliza Baird), except where listed otherwise on page 352

contents

INTRODUCTION

When you look in the mirror, believe it or not, you are basically looking at what you have eaten during the past year or so! Your body is fundamentally made up of light, air, and water—plus the nutrients (vitamins, minerals, essential fats, carbohydrates, and so on) that you absorb from your diet. In the West almost everyone has access to a huge array of foods, yet we are facing a modern epidemic—it's called malnutrition. This is because a large proportion of the "stuff" we eat is not technically food at all! In the dictionary "food" is defined as a substance that delivers nutrients to the body, which in turn, utilizes them for biological and chemical changes in order to assist growth, repair, and maintenance. The problem today is that many of the most commonly eaten "foods" tend to be so overly processed, refined, and/or packed with saturated fats and sugars, that they are often devoid of any health-giving nutrients whatsoever. And over-consumption of these types of foods is without doubt contributing to the tidal wave of late-onset (type-2) diabetes, cancers, heart disease, and most other chronic degenerative conditions that we are experiencing today.

Yet, if I told you that as much as 85 percent of our health problems, including many chronic degenerative conditions associated with aging, such as late-onset diabetes, arterial and liver disease, could be prevented or cured by simply changing your diet — would you believe me? Even the World Cancer Research Fund states that as many as 40 percent of breast cancer cases, that's around 18,000 annually in the UK alone, could be avoided by following a healthier lifestyle and diet.

Fresh vegetables contain an array of nutrients that your body requires so that it can thrive and age gracefully.

This concept has been understood for some time. Hippocrates (468–377 BC) famously suggested that we should "Let food be thy medicine and medicine be thy food," whereas the Roman poet Lucretius (c. 95–55 BC) wisely noted that "One man's meat is another man's poison." And he was right too; for example, tomatoes, when cooked, are the richest source of the carotenoid lycopene, which has been shown to reduce the risk of prostate cancer. Tomatoes can also reduce the harmful effects of radiation exposure and contain p-coumaric acid and chlorogenic acid, which block potent cancer-causing compounds found in processed meats such as bacon, ham, and tobacco smoke. Yet, for anyone suffering gut problems (see Chapter 5) or conditions like arthritis, this fruit—which is from the deadly nightshade family—can exacerbate symptoms. Of course, your genes and lifestyle also play a part, but in the majority of cases you can load the dice of fate more in your favor by eating a good diet and living a healthier lifestyle.

Garlic has liver-cleansing properties, as well as giving depth of flavor to dishes.

Tempting recipes that your body will love

This is not to say that you cannot have some fun along the way, as you will discover when you see our delicious healthy cake recipes made with plant sugars, which transform them into healthier treats for all the family. Very few people live on salads all the time, but if we could all take more responsibility for our health and find a greater balance in our diet, we could live longer, healthier lives. This is what this book is all about. There are thousands of healthy recipes, and if we tried to include them all this would not be an easy book to use but a weighty encyclopedia—therefore our aim is to inspire you to experiment more with a greater variety of foods and notice the considerable difference that small changes can make to your health.

My co-author, naturopath Stephen Langley, and I are concerned firstly with treating the person, rather than the illness, by using foods that help treat the underlying condition, although they are not necessarily a cure-all for everybody. This approach is more in keeping with Hippocrates' other tenet, "First use food. If that doesn't work, use herbs. If that doesn't work then (and only then) use intervention."

Not all oils are equal when it comes to nutrition, but there are many good ones to choose from. Together with vinegars and fresh herbs, they enliven food with taste as well as health-giving nutrients.

Clearly, much modern-day medicine has lost touch with its founding father, because, firstly, food and secondly, herbs, as stated by Hippocrates, are often ignored in favor of intervention—drugs, surgery, and so on. Although orthodox medicine certainly saves lives, and certain drugs can prop people up for longer periods, in a large majority of cases, this type of intervention is unnecessary and potentially damaging to the body.

And because what you eat can radically alter how you feel, we have arranged the recipes into 16 chapters, and in the introductory pages for each chapter you can find a great deal of important information. If you take a few minutes to read these introductions before checking out our delicious recipes, you will more fully understand how and why your diet can help to heal and protect you. For example, in Chapter 15, Eat to Stay Young, starting on page 306, you will discover why it is that in the West we urgently need to eat more alkaline-forming foods, and why eating more green super-foods aids this process. Also, find out why antioxidants such as vitamins A, C, and E are crucial in slowing the aging process, plus lesser known facts, such as why the amino acid L-carnosine, found in certain meats, can help to slow the aging process, while also keeping your skin looking younger for far longer!

You will also learn why, as we age, our diets need to be continually refined as enzyme production that aids in the absorption of vital nutrients slows down—and how to counteract this process. In the Anti-Allergy Foods and Healthy Digestive System chapters you can ascertain which foods trigger the most health problems and find out how to reduce or eliminate many food sensitivities by keeping your gut in better working order.

The foods with extra-special qualities

As you browse through each chapter, discovering the best foods for healthy bones, brain, kidneys, heart, gut, immune system, skin, hair, and so on, you may note that certain foods appear time and again. These super-foods—such as oily fish, flaxseeds, and specific fruits, vegetables, and whole grains—contain good amounts of a wide range of important nutrients.

In the Anti-cancer Foods chapter read about the most effective super-foods that can help prevent cancers. These include fresh rosemary, parsley, papaya, mango, and red grapes, plus apricots, green tea, broccoli, cauliflower, bok choy (pak choi), and more.

You will also discover the crucial part that vitamin D plays in preventing a host of health conditions and how to boost levels naturally.

Additionally, throughout the book we have added hundreds of small but important health tips to further enhance your day-to-day health, and "Food as Medicine" boxes to give you an understanding of why certain foods are beneficial for that particular area of health.

Because many foods and drinks now contain pesticides and herbicides, as well as hormone and antibiotic residues, Stephen and I advocate eating organic, freshly and locally grown foods whenever possible. Your body has the wisdom and intelligence to heal itself—it just needs the raw materials to do the job!

Spices transform foods—and some have very positive benefits to your health as well. Use them with meat, poultry, and fish and, of course, pulses—one of the most healthy forms of protein.

Remember that self-healing doesn't happen overnight with a couple of "nutritious" meals. It's an ongoing habit for the rest of your long life. If you are currently experiencing some health challenge, then just by turning to the relevant chapter, reading the introductory pages and then utilizing the recipes, you are taking an important first step towards living a younger life—for longer! Every 120 days your blood cells are completely renewed, so you should aim to adopt this new way of eating for at least this length of time if you want to experience positive results and a whole new you!

We wish you an abundance of health and happiness.

Bon appétit!

Hazel Courteney and Stephen Langley

Hazel Courteney is an award-winning, respected health and metaphysical writer and speaker based in the UK. In 1997 she was voted Health Journalist of the Year for her alternative columns in the *Sunday Times* and the *Daily Mail*. This is her third cookery book. Hazel has also written two best-selling health books and three highly acclaimed spiritual metaphysical books. For more information on Hazel's work, log on to her website www.hazelcourteney.com

Other books by Hazel Courteney include:
500 of the Most Important Health Tips You'll Ever Need: An A–Z of Alternative Health Hints for over 250 conditions; Stay Younger Longer: An Ultimate A–Z Anti Ageing Guide, Divine Intervention; The Evidence for The Sixth Sense; Countdown to Coherence; Mind and Mood Foods; Body and Beauty Foods.

Stephen Langley MSc, ND, DipHom, DBM, DipAc, DCH, OMD is a registered naturopath, homeopath, acupuncturist, doctor of Chinese medicine, and medical herbalist with over 25 years of clinical experience. He lectures and teaches naturopathic medicine at the College of Naturopathic Medicine (CNM) in London, Bristol, Manchester, Dublin, and Galway. Stephen has studied holistic medicine in China, India, the US, Australia, Tibet, and Japan. He can be reached via his busy health practice in London on 020 7631 0156.

larder list

Staples to keep in your larder.

Stephen and I are keen advocates of organic foods, which contain fewer pesticides, herbicides, and additives. Choose organic where possible.

We are fully aware of the huge numbers of people now experiencing sensitivities to various foods such as gluten, dairy (from cows), and yeast. Our larder list reflects this growing problem, and you will discover more on this subject in our recipes.

Check regularly to make sure all foods in your storecupboard are in date.

Beans and pulses
Alfalfa (sprouts)
Black beans
Black-eyed peas
Chickpeas
Great Northern beans
   (cannellini) beans
Kidney beans
Lentils
Lima (butter) beans
Mung beans (and their sprouts)
Navy (haricot) beans
Split peas (yellow or green)

Dried fruits
Apricots (preferably
unsulfured)
Cranberries
Dried plums (prunes)
Figs
Goji berries
Raisins

Fats and oils
There are many good oils to use in salad dressings and cooking, but be aware that heating changes their properties and many can become unstable at high temperatures, posing a potential health risk if used consistently. We use different oils and fats depending on the way the food is being cooked, and you will discover more about healthier fats and oils throughout the book. As a general rule, always choose organic, unrefined oils and store them in a cool dark place.

Almond butter
Avocado oil
Butter (organic, unsalted) or ghee
Canola (rapeseed) oil
Chili oil
Coconut butter/oil (raw, unrefined and organic)
Flaxseed oil
Olive oil (extra-virgin)
Peanut oil
Pumpkin seed butter
Safflower (look for ones with a high oleic content)
Sesame seed oil
Sunflower oil (look for ones with a high oleic content)
Tahini (sesame-seed paste)
Walnut oil

Flour and noodles

Gluten-free flours:
Almond flour
Buckwheat flour and noodles
Coconut flour
Egg noodles
Gluten-free breadcrumbs
Gluten-free flour and gluten-free noodles
Rice flour

Low-gluten flours:
Kamut flour and noodles
Spelt flour and noodles

Grains

Amaranth, millet, quinoa, and buckwheat are gluten-free, and much more readily absorbed. Other grains, such as kamut and spelt, have low levels of gluten and are less likely to inflame the gut. If you are gluten-intolerant avoid the low-gluten grains altogether.

Amaranth
Buckwheat
Corn
Cornmeal (polenta)
Couscous (made from millet)
Kamut
Millet
Oats (oatmeal/porridge—choose gluten-free, which are less likely to trigger bloating in sensitive individuals)
Quinoa
Rice (basmati, brown long-grain, brown risotto, jasmine, and wild).
Spelt

Herbs and spices

Keep dried herbs and spices in your storecupboard for all-year use, but use fresh herbs when you can.

Apple pie (mixed) spice
Basil
Bay leaves
Cardamom pods
Chili powder
Chives
Cilantro (fresh coriander)
Cinnamon
Cloves
Coriander
Cumin
Dill
Garlic
Ginger
Lemon grass
Mint
Nutmeg
Oregano
Paprika
Parsley
Rosemary
Sage
Star anise
Tarragon

Thyme
Turmeric

Nuts and seeds

Numerous people have nut intolerances—you will know if you have and will delete these from your list. Yet, for the majority of us, nuts and seeds are rich sources of minerals and essential fats, and they play an important part in a balanced diet. Buy organic, because nuts (and dried fruits) tend to be high in pesticides, herbicides and additives.

Almonds
Brazil nuts
Cashew nuts
Flaxseeds (linseeds)
Hazelnuts
Peanuts
Pecan nuts
Pine nuts
Pistachio nuts
Pumpkin seeds
Sesame seeds
Sunflower seeds
Walnuts

Pastas

The majority of our pasta dishes will suit most types of pasta. There is a huge variety of pastas available, many of which are non-wheat and gluten-free (check the labels, if you have a sensitivity). Experiment, and choose from penne, spaghetti, fettuccine, angel hair, and others.

Gluten-free pastas:
Buckwheat pasta
Quinoa pasta
Millet pasta
Rice (vermicelli) pasta

Low-gluten pastas:
Kamut pasta
Spelt pasta
Spinach pasta (make sure it is made with a gluten-free grain)

Whole-wheat (wholemeal) pasta contains gluten

Sugars

If not burned during exercise, sugar converts to fat in the body. Excess refined sugars trigger inflammation, weight gain, and blood-sugar problems. This is why we have used healthier sugars that can be used in moderation.

Agave syrup, organic and unrefined (a plant-based sugar that has a minimal effect on blood sugar levels, but only if you use the unrefined organic versions). See also page 23.
Honey, raw (untreated) or manuka honey
Maple syrup (organic)
Molasses (blackstrap)
Sugar (organic cane)
Xylitol (a plant-based sugar that has a minimal impact on blood sugar levels)

Vinegars

Apple cider vinegar
Balsamic vinegar
Pomegranate vinegar
Red wine vinegar
Rice vinegar
Umeboshi plum vinegar
White wine vinegar

Miscellaneous

Arrowroot
Baking soda (bicarbonate of soda)
Chocolate and unsweetened cocoa powder (organic dark)
Coconut milk
Curry paste (green)
Custard powder (organic)
Harissa paste
Lecithin granules (from non-genetically modified sources)
Mayonnaise (low-fat)
Miso paste
Mustard (Dijon)
Mustard (whole-grain)
Olives (black)
Parmesan cheese
Peanut butter (organic, unsalted)
Pepper (black)
Pesto
Salt (Himalayan crystal)
Salt (organic sea)
Seaweed (dried), such as kombu
Seaweed (flakes), such as nori
Seaweed (powdered), such as kelp
Soy sauce
Tamarind paste
Tomato paste (purée)
Vanilla beans (pods)
Vanilla extract

PART I

STAY
HEALTHY

Keep your body in optimum condition by eating for your

heart, digestion, kidneys, and bones, as well as boosting your

immunity and avoiding foods that you are intolerant to.

A healthy diet will also help you to avoid cancer, as well as

male and female health problems.

anti-allergy foods

One in every four of us suffers from some kind of sensitivity, either to certain foods we ingest, the chemicals around us, or a combination of these factors—and these numbers are growing. Allergies, or sensitivities, to various foods or substances are the most common triggers for a multitude of symptoms: from coughing, itchy skin, skin rashes, joint problems, fibromyalgia, autoimmune conditions such as lupus, wheezing, runny nose, sneezing, watery eyes, chronic sore throats, and so on.

Intolerance or allergy?

The severest form of allergy triggers anaphylactic shock—a life-threatening condition that requires immediate medical attention. People with severe allergies—such as to peanuts—usually carry an injection of adrenaline to be injected immediately if they are exposed to the allergen.

The terms "intolerance" and "allergy" mean two different things. An allergy is an inflammation caused by the interaction of a foreign substance with the body's defense system. That is, a substance in the bloodstream that does not belong to the body will have antibodies attached to it, making it more recognizable by the immune system. It is termed an allergy if the body overreacts and produces too many histamine-like chemicals. There are other less aggressive forms of allergic reaction, such as delayed onset allergy when a hay fever sufferer has a runny, itchy nose that can be triggered by an allergen being inhaled, ingested, or touched.

Intolerance, however, does not produce the same "markers" in the bloodstream as seen in an allergy. It is really the body's inability to properly process or assimilate a particular food. An example is a lactose intolerance, when the person lacks the enzyme, lactase, to break down milk sugars, which can trigger symptoms such as diarrhea and bloating. Intolerances are mostly confined to food whereas allergies can include food as well as other factors.

Pollutants and inhalants such as cigarette smoke can inflame the lungs and allow larger molecules, such as pollens, to enter the bloodstream. Similarly, the delicate lining of the small intestine can become inflamed, making it permeable. Larger, undigested food molecules and toxins can then pass through the gut wall into the bloodstream. This affects both the liver and the lymphatic system and places a greater strain on the immune system. The undigested food molecules are treated by the body as foreign invaders and provoke an immune reaction as though it were an infection. The body then sends antibodies to fight it. Known as "leaky gut," this problem is now recognized as a major trigger for most food intolerances and allergies and, in some people, migraines, malabsorption issues, IBS, colitis, osteoporosis, Crohn's disease, Candida, and most autoimmune illnesses.

Lectins (proteins that attach to carbohydrates), for example, are commonly involved with damage to the delicate villi of the small intestine. They are particularly concentrated in gluten, eggs, corn (maize), dairy milk, and the nightshade family—potatoes, tomatoes, eggplant (aubergine), and bell peppers (capsicums). Removing these from the diet allows the gut to heal, alleviating allergy-type symptoms. In time, you may be able to reintroduce some of them into your diet.

How to find the culprit foods

There are a number of tests available to check allergies. A skin test is often used to show up allergies to pollens, grasses, or certain foods, such as yeasts. A blood allergy test (called ELISA) is an accurate way of identifying the allergen, as well as showing how strong the reaction is. Intolerances won't be picked up through allergy testing, but a urine test for gut permeability will show up any breach in the small intestine, and this could be a major factor for the intolerance.

Eliminating foods that commonly cause inefficient breakdown in the gut, or which overload the liver, is a good start. Gluten in wheat is a common one, as are milk and soya foods (see list). Simply eliminating gluten and cow's milk products can have a profound effect on your health. You need to become your own food detective—read labels carefully! Yeast and refined sugars are a problem for many people because they can promote a "leaky gut" through Candida infestation—a yeast fungal overgrowth. A way of helping your body deal with any intolerance is to "ferment, sprout, or soak." This aids digestion by deactivating enzyme inhibitors or by reducing the food's lectin effect.

Keep an honest food diary over several weeks, writing down everything you eat. Note when and what symptoms arise. If, for example. within an hour of ingesting cow's milk or yogurt, you feel full and/or bloated, try eliminating it for one week and see what happens.

By eating more of the right foods, you can heal your gut and live a healthier, happier life. Certain foods have natural anti-inflammatory or healing properties. They include apples, onions, garlic, cranberries, and blueberries, whose anti-inflammatory properties act as an antihistamine. Pineapple and papaya are rich in healing enzymes. Beets (beetroot), peas, radishes, and fennel are liver cleansers that support gut health. Beans, peas, and lentils, sunflower, flax, and pumpkin seeds are all excellent sources of fiber to help keep your gut healthy.

The foods listed below are the most common allergenic foods with some alternatives.

Wheat Choose spelt, amaranth, or kamut, or ideally gluten-free foods.

Corn (maize) Eat brown rice, millet, buckwheat, amaranth, or quinoa.

Refined sugars and syrups Choose xylitol instead. Organic agave nectar (syrup) is sweeter than sugar, but it has a high fructose content, which is processed in the liver, so it is not suitable for those with fructose intolerance or malabsorption problems. Also try a little blackstrap molasses, organic maple syrup, or a good-quality honey, such as cold extracted or manuka.

Soya Eat only fermented foods such as tamari, miso and natto. Tofu is not a fermented food, although some people can tolerate it. Soy milk is not suitable for children under five, as the soya is in a raw (unfermented) state. Some adults suffer reactions to it due to its lectin content.

Dairy from animal sources Try organic almond, rice, or oat milk. You can also use coconut milk—preferably reduced-fat.

Potatoes Choose sweet potato instead.

Seafood Try avoiding shellfish first—most people can tolerate white fish.

Other common allergenic foods Nuts, eggs, yeast, tomatoes, bell peppers (capsicums), eggplants (aubergines), oranges and mushrooms.

A few of the foods on this list appear in some of the recipes in this chapter, but should be avoided if you find you are intolerant of them.

chicken rice soup

serves 4

2 tbsp virgin coconut oil

2 garlic cloves, coarsely chopped

5 cups/1.2 liters chicken stock

3 cups/350g cooked brown basmati rice (from about 1 cup/200g uncooked rice)

1lb/450g boneless, skinless chicken breasts or thighs, thinly sliced

1 tsp chopped preserved vegetables (tang chi)

2 tbsp Thai fish sauce

2 tbsp reduced-salt soy sauce

1 tsp xylitol

1in/2.5cm fresh root ginger, peeled and cut into fine shreds

½ tsp ground white pepper

to serve

1 scallion (spring onion), diagonally sliced

sprig of fresh dill

1 Heat the coconut oil in a small frying pan, add the garlic, and sauté until golden brown.

2 Set the frying pan aside to allow the garlic to flavor the oil, then pour into a cup and reserve both the oil and the garlic.

3 Heat the stock in a large pan, add the cooked rice and slices of chicken, and bring to a boil.

4 Stir in the preserved vegetables, fish sauce, soy sauce, xylitol, ginger, and white pepper, and simmer gently for about 30 seconds, or until the chicken is cooked through.

5 Transfer to a serving bowl and trickle over a little of the reserved garlic oil.

6 Top the soup with finely sliced scallion, and a sprig of dill.

Food as Medicine

• **Brown rice** is a more healthy option than quick-cook white rice. Brown rice, in addition to being gluten-free, has a relatively low glycemic index. This means that it releases glucose in the blood more slowly than white rice, thereby moderating blood sugar levels. Red rice is also a healthy alternative and is known to help reduce levels of LDL cholesterol.

• **Eat organic** if you suffer from food sensitivities as this will reduce your toxic load. Organic foods tend not to contain chemical-based herbicides, pesticides, or hormone residues. This in turn helps support your liver, which is the main organ of detoxification in the body.

health TIP

◉ **Excess refined sugars** in the diet convert to fat inside the body if not burned up during exercise. If you have a sweet tooth, replace refined sugars with the plant extract xylitol, which looks and tastes like ordinary sugar, but has a low glycemic index. Available from health shops and some supermarkets worldwide.

hot-and-sour chicken noodle bowl

serves 4

90g/3oz soba (buckwheat) noodles

1 tbsp sunflower oil

450g/1lb chicken breast strips

5 cups/1 liter vegetable or chicken stock

1 fresh red chili, sliced

2in/5cm piece fresh root ginger, peeled and quartered

1 lemongrass stalk, slightly crushed

2 kaffir lime leaves

3 tbsp Thai fish sauce

6oz/175g button mushrooms, halved

juice of 1 lime

a handful of fresh bean sprouts, rinsed

2 tbsp chopped fresh cilantro (coriander)

Food as Medicine

• **Limes** are high in vitamin C. In the 1700s they were successfully used to prevent scurvy, caused by a vitamin C deficiency. Limes are also an excellent source of the mineral potassium. They stimulate the digestive juices to aid digestion, and their high limonene content promotes liver detox-ification of harmful chemicals.

• **Ginger** is a natural painkiller, as it has potent anti-inflammatory properties. It also calms the stomach, and reduces heartburn as well as the nausea associated with morning and motion sickness. Ginger aids the circulation, because it naturally thins the blood making it less "sticky" and helps protect against conditions such as Alzheimer's and arthritis.

1 Prepare the noodles following the instructions on the packet until tender, then drain and rinse under cold running water until cool.

2 Meanwhile, heat the oil in a wok and stir-fry the chicken over a high heat for 4 minutes until browned. Remove and set aside.

3 Put the stock, chilli, ginger, lemongrass, kaffir lime leaves, and fish sauce in a separate pan and bring to the boil. Reduce the heat then simmer for 5 minutes. Add the mushrooms, lime juice, and chicken and cook gently for a further 4–5 minutes until the chicken is cooked through. Remove the lemongrass, kaffir lime leaves, and ginger.

4 Divide the noodles and bean sprouts between four shallow bowls. Ladle the soup and vegetables on top, and scatter over the cilantro.

health TIP

○ **Keep in mind** that the foods you tend to eat/and or crave the most are usually at the root of many food-sensitivity issues. Keep a food diary and note when symptoms, such as bloating, are worse. The largest culprits tend to be wheat (this is why we recommend soba noodles, which are made with buckwheat, but you could also use rice noodles), gluten, corn, and dairy produce.

oriental seaweed salad

serves 4

1oz/30g arame seaweed

8oz/225g radishes, thinly sliced into rounds

1 small cucumber, halved, seeded and cut into half-moons

3½oz/100g sugar snap peas, thinly sliced

1 scallion (spring onion), shredded

2 tsp toasted sesame seeds, for sprinkling

DRESSING:

2 tbsp light olive oil

2 tsp sesame oil

4 tsp rice wine vinegar

2 tsp tamari

1 Put the arame in a sieve and rinse under cold running water. Put in a bowl and cover with more cold water. Leave to soak for 5 minutes – the arame should double in volume. Drain and put in a pan.

2 Cover the arame with cold water and bring to the boil. Reduce the heat and simmer for 20 minutes until tender, then drain.

3 In the meantime, mix together the ingredients for the dressing in a small bowl or screwtop jar.

4 Combine the arame, radishes, cucumber, and sugar snap peas in a serving bowl. Spoon the dressing over and sprinkle with the spring onion and sesame seeds before serving.

Food as **Medicine**

- **Seaweeds** are sea vegetables that provide all the necessary vitamins, minerals, and trace elements necessary to support life in a particularly bio-available form. They are nature's best source of iodine in addition to being high in the minerals magnesium and calcium, plus the B group vitamin, folic acid.

- **Sesame seeds** are a rich source of the minerals calcium, iron, magnesium, and zinc, as well as containing good amounts of omega-6 essential fats. They contain protein, particularly the amino acid tryptophan— which aids natural sleep. In addition, they are a source of the B group vitamins.

japanese steamed fish

serves 4

3 tbsp mirin and 4 tbsp shoyu

1lb/450g salmon filet

9oz/250g soba or green tea noodles,

5 cups/1.2 liters vegetable stock

1in/2.5cm piece fresh root ginger, peeled and grated

handful of fine green beans, cut into thirds

handful of long-stem broccoli, trimmed

2 zucchini (courgettes), sliced diagonally

1 tbsp sunflower oil

2 scallions (spring onions), sliced diagonally

4 toasted nori strips, crumbled

1 Mix together 2 tbsp mirin and 2 tbsp shoyu. Add the salmon, spoon over the marinade then marinate, covered, in the refrigerator for 30 minutes. Cook the noodles according to the instructions, then set aside.

2 Bring the stock to a boil. Reduce the heat and add the ginger, beans, broccoli, and remaining mirin and soy sauce. Simmer for 4 minutes then add the zucchini and simmer for 2 minutes. Heat the oil in a large, non-stick frying pan. Reduce the heat a little and add the salmon, skin-side up, and cook for 3–4 minutes on each side.

3 Divide the noodles among four large, shallow bowls and ladle over the stock and vegetables. Top with the salmon, then scatter over the scallions and crumbled nori.

turkish quinoa pilaff

serves 4

⅔ cup/125g red or regular quinoa, rinsed

2 cups/450ml vegetable stock

2 tbsp olive oil

1 large onion, chopped

2 garlic cloves, finely chopped

1 red bell pepper, seeded and diced

¾ cup/100g canned chickpeas, drained and rinsed

1 tsp ground turmeric

1 tsp ground cumin

2 tsp ground coriander

seeds from 3 cardamom pods, crushed

10 unsulfured, ready-to-eat dried apricots, roughly chopped

2 handfuls of fresh cilantro (coriander), chopped

a handful of fresh mint, chopped

7oz/200g feta cheese, cubed

sea salt and ground black pepper

1 Put the quinoa in a pan and cover with the stock. Bring to the boil then turn down the heat to its lowest setting, cover with a lid, and simmer for 10–15 minutes until tender. Drain and set aside.

2 In the meantime, heat the olive oil in a nonstick pan over a medium heat. Cook the onion for 5 minutes, stirring occasionally. Add the garlic, red bell pepper, and chickpeas, and cook for a further 3 minutes then add the spices and apricots.

3 Continue to cook for 1 minute before adding the cooked quinoa. Stir until combined and heated through. Season with salt and pepper.

4 Transfer the pilaff to a bowl and stir in the coriander and mint. Serve topped with the feta.

Food as Medicine

• **Quinoa** was called "The mother of all grains" by the Incas. Although not technically a grain, it has a high protein content, particularly the amino acid lysine, which is crucial to the production of antibodies and the energy that supports immune function. In addition to being gluten-free, quinoa provides good amounts of iron, calcium, and the B group vitamins.

• **Turmeric** In countries where curries are popular, including Okinawa, there is a far lower incidence of conditions such as dementia, which is linked to inflammation in the brain. This is because turmeric, one of the main spices used in curry dishes, contains a substance called curcumin, which has highly anti-inflammatory properties.

health TIP

• **Eat cilantro** (coriander)— it helps to remove toxic metals from the body— including aluminum, lead, mercury, and cadmium. It also reduces flatulence and its essential oils have anti-inflammatory properties.

buckwheat pancakes with slow-cooked vegetables

serves 4

scant ½ cup/60g buckwheat flour

scant ½ cup/60g whole-wheat spelt flour

¼ tsp sea salt, plus extra to taste

1 cup /250ml plus 2 tbsp rice milk

2 eggs, lightly beaten

sunflower oil, for frying

5oz/150g soft goat's cheese, crumbled

SLOW-COOKED VEGETABLES:

scant ½ cup/100ml olive oil, plus extra for frying

6 large shallots, quartered,

1 eggplant (aubergine), cut into bite-size pieces

1 large fennel bulb, cut into 8 wedges

4 tbsp fresh apple juice, not from concentrate

1 tbsp balsamic vinegar

ground black pepper

1 Sift both types of flour and the salt into a large bowl and stir until combined. Combine the rice milk and 3 tbsp water in a pitcher and whisk in the eggs. Make a dip in the center of the flour and gradually whisk in the liquid to make a runny batter the consistency of light (single) cream. Leave to rest, covered in the refrigerator for 30 minutes.

2 To make the slow-cooked vegetables, heat the olive oil in a deep pan over a medium heat. Sauté the shallots for 7 minutes, stirring occasionally, until softened. Turn the heat to low, and add the eggplant and fennel. Stir until combined, cover with a lid, and cook for 25 minutes, stirring occasionally to prevent the vegetables sticking.

3 Add the apple juice and balsamic vinegar, then season to taste. Stir and cook, uncovered, for a further 10 minutes until the vegetables are very soft and the sauce has reduced and thickened. Keep warm, covered, while you cook the pancakes.

4 Heat a medium-size, nonstick frying pan and pour in a little sunflower oil. Using a crumpled piece of kitchen paper, wipe the oil over the base of the pan until lightly coated. Pour about 2 tbsp of the batter into the pan and swirl so that it coats the pan in a thin, even layer. Cook for about 2 minutes or until set and slightly golden, then use a spatula to flip the pancake over and cook for another minute or so.

5 Keep the pancake warm while you cook the remaining 11 pancakes. To serve, place three pancakes on each serving plate. Spoon the vegetables on top, then scatter over the goat's cheese.

Food as Medicine

• **Buckwheat**, a common part of the Japanese diet, is gluten-free and contains one of the highest sources of rutin—a flavonoid (plant chemical) that helps strengthen the capillaries and veins. It also contains omega-3 fats and helps the gut to produce more friendly bacteria to aid gut health.

buckwheat noodles in miso ginger broth

serves 4

6oz/175g dried buckwheat noodles

1 tsp toasted sesame oil

1 tbsp safflower oil

1 red onion, finely chopped

1 red chili, seeded and finely chopped

1in/2.5cm fresh root ginger, peeled and grated

¼ cup/60ml reduced-salt soy sauce

4 cups/1 liter vegetable stock

6oz/175g green beans, trimmed

6oz/175g carrots, cut into matchsticks

2 cups/115g thickly sliced oyster mushrooms

8oz/225g bok choy (pak choi), cut into thick rounds

3 tbsp miso paste

4oz/115g enoki mushrooms, root base removed

1½ cups/175g bean sprouts, rinsed and drained

7 scallions (spring onions), cut lengthways into strips

Food as Medicine

• **Miso** contains all the essential amino acids and, being fermented and rich in enzymes, it supports healthy bacteria in the gut. It also offers protection against radiation poisoning and, because of its isoflavone content, it helps to reduce hot flashes associated with the menopause.

1 Cook the noodles according to the pack instructions, then rinse well.

2 Put the sesame and safflower oils, onion, chili, ginger, and soy sauce in a large pan. Cook gently for 10 minutes, or until the onion is soft, then stir in the stock and beans.

3 Bring gently to a boil, then add the carrots and oyster mushrooms. Continue cooking for 2–3 minutes, then add the bok choy and cooked noodles. Again, continue simmering for 1–2 minutes.

4 Add the miso, enoki mushrooms, bean sprouts, and scallions to the pan, then serve immediately while the vegetables are still crunchy and vibrant in color.

health TIP

◉ Natural-source carotenes, found abundantly in carrots, convert to vitamin A in the body. This vitamin is vital for supporting mucous membranes, such as the lungs and gut lining, as well as helping to protect the delicate tissues in the eyes against conditions such as macular degeneration.

summer pasta

serves 4

1lb 5oz/600g (broad) beans, shelled

1lb/450g wheat-free spaghetti

6 tbsp extra-virgin olive oil

4 garlic cloves, thinly sliced

20 cherry tomatoes

1 cup/175g small black olives

6oz/175g char-grilled artichokes, halved

2 x 4oz/125g balls buffalo mozzarella, torn into bite-size pieces (optional)

a handful of fresh basil leaves

Parmesan shavings, to serve (optional)

sea salt and ground black pepper

1 Steam the fava beans for 3 minutes or until tender. Refresh under cold running water, then gently squeeze the beans out of their gray outer shell to reveal a bright green bean inside. Set aside.

2 Cook the spaghetti in a large pan of boiling salted water according to the pack instructions until al dente. Drain the pasta, reserving 6 tbsp of cooking water.

3 In the meantime, heat the oil in a large pan over a medium-low heat. Fry the garlic for 30 seconds before adding the tomatoes. Cook, turning the tomatoes occasionally, until starting to soften and blister. Add the olives, artichokes, and cooked fava beans and heat through.

4 Add the pasta to the pan with the reserved cooking water and mozzarella, then toss until combined. Divide among four large, warm shallow bowls and season to taste. Scatter over the basil and Parmesan before serving.

Food as Medicine

● **Wheat-** and gluten-free pastas made from foods such as quinoa, corn, or rice are beneficial, because gluten can damage the delicate villi on the gut wall and affect nutrient absorption. Spelt-based pastas are also lower in gluten, but are not suitable if you have a severe gluten intolerance. Wheat-free pastas are also better for balancing blood sugar.

health TIP

○ **Some people** may have a sensitivity to corn, so it's important to check labels, as many gluten-free foods are high in cornstarch (maize flour) and/or syrups. This is especially true when it comes to breads, cereals and some alternative non-dairy "milks" such as almond milk. Remember to keep that all-important food diary and note when symptoms are worse. It really is crucial to have an intolerance test, if you suffer with food sensitivities, and to avoid any offending foods.

Food as Medicine

- **Cinnamon** helps to balance blood sugar by delaying the rate at which food leaves the stomach. It also stimulates the insulin receptors, benefiting people with type-2 diabetes. This spice is a powerful antioxidant with anti-fungal action, especially to the yeast/fungal overgrowth *Candida albicans*. It also prevents blood platelets from sticking and is a rich source of manganese.

- **Butternut squash** is a rich source of carotenoids (phytonutrients), which have antioxidant properties, and it contains more beta-carotene (which converts to vitamin A in the body) than pumpkin. It also contains plenty of fiber, is high in vitamin C and provides good amounts of the B vitamins, plus potassium.

moroccan seven-vegetable tagine with quinoa

serves 4

2 tsp ground cumin

2 tsp ground coriander

a pinch of saffron threads

1 cinnamon stick or ½ tsp ground cinnamon

2 garlic cloves, crushed

1 tbsp grated fresh root ginger

1 onion, thinly sliced

grated zest and juice of 1 unwaxed lemon

2 carrots, diced

3½oz/90g small turnips, halved or quartered

2½ cups/550ml boiling water

1lb/450g peeled and diced butternut squash

1 cup/225g ready-to-eat dried apricots

1 eggplant (aubergine), cut into 1in/2.5cm dice

1 tsp olive oil

2 zucchini (courgettes), halved and sliced thickly

2 tomatoes, quartered

sea salt and ground black pepper

TO SERVE:

1⅓ cups/225g quinoa

1¾ cups/425ml boiling water

a pinch of salt

health TIP

○ **Try to sit down** when you eat your meals, and chew your food thoroughly. Remember that digestion begins in your mouth and that your stomach doesn't have teeth! If you eat on the run, your digestion won't work as efficiently and, over time, you can develop what is known as a "leaky gut" which, in turn, can trigger food sensitivities.

1 Put the dried spices in a tagine or flameproof Dutch oven (casserole) with the garlic, ginger, onion, and lemon zest and juice. Add the carrots, turnips, and boiling water, stir well and bring to a simmer. Cover and cook for 5 minutes.

2 Once the tagine is underway, put the quinoa in a pan with the boiling water and salt. Bring to a boil, stir once, then cover, reduce the heat and cook gently for 15 minutes, or until the quinoa is tender and has absorbed all the liquid.

3 Stir the butternut squash and apricots into the tagine, cover the pan and cook for 10 minutes. Meanwhile, toss the eggplant with the olive oil and seasoning, spread out on a baking sheet and roast in a preheated oven at 400°F/200°C/Gas 6 for 15 minutes or until softened and golden brown.

4 Add the zucchini and tomatoes to the tagine, cover again, and cook for a further 5 minutes. Mix the roasted eggplant into the tagine, just before serving with the cooked quinoa.

marinated lamb with garlic-yogurt sauce

Food as Medicine

● **Lamb**, particularly organic "pasture-fed" produce, is a good source of mono-unsaturated and omega-3 fatty acids. It is one of the least allergenic of all foods, meaning that practically everybody can eat it without it causing an allergy-type response. It is an excellent source of protein, high in the amino acid tryptophan, plus iron and B vitamins, especially B_{12}, B_6 and folic acid— necessary for lowering toxic homocysteine levels.

serves 4

3 tsp harissa paste

2 tbsp lime juice

1 tsp ground coriander

1 tbsp olive oil

4 lean lamb steaks, about 6oz/175g each

4 wheat-free flatbreads

1 large carrot, grated

3 tbsp chopped fresh mint

3 tbsp chopped fresh cilantro (coriander)

2 tbsp chopped fresh chives

4 tomatoes, seeded and diced

2 tbsp pumpkin seeds

sea salt and ground black pepper

GARLIC YOGURT SAUCE:

scant ½ cup/100ml plain (natural) sheep's yogurt

juice of ½ lemon

1 garlic clove clove, crushed

1 tsp olive oil

1 Mix together the harissa paste, lime juice, ground coriander, and olive oil in a large, shallow dish, then season with salt and pepper to taste. Add the lamb and spoon the marinade over, turning the lamb until well coated. Leave to marinate, covered, in the refrigerator for at least 1 hour or preferably overnight.

2 Mix together the ingredients for the garlic yogurt sauce, and season. Stir in 1 tbsp of water if it's very thick – it should be the same consistency of light (single) cream.

3 Lift out the lamb from the marinade and discard any marinade remaining in the dish. Heat a large griddle pan over a high heat. Griddle the lamb steaks for 3 minutes on each side, or until cooked to your liking. Remove from the heat and leave on a warmed plate to rest, covered, for 5 minutes.

4 Warm the flatbreads in a low oven. Divide the flatbreads among four plates and top with the carrot. Scatter over the herbs, tomatoes, and pumpkin seeds. Cut the lamb into slices and lay on top of each flatbread, then spoon over the garlic yogurt sauce. Serve the bread flat or folded in half, as you prefer.

asian salmon with rice noodles

serves 4

4 salmon steaks, about 4oz/115g each

2 tsp Chinese five spice powder

275g/10oz rice vermicelli noodles

2 tbsp reduced-salt light soy sauce

2 tsp good-quality honey, such as cold extracted or manuka

1in/2.5cm piece fresh root ginger, peeled and grated

2 garlic cloves, crushed

1 large carrot, about 4oz/115g, thinly sliced

1 large leek, about 4¼oz/130g, sliced

5 cups/350g sliced mushrooms

1 tbsp chopped fresh cilantro (coriander) (optional)

ground black pepper

1 Wash the salmon steaks and pat dry with kitchen paper. Rub the five spice powder into both sides of the fish and season well with black pepper. Set aside for 30 minutes.

2 Meanwhile, put the noodles into a bowl, cover with boiling water, and soak for 15 minutes. Drain, then add the noodles to a pan of boiling water, and cook for 1 minute. Drain and keep the noodles warm.

3 Cook the salmon steaks under a hot broiler (grill) for 7–10 minutes, or until thoroughly cooked, turning once halfway through.

4 Heat a nonstick pan. Add the soy sauce, honey, ginger, garlic, carrot, and leek to the pan and sauté the vegetables for 3–4 minutes, until beginning to soften. Add the mushrooms to the pan and sauté for a further 2 minutes.

5 Divide the noodles among four bowls or plates. Spoon the vegetables and their juices over the noodles and put the grilled salmon on top. Sprinkle with cilantro, if using, and serve.

health TIP

○ **Lectins** are a type of protein which, when eaten, can cause intolerances to sensitive digestive tracts. The most common offenders are gluten, cow's milk products, eggs, beans, tomatoes, eggplant (aubergine), bell peppers (capsicum), and potatoes. Cooking helps deactivate lectins to some degree, but if you are highly sensitive, avoid these foods. Keep a food diary and note when your symptoms are worse.

Food as Medicine

• **Salmon** is an easy protein to digest and exceptionally high in omega-3 fats, which are vital for good health. It uniquely provides a ratio of around 5:1 omega-3 to omega-6 essential fats, and is a great source of both vitamin D and selenium.

• **Honey** has a natural antimicrobial action due to its hydrogen peroxide content. Manuka UMF honey contains extra potency against many different bacteria because of the natural antibiotic properties of the manuka bush that the bees feed on.

red onion and rosemary farinata with tzatziki

serves 4–6

scant 1¼ cups/150g chickpea (gram) flour

½ tsp sea salt

5 tbsp olive oil

1 large egg, lightly beaten

scant ½ cup/50g pitted black olives, halved

1 heaping tbsp chopped fresh rosemary

1 red onion, thinly sliced

1 red chili, seeded and thinly sliced

sea salt and ground black pepper

TZATZIKI:

scant 1 cup/200ml plain (natural) sheep's or goat's yogurt

1 garlic clove, crushed

3in/7.5cm cucumber, halved, seeded and grated

2 tsp lemon juice

Food as Medicine

• Goat's and sheep's yogurt is absorbed more efficiently than cow's yogurt. This is because the shape of the protein molecule is different and the fat molecule is much smaller than in cow's milk products. In addition, not as much lactose is present, requiring less enzyme activity to break it down, so these yogurts are less likely to cause fermentation in the gut.

1 Put the chickpea flour and salt into a bowl and make a well in the center. Add scant 1⅔ cups/400ml tepid water and 2 tbsp of the oil, then the egg. Using a wooden spoon, gradually draw the flour into the wet ingredients to make a thick, smooth batter. Cover and leave to rest for 1 hour.

2 Preheat the oven to 425°F/220°C/Gas 7. Pour the remaining oil into a 13 x 9in/33 x 23cm baking pan and heat in the oven. When very hot, carefully remove from the oven. Skim any froth off the top of the batter, stir, then pour the mixture into the pan.

3 Scatter the olives, rosemary, onion, and chili over the top of the batter. Bake for 15–20 minutes, or until set and golden.

4 In the meantime, make the tzatziki. Mix together the yogurt, garlic, cucumber, and lemon juice. Season to taste, then chill until ready to serve. Serve the farinata cut into wedges or rectangular portions with the tzatziki on the side.

health TIP

○ **Fresh rosemary** contains many antioxidants and and it has been shown to possess powerful anti-cancer properties. Rosemary encourages better blood flow, particularly to the head, where it can help with memory. It relaxes the muscles, calms a stress headache, and increases bile production, aiding digestion.

steak with caramelized onions and squash

serves 4

3 tbsp olive oil

2 large red onions, sliced

2 tbsp balsamic vinegar

1 tsp xylitol

1 heaping tbsp fresh thyme

4 filets mignons, about 6oz/175g each

oregano leaves, to garnish

SQUASH:

2¾lb/1.25kg diced butternut squash

2 garlic cloves, peeled and halved

2 tbsp low-fat mayonnaise

sea salt and ground black pepper

1 Heat 2 tbsp of the olive oil in a nonstick pan and cook the onions over a medium heat for 5 minutes until beginning to soften. Reduce the heat to low, part-cover the pan with a lid, and cook for a further 15 minutes, stirring occasionally, until very soft.

2 Add the balsamic vinegar, xylitol, and thyme to the onions then stir in 3 tbsp of water and a pinch of salt. Cook, uncovered, for 2–3 minutes until sticky and caramelized, then set aside, covered, to keep warm.

3 In the meantime, make the squash mash. Cook the squash and garlic in boiling water for 10–14 minutes until tender. Drain, add the mayonnaise, and mash until smooth. Season and set aside, covered, to keep warm.

4 Brush the steaks with the remaining oil and season. Heat a griddle pan until very hot and cook the steaks for 2 minutes on each side or until cooked to your liking. To serve, divide the squash among four plates, top with a filet mignon and any pan juices, and a large spoonful of onions. Scatter over a few oregano leaves before serving.

Food as **Medicine**

- **Red onions** are high in quercetin, which acts as a natural antihistamine. They are a good source of the mineral chromium, which helps to regulate blood sugar. They also act as a prebiotic, helping the gut to manufacture more healthy bacteria.

- **Prunes** contain healthy soluble fiber, which helps to lower cholesterol and keep you regular! Prunes are high in potassium and a rich source of antioxidants, and their high vitamin C content makes iron absorption more efficient.

mixed fruit spread

makes 1 small jar

½ cup/115g ready-to-eat dried prunes, roughly chopped

½ cup/115g unsulfured ready-to-eat dried apricots, roughly chopped

1 tsp vanilla extract

1 Put the prunes, apricots, and vanilla in a pan and pour over a scant 1¾ cups/425ml water and bring to a boil. Turn down the heat, cover with a lid, and simmer for 40 minutes or until the fruit is very tender.

2 Transfer the fruit to a blender and process with 5 tbsp water to make a thick spreadable paste. Set aside to cool before spreading over toast or bread, or stirred into plain (natural) yogurt. Store in an airtight container in the refrigerator.

chapter 2

anti-cancer foods

Cancer is the second biggest killer after heart disease. Yet, the World Health Organization (WHO) has stated that 85 percent of adult cancers could potentially be avoided by a change in diet and lifestyle. Even those born with a genetic tendency to cancer can stack the odds in their favor by eating anti-cancer foods.

The rise in cancer rates has mirrored the increase in environmental toxins. Combine these with toxins such as cigarettes, alcohol, and drugs, plus sugars and man-made fats, and you have a toxic cocktail that constantly challenges our immune systems. The liver cannot detoxify this cocktail without enzymes, and to make enzymes we need minerals, which have to come from our diet. We are experiencing a double-whammy—many people eat foods that are deficient in minerals, while trying to detoxify toxins with a liver that is in short supply of these enzyme-producing protectors. No wonder cancer is on a continual upward curve. Thankfully, nature has provided us with a wealth of anti-cancer foods—we just have to eat more of them!

The cancer fighters

The brassica family contains a number of cancer-fighting chemicals that help to detoxify the liver. It also deactivates excess estrogens, which act as a trigger for hormonal-type cancers, such as cancer of the breast and uterus. Brussels sprouts, cauliflower, kale cabbage, rutabaga (swede),

kohlrabi, mustard greens, broccoli, radish, turnip, and bok choy (pak choi) are all great anti-cancer foods. The herb rosemary can also help reduce excess estrogen and is highly anti-cancerous.

Foods that assist liver detoxification include garlic, onions, scallions (spring onions), leeks, and shallots, as well as foods containing limonoids, such as lemons, oranges, noni, and limes.

Globe artichokes are also good because they encourage better bile flow. Parsley has been shown to shut down certain enzymes that stimulate the growth and spread of cancer cells, whereas watercress has been seen to protect against DNA damage. Another cancer fighter is paprika. Made from chili peppers, it contains capsaicin, which has demonstrated an ability to neutralize cancer-causing substances such as nitrosamines (from burnt meat).

Resveratrol—found in grapes, mulberries, peanuts, and red wine—appears to block the blood supply to cancer cells, as well as destroying them. The antioxidants found in fresh fruits and vegetables help to "mop up" excess free-radical production, triggered by ingesting toxins and burnt foods, as well as a generally poor diet, combined with the effects of stress, environmental pollution, and so on.

Antioxidants have protective qualities against genetic damage, and sources include bilberries, acai, goji berries, blueberries, blackberries, cherries, raspberries, strawberries, persimmon, pomegranates, beets (beetroot), purple kale, and red grapes.

Anthocyanins are major antioxidants grouped under several categories. The beta-carotenes found in orange fruit and vegetables, such as carrots, squash, guava, mangoes, apricots, sweet potatoes, pumpkin, cantaloupe melon, papaya, and tangerines, are excellent anti-cancer foods. Other carotenes are found in green leafy vegetables, such as spinach, collards (spring greens), kale, watercress, bok choy (pak choi), spring cabbage, and Swiss chard. Papaya and mango have been shown to have a dramatic anti-cancer effect. Lycopenes are yet another class of carotene and are found in cooked tomatoes, pink grapefruit, guava, and watermelon. Catechins, present in apples, berries, and green tea, are also anti-cancerous.

Vitamin D is important in helping to prevent and heal cancers. Foods sources are sardines, pilchards, herring, eel, and sunflower seeds.

The antioxidant mineral selenium works with vitamin E to help protect cells from damage, and selenium is also an important mineral for liver detoxification. Good selenium sources include pheasant, partridge, scallops, squid, Brazil nuts, cashew nuts, sunflower seeds, and lentils. For vitamin E, eat wheat germ, soy beans, avocados, millet, rice, cucumber, nuts, and sesame seeds. Research carried out on the Hass avocado has shown promising results against oral cancers.

Calcium, low levels of which are associated with colorectal cancers, is found in sesame seeds, chickpeas, almonds, goat's and sheep's milk products, green leafy vegetables, mung beans, and parsley. Also, eat sardines plus their bones.

High-fiber foods keep the bowel functioning more efficiently, reducing the body's toxic load. Whole grains, rice bran, fruit, and vegetables (especially raw with skins), and beans, peas and lentils are all excellent. Figs, in addition to being high in fiber, are alkaline and a good source of calcium and potassium plus vitamins A and C—a great super-food for fighting off cancer.

A notable nutrient that is effective against breast and colon cancer is curcumin, the yellow pigment found in turmeric. In Asia where the spice is regularly consumed, there is a significantly lower incidence of bowel cancer. This super-spice also helps to reduce inflammation, which can act as a trigger for many cancers.

Essential fats found in oily fish and seeds are highly anti-inflammatory. Organic mackerel, salmon, herring, pilchards, and sardines are perfect sources. Furthermore, pineapple contains a compound known as bromelain that also acts as a natural anti-inflammatory.

Different foods to discover

The Japanese diet tends to be high in fermented soya products, which contain plant chemicals called isoflavones, considered to be good for health. These are hailed as the reason why the Japanese experience a lower incidence of breast, bowel, and prostate cancers. As soya can be difficult to digest properly, choose fermented soya foods such as miso, natto, tempeh, and tamari, or in the coagulated form, tofu.

Research has uncovered anti-cancer properties among brown seaweeds, such as kombu. You can also try wakame, hijiki, nori, and any of the kelps or red algaes. Cultures whose diets consist of daily amounts of nitrilosides (a bitter component of food), have very low cancer rates. High levels are found in cassava (tapioca), mung and fava (broad) beans, wheat grass, millet, buckwheat, alfalfa, bamboo shoots, macadamia nuts, wild blackberries, plums, pears, peaches, cherries, and nectarines. Beta-glucans from mushrooms have a proven modulating effect on the immune system and have successfully been used as part of cancer treatment. Choose from shiitake, maitake, and reishi, as well as portabello (field) mushrooms.

A diet rich in organic rainbow-colored foods, plus fresh fish, sea vegetables, fermented soya products, and olive oil is ideal to help prevent and manage cancer.

indian yellow lentil soup with spicy mustard seeds

Food as Medicine

- **Garlic** is a powerful antioxidant with a host of health benefits. It is a natural antibiotic, an anti-oxidant, and also an anticoagulant. It is high in the trace element, germanium, which has been shown to be effective against cancers and to promote the release of nitrous oxide from blood vessel walls, thus encouraging better blood flow.

- **Ghee** is butter that has been clarified—heated to make a clear amber liquid. The milk solids are removed, making it practically lactose free, and therefore easier to digest. It has a higher percentage of the more healthy medium chain fatty acids than butter has, and enhances rather than impedes protein digestion; plus it encourages absorption of fat-soluble vitamins, such as vitamin E. Ghee also has a higher smoking point than butter, making it ideal for cooking and frying.

serves 4

1½ cups/350g yellow lentils (channa dhal) or yellow split peas

½ tsp ground turmeric

½ tsp cumin seeds

1 small dried red chili, seeded

boiling vegetable stock (see method)

¼ cup/60ml sheep's yogurt, to serve (optional)

salt

SPICY MUSTARD SEEDS:

3 tbsp corn or mustard oil or ghee

1 tbsp mustard seeds

1 tbsp cardamom seeds

1 onion, halved and finely sliced lengthways

2 fat garlic cloves, crushed

1 red chili, cored and finely sliced (optional)

1 Put the yellow lentils, turmeric, cumin, and chili in a pan, cover with 1 quart/1 liter cold water, and bring to a boil. Simmer, covered, until tender (the time will depend on the age and variety). Purée in a blender, in batches if necessary. Transfer to a clean pan and stir in enough boiling stock to make a thick, soupy consistency. Reheat to just below boiling point, then taste and adjust the seasoning.

2 To make the spicy mustard seeds, heat the oil or ghee in a frying pan, add the mustard and cardamom seeds, and stir-fry until they pop. Add the onion and cook until lightly browned. Add the garlic and chili, if using, and stir-fry for about 1 minute to release the aromas.

3 Serve the soup in bowls or cups, topped with a spoonful of spicy mustard seeds, and a dollop of plain yogurt, if you like.

health TIP

- **A vital nutrient** in the fight against all cancers is vitamin D, which is synthesized in the body when your skin is exposed to natural sunshine. As much as possible, enjoy about 15 minutes of sun daily, away from the midday sun, without sunscreen. In winter take 1000iu of vitamin D_3 daily to help keep your immune system in great shape.

carrot and lentil soup

serves 4

1¼ cups/275g red lentils

3 tbsp/40g butter

1 red onion, chopped

1 garlic clove, chopped

2 tbsp sun-dried tomato paste (purée)

1lb/450g carrots, grated

3 quarts/3 liters chicken stock

½ cup/120ml plain sheep's yogurt

a handful of fresh cilantro (coriander), chopped

1 Rinse and drain the lentils, then set aside. Heat the butter in a heavy-based pan over a high heat. When the butter is sizzling, add the onion and garlic, and cook for 4–5 minutes, stirring often. Add the sun-dried tomato paste and stir-fry for 1 minute. Add the carrots, lentils and stock to the pan, and bring to a boil. Cook at a rapid simmer for 40 minutes, until the lentils are soft.

2 Spoon the soup, in batches, into a food processor or blender and process until smooth. Return the soup to a clean pan and cook over a low heat for a few minutes, until heated through.

3 Serve with dollops of yogurt and the cilantro sprinkled on top.

Food as Medicine

• **Red lentils** are one of the oldest known foods. They cook quickly, are easy to digest, and have high antioxidant properties. Although not a complete protein, they do provide a good source of sustainable energy plus iron, magnesium, and B vitamins. High in fiber, they help lower cholesterol and regulate blood sugar levels.

• **Figs** are a rich source of manganese and copper, plus the alkaline-forming minerals calcium, potassium, sodium, and magnesium. This makes them a perfect blood-cleanser, and their high potassium content helps regulate blood pressure. In addition, the insoluble fiber acts as a laxative, keeping the bowels regular.

honey-roast figs

serves 4

5 tbsp good-quality honey, such as cold extracted or manuka

½ tsp ground cinnamon

3 tbsp fresh orange juice

zest of 1 orange

1 tbsp virgin coconut oil

12 figs

VANILLA YOGURT:

scant ⅔ cup/150m plain (natural) sheep's yogurt

1–2 tsp vanilla bean paste

1 Preheat the oven to 375°F/190°C/Gas 5. Put the honey, cinnamon, orange juice and zest, and coconut oil in a pan and heat gently, stirring frequently, until melted. Continue to cook for about 3–5 minutes until starting to thicken.

2 Using a small sharp knife, make a cut like a cross in the top of each fig, cutting halfway down to the base. Stand the figs upright in a roasting pan, opening them out slightly, and spoon the honey sauce over. Bake for 10–15 minutes until softened.

3 Put the yogurt into a serving bowl and stir in the vanilla bean paste, to taste. Serve the figs with any juices from the pan and a large spoonful of the vanilla yogurt.

mediterranean sardines

serves 4

4 tbsp olive oil

zest and juice of 1 small lemon

2 garlic cloves, crushed

2 tbsp fresh oregano, chopped

2 tbsp fresh thyme, chopped

8–12 fresh sardines, depending on size, heads removed, gutted, and cleaned

sea salt and ground black pepper

lemon wedges, to serve

1 Mix together the olive oil, lemon zest and juice, garlic, oregano and thyme in a shallow dish that is large enough to accommodate the sardines in one layer.

2 Arrange the sardines in the dish and turn in the marinade. Marinate, covered, for about 1 hour in the refrigerator.

3 Preheat the broiler (grill) to medium. Season the sardines and cook for about 8 minutes, depending on their size, turning once, until golden and crisp on the outside. Serve with lemon wedges.

Food as Medicine

• **Sardines** are one of the best food sources of vitamin D and the omega-3 fatty acid DHA. Serving them with watercress or arugula (rocket) would add a host of anti-cancerous nutrients to this dish, including natural-source carotenes plus vitamins C, B_1, B_6, K and E, and calcium, manganese, and zinc.

• **Globe artichokes** have concentrations of cynarin in their leaves, which helps to protect the liver against damage, promotes bile flow from the gall bladder, and lowers the production of LDL cholesterol. The form of fiber, called inulin, found in globe artichokes is a prebiotic, which feeds the gut's friendly bifidobacteria.

artichokes with garlic mayo

serves 4

4 globe artichokes, rinsed

juice of ½ lemon

GARLIC MAYONNAISE:

1 egg yolk

about 1 tbsp lemon juice

½ tsp Dijon mustard

scant ⅔ cup/150ml sunflower or other flavorless oil

1 garlic clove, crushed

sea salt and ground black pepper

1 To make the mayonnaise, put the egg yolk, 1 tbsp lemon juice, mustard, and a pinch of salt into a blender. Switch the motor on and slowly trickle in the oil until the mixture starts to emulsify and thicken; continue until all the oil has been incorporated. Transfer to a bowl, stir in the garlic, and season with pepper, then add more lemon juice, to taste.

2 Remove the tough outer leaves and stem from each artichoke. Cut off the top ½in/1cm then, using a pair of scissors, trim the outer leaves. Stir the lemon juice into a large bowl of water, then add the artichokes—this will prevent them discoloring.

3 Put the artichokes, stem-side down in a single layer in a steamer. Steam for 20–35 minutes, depending on their size, until tender (the artichokes are ready when the leaves can be pulled away easily). Remove the artichokes with tongs and drain upside down in a colander. Serve warm or at room temperature with the mayonnaise in small bowls on the side.

kitchiri with golden onions

serves 4

⅓ cup/60g red lentils, rinsed

scant 1¼ cups/225g brown basmati rice

2 bay leaves

4 cardamom pods, split

3 tbsp virgin coconut oil

2 onions, finely sliced

1 tsp xylitol

3 garlic cloves, chopped

2in/5cm piece fresh root ginger, grated

2 tsp cumin seeds

2 tsp coriander seeds, crushed

2 tsp fenugreek seeds

1 tsp turmeric

2 tsp garam masala

3 tbsp chopped fresh flat-leaf parsley

sea salt and ground black pepper

1 Put the lentils in a pan and cover with cold water. Bring to a boil then reduce the heat and simmer, part-covered, for 20–25 minutes until tender. Skim off any foam that rises to the surface during cooking, then drain.

2 In the meantime, put the rice in a pan. Pour in enough water to cover the rice by about ½in/1cm. Add the bay leaves and cardamom, then bring to a boil. Reduce the heat to its lowest setting, cover, and simmer for about 20–25 minutes until the water is absorbed and the rice is tender. Remove from the heat and set aside, covered, for 5 minutes.

3 To make the golden onions, heat half of the coconut oil in a nonstick frying pan and fry the onions for 10 minutes, covered, over a medium heat, shaking the pan occasionally. Remove the lid, stir in the xylitol, increase the heat and cook until golden, stirring frequently; set aside.

4 Heat the remaining coconut oil in a large pan and fry the garlic, ginger, cumin, coriander, and fenugreek seeds for 1 minute, then stir in the turmeric, garam masala, parsley, lentils, and rice. Turn until everything is coated in the spiced oil and warmed through. Remove the bay leaves and cardamom pods, and season to taste, before serving topped with the golden onions.

Food as Medicine

• **Coconut butter or oil** is best bought organic. At room temperature it's like a fairly soft spread, and tastes delicious on crackers. When heated it liquefies. As well as being anti-cancerous, coconut butter/oil helps to boost immune function, reduces inflammation, helps balance blood sugar levels and is used for healing skin conditions such as eczema. It also increases the metabolic rate, so aiding weight loss.

paprika chicken wraps

serves 4

4 boneless, skinless chicken breasts

2 tbsp olive oil

1 tbsp paprika

1 tsp sea salt

TO SERVE:

4 large, soft wheat-free tortillas

4 tbsp hummus (optional)

1 avocado, peeled, stone removed, and sliced (optional)

12 salad leaves

16 cherry tomatoes, halved

juice of 1 lemon, plus 2 extra lemons, halved, to serve (optional)

sea salt and ground black pepper

1 Butterfly the chicken breasts and open them out like a book. Put between two pieces of plastic wrap (clingfilm) and beat with the flat side of a cleaver, or tap with a rolling pin, to flatten them.

2 Put the chicken in a plastic bag and add the olive oil. Crush the paprika with a small mortar and pestle, then add with the salt to the plastic bag. Shake the bag to distribute the seasoning, and massage the chicken through the plastic bag to help coat it. Leave for at least 30 minutes or overnight in the refrigerator.

3 Preheat the broiler (grill), then put the chicken into the broiling pan. Cook until nicely golden on one side, about 5 minutes. Turn the chicken over and cook for 5 minutes on the other side. Remove the chicken from the pan and slice into ½in/1cm wide strips.

4 To make the wraps, spread a spoonful of hummus over each tortilla, then top with the avocado, if using, with the salad leaves, chicken strips, and tomato halves. Add a squeeze of lemon juice, then sprinkle with salt and pepper, roll up, and serve. Serve extra lemon halves on the side.

Food as Medicine

• **Olive oil** is an abundant source of oleic acid, a mono-unsaturated fatty acid, and contains a small amount of linoleic acid, an essential fatty acid. Both are important for cholesterol management. You can buy olive oils pressed with fresh rosemary, which adds a wonderful flavor to rice, pasta, and meat dishes—and rosemary is highly anti-cancerous.

• **Avocados** contain mono-unsaturated fat, which helps lower cholesterol. They are also high in the antioxidants vitamin E and glutathione, which is a potent anti-cancer nutrient.

health TIPS

- **Enjoy a glass of red wine** or diluted red grape juice with your meals. The skins of red grapes contain an important compound called resveratrol, which has been shown to help balance blood sugar and support heart function, and it is also highly anti-cancerous. Blueberries and pomegranates are also high in healthy resveratrol.

- **Scientists,** such as cell biologist Dr. Bruce Lipton in America, have demonstrated that your emotions and sustained thoughts can have a major impact on your health—so laugh a lot, and as much as possible think and act as positively as you can.

red salad with beets, red cabbage, and harissa dressing

serves 4–6

2–4 small whole heads of garlic

6–8 small beets (beetroot), unpeeled

about 3 tbsp olive oil

1 small red cabbage

2 tbsp white wine vinegar, cider vinegar, or lemon juice

2 red onions or 6 scallions (spring onions)

1 tbsp umeboshi plum vinegar, or to taste (optional)

sea salt and ground black pepper

2 medium red chilies, finely sliced (optional), to serve

HARISSA DRESSING:

½ cup/125ml cold-pressed extra-virgin olive oil

1 tbsp harissa paste or 1 tsp chili oil

1 Preheat the oven to 400°F/200°C/Gas 6. Cut the top off each garlic —you will be able to see all the cloves. Put the beets and garlic in a small baking dish, add 2 tbsp olive oil, and turn to coat on all sides, then sprinkle with salt and pepper. Drizzle the remaining oil over the garlic. Roast for 30–45 minutes or until the beets and garlic are tender (you may have to remove the beets earlier). Baste the beets and garlic several times during cooking. When cooked, remove from the oven and cut the beets into four wedges (peel them or not, as you like).

2 About 15 minutes before the beets are cooked, cut the cabbage into quarters and remove the white core. Cut the quarters into fine slices and put into a bowl. Sprinkle with vinegar, then toss the cabbage with your hands until coated.

3 Cut the red onions into fine wedges, put into a bowl, and pour over boiling water to cover. Drain just before using. If using scallions, chop them coarsely.

4 When ready to serve, pop the roasted pulp out of 4 garlic cloves and put into a serving bowl. Add the extra-virgin olive oil and harissa or chili oil and beat with a fork. Drain the onions, pat dry with paper towels, then add to the bowl. Sprinkle with umeboshi plum vinegar, if using. Add the cabbage and beets, and toss gently.

5 Taste and adjust the seasoning and top with the chilies, if using. Put the heads of garlic on the side of the serving dish for people to press out the delicious flesh themselves.

Food as Medicine

• **Red cabbage** is high in chlorine and sulfur, which help to expel wastes, keeping the blood clean. It also contains phytonutrients, such as indole-3-carbinol, which encourage the excretion of excess estrogens known to trigger hormonal cancers. Anthocyanins (the chemicals that give the plant its color) provide antioxidant protection to the body.

sprouted bean, radish, and broccolini salad

serves 4

3 tbsp pumpkin seeds

9oz/250g broccolini, trimmed

1 small cucumber, halved, seeded, and sliced into half-moons

10 radishes, sliced into rounds

1 small red onion, diced

2 handfuls of mixed sprouted beans

DRESSING:

4 tsp tamari

1 tbsp sesame oil

1 tbsp hemp oil

¾in/2cm piece fresh root ginger, grated

juice of ½ lime

1 Put the pumpkin seeds into a large, dry frying pan and toast over a medium heat, tossing the pan regularly, for about 3 minutes or until the seeds start to color and begin to pop. Remove from the heat and leave to cool.

2 Mix together the ingredients for the dressing, then set aside.

3 Put the broccoli, cucumber, radishes, and red onion in a bowl. Scatter the sprouted beans over the top. Pour the dressing over and turn the salad until everything is coated. Scatter over the pumpkin seeds before serving.

health TIP

- **Most cancers** (and Western diseases such as arthritis) thrive in an over-acid environment, so it's worth making the effort to include more green foods in your diet. Eat broccolini, cucumber, sprouted beans, asparagus, pea shoots, alfalfa, and watercress or arugula (rocket). They will all help to alkalize your blood, keeping you healthier.

Food as Medicine

- **Broccoli** is a cruciferous vegetable—as are Brussels sprouts, cauliflower, kale, cabbage, radish, turnip, mustard greens, rutabaga (swede), kohlrabi, and bok choy (pak choi). This family of foods contain a number of cancer-fighting chemicals, which not only repair DNA damage, but also encourage better liver detoxification by deactivating cancer-causing excess estrogens. Broccoli's iron content is well absorbed due to its high vitamin C levels.

tofu and shiitake mushrooms on crispy black rice patties

serves 4

1lb/450g deep-fried tofu, patted dry and cubed

2 tbsp reduced-salt soy sauce

1 tsp chili oil

2 tbsp virgin coconut oil

10oz/275g carrots, cut into matchsticks

8oz/225g shiitake mushrooms, thickly sliced

2 tbsp hoisin sauce

1 tbsp rice vinegar

1 tbsp sesame oil

9 scallions (spring onions), cut into 1in/2.5cm strips

sea salt and ground black pepper

RICE PATTIES:

1 cup/200g uncooked black rice (not wild rice)

1 tbsp reduced-salt soy sauce

1 tsp sweet chili sauce

1 egg yolk

4 tbsp spelt flour

a handful of fresh chives, thinly sliced

a handful of cilantro (coriander) leaves, finely chopped

sea salt and ground black pepper

virgin coconut oil, for frying

TO FINISH:

1 large bok choy (pak choi), thickly sliced

coarsely chopped fresh cilantro (coriander), to serve

1 To make the patties, put the rice and soy sauce in a pan and cook according to the pack instructions. When cooked, drain through a colander and rinse until the water runs clear. Put the rice into a bowl and mash with the chili sauce, egg yolk, flour, chives, cilantro, salt, and pepper. Roll into 12 balls and flatten into patties. Heat about ½in/1cm oil in a wok or large frying pan. When the oil is hot, drop in the patties a few at a time, and cook for a few minutes on each side until crisp and golden. Drain on paper towels and keep them warm. Preheat the oven to 400°F/200°C/Gas 6.

2 Mix together 1 tbsp of the soy sauce and chili oil in a bowl. Add the tofu and turn until coated. Put the tofu on a non-stick baking sheet and cook in the oven at for 20 minutes, turning once. Heat the safflower and sesame oils in a wok or frying pan. Heat the coconut oil in a wok or frying pan over a high heat. Stir-fry the carrots and mushrooms for 2–3 minutes or until tender but still with some bite to them. Add the hoisin, the remaining 1 tbsp soy sauce, the rice vinegar, and about ¾ cup/175ml water. Continue cooking for 2 minutes. Stir in the sesame oil, scallions, roasted tofu, and season to taste.

3 Using a separate wok or a large frying pan, stir-fry the bok choy for 2–3 minutes, until cooked, but still a little crunchy. Put three patties on each plate, with a mound of bok choy and the tofu and mushrooms spooned alongside. Sprinkle chopped cilantro over the top and serve.

Food as Medicine

• **Soy beans** are high in usable protein (around 34 percent) and are often called "the meat of the earth." In addition, they have anti-cancer compounds in the form of phytoestrogens but, owing to their lectin content, they can be difficult to digest and assimilate unless fermented or sprouted. Eat only fermented soya products such as tamari, natto, or tempeh. Avoid using raw (unfermented) soya products, such as soy milk, especially for children.

tofu and black bean stir-fry

serves 4

3 tbsp salted black beans, rinsed

2–3 tbsp virgin coconut oil

14oz/400g tofu, patted dry and cut into ½in/1cm slices

1in/2.5cm piece fresh root ginger, peeled and cut into matchsticks

2 large garlic cloves, finely chopped

1 cup/100g frozen edamame beans

3½oz/100g sugar snap peas

3½oz/100g baby corn, halved lengthways

2 tbsp tamari

1 tsp sesame oil

2 scallions (spring onions), sliced diagonally

ground black pepper

1 Put the salted black beans in a small bowl and cover with hot water. Leave to soak for 30 minutes. Drain, reserving 4 tbsp of the water.

2 Heat a wok or large frying pan over a high heat. Add 2 tbsp coconut oil and, when melted, add half the tofu. Fry for 3 minutes on each side until golden. Remove from the wok and fry the remaining tofu, adding more coconut oil, if necessary. Set the tofu aside.

3 Add the ginger, garlic, edamame beans, sugar snap peas, and baby corn, then stir-fry for 2–3 minutes until slightly tender. Next add the black beans, reserved soaking water, tamari, sesame oil, and tofu, and cook for a further 2 minutes until heated through. Season with pepper and serve sprinkled with scallions.

health TIP

○ **When stir-frying,** do not allow any oil you use to start smoking, as "burned" foods produce HCAs (heterocyclic amines), which are known to trigger cancers. Never use mass-produced refined oils, which have been hydrogenated. Buy good-quality peanut oil, coconut oil, or ghee butter for stir-frying.

Food as Medicine

● **Black beans** are a good source of protein and soluble fiber, important for bowel health, blood sugar regulation, and cholesterol management. They contain more antioxidants in the form of flavonoids than all other beans, due to their darker coating, and they are a high source of the trace mineral molybdenum, important for helping the liver detoxify sulfites and the by-products of the fungus *Candida albicans*.

spice-crusted fish with cauliflower

serves 4

2 tsp ground cumin

2 tsp ras-el-hanout

2 tsp dried thyme

1 tsp paprika

4 thick skinless white fish fillets

2 tbsp olive oil

1 tbsp chopped fresh cilantro (coriander)

sea salt and ground black pepper

steamed green beans, to serve

CAULIFLOWER:

2 large shallots, finely chopped

1 tbsp olive oil

2 garlic cloves, crushed

1¼lb/600g cauliflower florets

about 1¼ cups/300ml hot vegetable stock

2 tbsp thick plain (natural) sheep's yogurt

1 Preheat the oven to 400°F/200°C/Gas 6.

2 Mix together the cumin, ras-el-hanout, thyme, and paprika, then season. Spoon the spice mixture over one side of each fish fillet until covered, pressing it down slightly with your fingers.

3 Heat the oil in a large, nonstick frying pan and sear the fish fillets, spice-side down, for about 2 minutes or until beginning to color and turn crisp. Turn the fish over and put into a baking pan. Roast for a further 10–12 minutes, depending on the thickness of the fish, until cooked through.

4 To make the cauliflower, sauté the chopped shallots in the oil for 6 minutes, stirring regularly, until softened. Add the garlic and cook for another minute.

5 In the meantime, steam the cauliflower for about 4 minutes or until tender. (Alternatively, cook in boiling water until tender, then drain.) Tip the shallots and garlic into a blender with the steamed cauliflower, stock, and yogurt, then blend to a smooth purée – adding more stock, if necessary. (Alternatively, mash with a potato masher.) Reheat gently in the pan and season to taste.

6 Divide the cauliflower among four serving plates, top with a fillet of fish, and scatter over cilantro. Serve with green beans.

Food as Medicine

- **Oily fish**, particularly organic salmon, mackerel and sardines, are an easy form of protein to digest. They are high in the anti-inflammatory omega-3 fatty acids, which have shown an ability to slow the rate of cancer growth, particularly relating to cancer of the breast.

sweet-and-sour fish

serves 4

1 sea bass, about 1lb/450g

peanut or safflower oil, for brushing

SWEET-AND-SOUR TOPPING:

2 tsp cornstarch (cornflour)

2 tbsp virgin coconut oil

2 garlic cloves, finely chopped

½ cup/115g pineapple chunks, fresh or canned

about 3in/7.5cm cucumber, quartered lengthways, then thickly sliced crossways

1 small onion, halved, then thinly sliced

2 small tomatoes, quartered

3 medium scallions (spring onions), coarsely chopped into 1in/2.5cm lengths

2 large fresh red chilies, sliced diagonally

2 tbsp Thai fish sauce

1 tbsp reduced-salt light soy sauce

½ tsp xylitol

½ tsp ground white pepper

1 Make several diagonal cuts into each side of the fish.

2 Preheat the broiler (grill) to very high and line the broiler pan with foil. Brush the fish with oil and broil (grill) for 10–12 minutes, turning once, or until it is opaque and cooked through.

3 When the fish is almost cooked, make the sweet-and-sour topping, mix the cornstarch with ⅓ cup/75ml water in a small cup, and set aside.

4 Heat the oil in a wok or frying pan, add the garlic and stir-fry until golden brown. Stirring constantly, add the pineapple, cucumber, onion, tomatoes, scallions, chilies, fish sauce, soy sauce, xylitol, and pepper.

5 Stir the cornstarch mixture to loosen it, then add it to the vegetables, and stir briefly to thicken the sauce. Transfer the fish to a serving dish. Pour the topping over the fish, then serve.

Food as Medicine

- **Pineapple** contains the enzyme bromelain, which acts as a digestive aid, helping to break down proteins, especially meat (think of ham and pineapple!). In addition, the enzyme is anti-inflammatory, and prevents blood platelets from sticking together. Bromelain has also shown anti-tumor activity in laboratory tests.

health TIP

○ **Natural-source carotenes** found in carrots, apricots, papaya, asparagus, sweet potatoes, pumpkin, parsley, spinach, watercress, spring greens, and mangoes are highly protective against cancers. Lycopene, a carotene found in tomatoes, helps to protect against cancer of the colon and prostate, especially when cooked in a little oil.

health TIPS

● **Drink more organic** green and white teas, which contain powerful antioxidants that are highly protective against many cancers. If you find these teas a little bitter, add a small amount of good-quality honey, such as cold extracted or manuka, to sweeten them.

● **As much as possible,** eat fresh organic foods, because many non-organic foods can be laced with more than 300 pesticides that are either known carcinogens or are hormone disrupters. Also, use organic skin creams, because toxins can also be absorbed through the skin!

thai fruit salad

serves 4

1 small ripe papaya

½ pineapple

1 ripe mango

4 rose apples (optional) or regular apples

1 ripe guava

1 tbsp lemon or lime juice

10 mint leaves, finely chopped, to serve

1 Peel, halve, and seed the papaya. Cut the flesh into small cubes.

2 Peel, core, and cube the pineapple.

3 Cut the cheeks off the mango, cut the flesh in diamond shapes down to the skin, turn the cheeks inside out, then scoop off the cubes of mango with a fork.

4 To prepare the apples, cut them in half, cut out the cores, and cut the flesh into small cubes.

5 Cut the guava in half, scoop out and discard the seeds, then cut the flesh into small cubes.

6 Arrange the fruit in a bowl. Add the lemon or lime juice, and chopped mint. Mix well and chill in the refrigerator before serving.

Food as Medicine

- **Papaya** is especially good if eaten before a meat dish because it's enzyme, papain, helps to break down heavy proteins. It has also been shown to be effective against a wide range of cancers, where the enzyme has helped to dissolve away the coating surrounding cancer cells.

- **Mango**, high in polyphenols and beta-carotene, it has also been seen to destroy both colon and breast cancer cells in lab tests.

fresh virgin mary

serves 1

6 ripe tomatoes

3 celery sticks

1 garlic clove (optional)

1 red chili, seeded

ice cubes

a large pinch of celery salt (optional)

1 To skin the tomatoes, cut a small cross in the base, put into a large bowl and cover with boiling water. Leave for 1 minute, then drain and pull off the skins.

2 Juice the tomatoes, celery, garlic (if using) and chili. Pour into a jug of ice, stir in the celery salt, if using, then serve.

chapter 3

foods for good vision

The eyes—just like our skin—are very much a barometer of our internal health. What we eat or drink and how much sleep we have had will be mirrored in our eyes. Eye problems are highly varied, ranging from simply being tired to suffering blurred vision, redness, and dark circles. Generally, if the whites of your eyes look yellowish, it denotes that your liver is somewhat toxic and you need to clean up your diet. Dark panda-like eyes are linked to a lack of sleep, low iron levels or an underactive thyroid. And if you see small shapes floating in your vision, this again can indicate poor liver function, and possibly Candida, a yeast/fungal overgrowth. Again, it's down to what you eat.

Puffy or "baggy" eyes can signify that the lymph glands in the head and neck are not draining adequately. Too much salt in the diet can trigger puffy eyes, as can food intolerances. If your eyes are bloodshot, you may have eyestrain or trauma to the eye, or have allergies, be lacking in sleep, or have been exposed to contaminants, either externally or internally (such as alcohol).

As we age, a combination of free-radical damage from sunlight, genetic factors, lack of nutrients from our diet, and the process of aging can trigger a host of eye conditions. Macular degeneration (AMD), for example, is now the leading cause of blindness in people over 55. The macula is the small, central part of the retina and has highly specialized nerves that help us to read and recognize objects and faces. In AMD, vision becomes blurred and begins to close in. Apart from the aging process, smoking, high blood pressure, a diet high in saturated fat, and/or a family history can all contribute. AMD is more common in light-colored irises than dark.

The second leading cause of blindness is glaucoma, a condition in which the optic nerve becomes damaged caused by increased pressure from a build-up of fluid in the eye. As the field of vision is progressively lost, tunnel vision can occur, if not corrected. The partial loss of the visual field can sometimes go unnoticed for considerable periods of time and is the reason why it is important to have your eyes checked by an ophthalmologist. Contributing factors include aging, trauma, steroid use, altered blood flow to the head (related to blood pressure, for example), African descent, and family history.

Diet and exercise for eye health

To improve bloodflow to the head and eyes, you need to include essential fatty acids and magnesium in your diet. Essential fatty acids (omega-3s) found in oily fish reduce oxidative damage through their anti-inflammatory action, in addition to keeping blood thinner. Choose fish such as mackerel, salmon, herring, or sardines. Vegetarian sources are hemp and flax seeds. High amounts of DHA, a component of omega-3 fats, are also found in the retina of the eye.

Magnesium helps to relax the muscles connected to the eye—in fact, involuntary "eye twitching" is one of the first signs of a severe magnesium deficiency. Foods rich in magnesium include chlorophyll-rich green leafy vegetables, plus kelp, almonds, beans (black, white, and soy), broccoli, and fish such as halibut.

Exercises that stretch the neck and shoulders should be a daily routine to help with blood flow to the head and neck. Yoga or Pilates is suitable.

Cataracts are also more common with age and are responsible for roughly half the world's blind population. A cataract is a clouding of the lens, whereby light is obstructed much like a film covering the lens. It usually affects both eyes, although one will generally degenerate faster. The condition is insidious with slow visual loss, potentially leading to blindness. Other risk factors are high blood pressure, diabetes, ultraviolet (UV) light, radiation, and iodine deficiency.

L-carnosine has been shown to be effective in slowing down this degeneration. It is found in animal foods, particularly muscle meat. Organic lean beef, chicken, and turkey are all good.

Dark purple fruits and vegetables—bilberries, blueberries, red grapes, blackberries, cherries, pomegranates, beets (beetroot) and purple kale— are rich in anthocyanosides. These powerful plant chemicals target blood vessels, particularly those in the eyes.

Over time, UV light can damage the delicate structures of the eye causing cataracts and possibly macular degeneration. The macula is yellow because of pigments made up of two types of carotenes—lutein and zeaxanthin. Due to their ability to absorb blue light, both lutein and zeaxanthin help protect the photoreceptor cells of the macula (found at the back of the retina) from being damaged through exposure to UV light. Lutein and other carotenoids are found in kale, raw spinach, spring greens, watercress, turnip greens, broccoli, Brussels sprouts, Swiss chard, bok choy (pak choi), pistachio nuts, kiwi fruit, peas, and egg yolks.

Zeaxanthin can be obtained from orange fruits and vegetables, such as pumpkin, carrots, sweet potatoes, butternut squash, persimmons, cantaloupe melon, papaya, mangoes and apricots.

Avoiding damaging oxidation

Hyaluronic acid (HA) is a naturally occurring component of connective tissue found in the joints, ligaments, tendons, and eyes, and levels fall over time due to aging and oxidation.

Magnesium, vitamin C, and zinc are necessary for the production of this important component, but these minerals will be missing from any overly processed diet. Without adequate levels of HA, soft tissues, including the eyes, are more prone to trauma and destruction, thereby losing their ability to remain supple.

Vitamin C is necessary to manufacture HA in the body and good sources include bell peppers, limes, and kiwi fruits.

Zinc is found in flax, pumpkin, sunflower, and sesame seeds, peanuts, pecan nuts, pine nuts, oysters, crab, and shellfish.

Natural source, full-spectrum vitamin E can also help to prevent or reduce the damaging effects of oxidation, particularly the delicate nerve fibers of the eye. Good sources of vitamin E are cod liver oil, wheat germ, soy beans, avocados, millet, rice, cucumber, nuts (especially pecan nuts, almonds, hazelnuts and Brazil nuts), and sesame seeds.

Remember that both alcohol and caffeine leach precious water-soluble nutrients and antioxidants out of your body. Maintain as much of the antioxidant bounty as possible from fresh vegetables by lightly steaming them or eating them raw.

To keep your eyes sparkling into old age, eat a diet rich in the above antioxidants, essential fats, minerals, and other plant chemicals. Eliminate constipation, by eating fiber-rich foods and drinking plenty of water. Take regular exercise and you can greatly reduce or slow down the onset of the three major eye conditions.

carrot and ginger soup with lime and clementines

serves 4

2 tbsp/30g butter or ghee

2 tbsp olive or sunflower oil

2 onions, chopped

1in/2.5cm piece fresh root ginger, finely chopped

1lb/450g carrots (about 4–6), finely sliced

1 quart/1 liter chicken stock or water

juice of 5 clementines (about ¾ cup/175ml)

sea salt and ground black pepper

shreds of lime and clementine zest, to serve

1 Heat the butter and oil in a pan, add the onions and a pinch of salt, and cook until softened and golden. Add the ginger and carrots, and sauté for a few minutes more.

2 Add the stock or water and the clementine juice, then season with salt and pepper. Bring to a boil, then simmer until the carrots are tender, about 20 minutes.

3 Strain into a pitcher (jug), then put the solids into a blender with 1–2 ladlefuls of strained liquid. Purée, adding extra liquid if necessary. When smooth, add the remaining liquid and purée again.

4 Reheat the soup if necessary, taste and adjust the seasoning, then serve the soup in bowls and top each with the shreds of lime and clementine zest.

Food as Medicine

- **The fats** in this recipe are cooked at a low temperature, but if you are using high heat for frying, choose ghee or organic coconut oil preferably, which are stable at high temperatures. You can use olive oil for cooking at a lower heat, but minimize your use of refined sunflower, safflower, and corn oils, and other polyunsaturates (found in many margarines), which become unstable at high temperatures.

health TIPS

- **If you have** dark panda-like circles under your eyes, even if you are getting sufficient sleep, you may have an underactive thyroid or low iron levels. It is well worth having a check-up. And if the whites of your eyes tend to look yellowish, this usually indicates that your liver is somewhat toxic and you need to clean up your diet.

- **If you are** sleeping well, but still find that you have circles under your eyes after having three or four good nights' sleep, eliminate wheat for a week and see if this helps. If there is no change, also try eliminating cow's milk from your diet. These are the most common triggers.

ribbon vegetable and hummus wraps

serves 2

2 whole-wheat chapati wraps

4 tbsp hummus

1 carrot

½ red, orange, or yellow bell pepper, seeded and thinly sliced

1 scallion (spring onion), sliced

a handful of watercress or arugula (rocket), rinsed

1 Gently warm the chapati wraps to make them more flexible, either by dry-frying for a few seconds on each side in a frying pan, or in the microwave for 10 seconds on high.

2 Spread each one with 2 tbsp hummus. Use a vegetable peeler to shave the carrot into ribbons, then divide these among the wraps. Add the pepper slices, scallion, and watercress or arugula, then roll up the wraps and cut in half to serve.

Food as Medicine

• **Beta-carotenes** are antioxidants with an affinity for mucous membranes, particularly the eyes. They are found in orange fruits and vegetables, such as carrots, squash, mangoes, apricots, sweet potatoes, and pumpkin, as well as green leafy vegetables, such as spinach, kale, watercress, arugula (rocket) and bok choy (pak choi).

• **Make delicious sandwiches and wraps** with fish. Studies have confirmed that omega-3 fatty acids help to prevent and reduce the incidence of dry eyes. Cold water fish, such as herring, salmon, mackerel, and sardines are the best sources. When possible, choose organic fish in order to minimize your exposure to pollutants.

pumpkin soup

serves 4

2lb/900g diced pumpkin or squash

3 tbsp olive oil

1 large onion, chopped

1 celery stick, chopped

1 large carrot, sliced

1¼ quarts/1.25 liters chicken stock

2 bay leaves

2 long fresh rosemary sprigs

1 large potato, cut into chunks

sea salt and ground black pepper

¼ cup/60 ml plain (natural) sheep's, goat's, or dairy-free yogurt

4 tsp toasted pumpkin seeds

1 Preheat the oven to 400°F/200°C/Gas 6. Put the pumpkin in a bowl with 2 tbsp oil and turn until coated. Transfer to a roasting pan and roast for 30 minutes or until tender.

2 In the meantime, heat the remaining oil and fry the onion, celery, and carrot for 5 minutes, stirring occasionally. Add the chicken stock, bay leaves, rosemary, and potatoes, and bring to a boil. Turn down the heat and cook, part-covered, for 20 minutes or until tender.

3 Remove the herbs, then add the roasted pumpkin to the soup. Using a hand-held blender, purée the soup until smooth. Season to taste and reheat to just below boiling point. Ladle into heated soup bowls, top with a swirl of yogurt and a sprinkling of pumpkin seeds before serving.

north african beans with pomegranate dressing

Food as Medicine

- **Fresh vegetables**, herbs, and fruits contain vitamin C, which is essential for good health. When we eat adequate amounts of vitamin C, as well as foods rich in zinc (such as nuts, seeds, and oysters,) and magnesium, (such as green, leafy vegetables and kelp,) our body is able to manufacture hyaluronic acid, which is important for healthy eyes and joints. Homemade chicken soup cooked using the skin and carcass is a direct source of hyaluronic acid.

serves 4

1¼ cups/250g dried mung beans, soaked overnight

1 small red onion, diced

1 carrot, grated

1 zucchini (courgette), diced

3 tbsp chopped fresh mint

3 tbsp chopped fresh cilantro (coriander)

4 tbsp pomegranate seeds

POMEGRANATE DRESSING:

2 tbsp pomegranate molasses

juice of 1 small lemon

3 tbsp extra-virgin olive oil

sea salt and ground black pepper

1 Drain and rinse the mung beans and put in a pan. Cover with plenty of cold water, then bring to a boil. Reduce the heat to low, cover with a lid, and simmer for about 50 minutes or until tender. (The freshness of the dried beans will influence how long they take to cook.) Drain and transfer to a serving bowl.

2 Add the onion, carrot, and zucchini to the mung beans. Mix together the ingredients for the dressing, then season. Pour the dressing over the beans, and turn gently until combined.

3 Scatter over the herbs and turn gently again, then sprinkle with the pomegranate seeds before serving.

health TIP

- **If you tend** to spend a lot of time at a computer screen, every hour or so look into the far distance for 10–20 seconds, then slowly bring your focus back to a finger or pencil held at arm's length. This helps to stretch your eye muscles.

venison with dark berry sauce

serves 4

1 tbsp olive oil

4 venison loin steaks, about 5oz/150g each

sea salt and ground black pepper

DARK BERRY SAUCE:

⅓ cup/75ml fresh orange juice

1–2 tbsp pure maple syrup or good-quality honey, such as cold extracted or manuka, to taste

1 star anise

1 tsp ground allspice

5oz/150g blackberries

zest of 1 orange

Food as Medicine

- **Organic** beef, venison, chicken, and turkey are good sources of L-carnosine, a combination of two amino acids found in animal foods, particularly muscle meat. Studies have shown it to be effective in slowing down the progression of cataracts.

- **Green leafy** vegetables should accompany every meal. They are high in chlorophyll and, as a result, rich in magnesium. Magnesium is a smooth muscle relaxant that helps to increase blood flow to the head and relaxes the eye muscles. Involuntary twitching of the eye is one of the first signs of a magnesium deficiency.

1 To make the dark berry sauce, put the orange juice, maple syrup or honey, star anise, and allspice in a pan and bring to a gentle boil. Turn down the heat and stir over a gentle heat until combined.

2 Add the blackberries and orange zest, and cook gently for 5 minutes until softened and the sauce has reduced. Taste for sweetness, and add a little extra maple syrup, if necessary.

3 Meanwhile, heat the oil in a large, nonstick frying pan over a medium heat. Season the venison, then cook for 2–3 minutes each side or until cooked to your liking—you may need to do this in two batches.

4 Serve the venison accompanied by the dark berry sauce.

health TIP

- **To reduce your chances** of contracting AMD (age-related macular degeneration) cut down on refined sugars and foods high in saturated fat. To avoid cataracts, wear sunglasses and a hat when in bright sunlight. Taking regular exercise, and receiving acupuncture, can help to increase the circulation to the eye area. Smokers increase their risk of developing AMD by more than two and a half times that of those who do not smoke.

roasted winter ratatouille

serves 4

1 carrot, cut into matchsticks

12oz/350g butternut squash, cut into large bite-sized pieces (about 2½ cups)

2 turnips, cubed

4 Jerusalem artichokes, cubed

4 large shallots, halved lengthways with the stem intact

3 tbsp olive oil

a small handful of sage leaves

2 tbsp tamari

1 tbsp balsamic vinegar

¼ tsp dried chili flakes

8 vine-ripened tomatoes, seeded and quartered

sea salt and ground black pepper

1 Preheat the oven to 400°F/200°C/Gas 6. Put the carrot, butternut squash, turnips, Jerusalem artichokes, and shallots in a bowl, then add the olive oil and turn until coated. Transfer the vegetables to two large roasting pans, scatter over a few sprigs of sage, and roast for 20 minutes, turning occasionally until beginning to soften.

2 Reduce the oven temperature to 350°F/180°C/Gas 4. In a bowl, mix the tamari, balsamic vinegar, and chili flakes with 1 scant cup/200ml water. Remove the sage and pour the mixture over the vegetables. Scatter over the tomatoes then cover the dish with foil.

3 Return the dish to the oven and roast for a further 1 hour, turning occasionally, until the vegetables are very tender. Before serving, scatter over a few sage leaves and season with salt and pepper.

Food as Medicine

• **Globe artichokes** are one of the highest food sources of antioxidants. They contain the eye-protecting flavonoids lutein and zeaxanthin, both important against UV damage. In addition, they are a good source of cynarin, which promotes bile, and silymarin, which encourages better liver function, thus enhancing blood quality.

• **Tomatoes** contain lycopene, a type of carotene, which makes the fruit red—the redder the tomato, the higher the lycopene content. Together with other antioxidants, including vitamins C and A, lycopene can help to reduce age-related macular degeneration. Adding olive oil to the cooked tomato enhances its absorbability.

health TIP

○ **Enjoying some freshly** cooked organic chicken or turkey (especially the dark part of the meat with the fat trimmed off) with this ratatouille will help your eyes, as these meats contain the amino acid taurine, which not only supports the retina, but also helps to prevent cataracts.

pesto and spinach frittata

serves 4

2 tbsp extra-virgin olive oil

2 onions, sliced

3 large garlic cloves

2oz/50g arugula (rocket)

150g/5½oz young spinach

1 tbsp fresh chopped oregano

6 tbsp fresh basil pesto

6 eggs, lightly beaten

3oz/75g soft goat's cheese, cut into large bite-size pieces

5 tbsp freshly grated Parmesan

ground black pepper

health TIP

O **Your eyes need** plenty of vitamin C to help make collagen, which strengthens the capillaries that nourish the retina and protects against UV light damage. If you don't eat five pieces of fresh fruit and vegetables daily, take at least 1g of vitamin C daily in divided doses with food to help support your eyes and immune system.

1 Heat the olive oil in a medium nonstick frying pan over a medium heat. (Make sure the handle is heatproof.) Fry the onions for 7 minutes, stirring regularly, until softened. Add the garlic and cook for 1 minute.

2 Add the arugula, spinach, and oregano, and cook over a medium-low heat, turning the leaves continuously, until wilted – this will take about 2–3 minutes. Remove the pan from the heat.

3 Preheat the broiler (grill) to medium-high.

4 Stir the pesto into the beaten eggs, season with pepper, and pour over the onion mixture until evenly covered. Return the pan to the heat and cook for 1 minute until beginning to set, then scatter over the goat's cheese. Cook for a further 2 minutes until half-set.

5 Scatter the Parmesan over the top and put under the broiler for 3–5 minutes until just set. Leave to stand for 5 minutes before cutting into wedges to serve.

Food as Medicine

• **Rutin** is a flavonoid found in buckwheat, the rind of citrus fruit, and in mulberries and cranberries. Rutin strengthens the capillaries and inhibits an enzyme in the eye called aldose reductase, which leads to oxidation of the delicate blood vessels, thereby slowing the progression of some eye diseases.

peaches with pistachio nuts and dates

serves 2

3 tbsp thick organic yogurt

1 tsp grated orange zest

10 pistachio nuts or other favorite nuts, roughly chopped

2 pitted (stoned) dates, finely chopped

2 ripe peaches or nectarines

1 Preheat the broiler (grill) to medium and line a broiler (grill) pan with foil. Meanwhile, mix together the yogurt, orange zest, pistachio nuts, and dates in a small bowl.

2 Cut the peaches in half lengthways, twist to separate the fruit into halves, then pry out the pit (stone).

3 Spoon the mixture into the peach centers. Broil (grill) for 6–7 minutes until the mixture starts to turn golden and the fruit softens.

Food as Medicine

• **A glass of wine with your meal** is good for your eyes too! The chemical resveratrol is produced by the skins of certain plants in response to a fungus. It is most noticeably found in the skins of red grapes (particularly the muscadine variety), mulberries, and, to a lesser degree, peanuts. Many studies have shown its antioxidant effect in protecting the skin and eyes.

• **Cherries** are high in anthocyanins (the red pigment) and, like red grapes, are anti-inflammatory and a strong antioxidant. In addition, they are high in vitamin C, protecting the eyes from UV damage as well as helping to remove excess uric acid from the blood.

pear and cherry crumble

serves 6

4 just-ripe pears, peeled, cored, and cut into bite-size pieces

9oz/250g frozen dark cherries

1/2 tsp ground cinnamon

CRUMBLE TOPPING:

5 tbsp/75g unsalted butter

1 1/4 cups/150g whole-wheat spelt flour

2 tbsp xylitol

2 tbsp rolled oats

4 tbsp chopped pecan nuts

1 Preheat the oven to 350°F/180°C/Gas 4. Put the pears, cherries, and cinnamon into a pan and bring to boiling point. Turn down the heat, part-cover, and simmer for 5 minutes or until the fruit is tender. Spoon the fruit and juices into a pie pan.

2 To make the crumble topping, rub the butter into the flour until it resembles very coarse bread crumbs (don't rub it in too much or the crumble won't be crisp when cooked). Stir in the xylitol, oats, and chopped pecan nuts.

3 Scatter the crumble over the fruit, then bake for 30–35 minutes until crisp and golden on top.

health TIPS

- **Late-onset diabetes** (type-2 diabetes), now found even in young people, is mainly triggered by eating too much refined sugar and fats, and being overweight. It can lead to serious eye problems. If you reduce your intake of refined sugars, processed saturated fats, and white foods—as well as adding more cinnamon to your desserts—you can reduce excess glucose levels in the blood.

- **Puffiness** and bags under the eyes can denote kidney problems and a build up of toxins in the body, and it can also signify that sodium and potassium levels are out of balance. Reducing sodium-based salt and taking 99mg of potassium daily for a week or so should help to reduce this problem. Drinking plenty of water, while avoiding wheat and animal dairy foods for a few days should also help.

chapter 4

feed your bones and teeth

Osteoporosis silently threatens men and women. One in two women and one in five men over the age of 50 will break a bone through osteoporosis. Also, thanks to many people's highly stressed lifestyles, combined with their over-consumption of sugary, refined foods, and a host of other factors, we are now at risk of experiencing a health time-bomb. Binge drinking is triggering early onset osteoporosis in both men and women, and is just one example which shows that what you put into your mouth is crucial to the future health of your bones.

Bone mass peaks in your mid twenties, but, if you live a fast-paced lifestyle and tend to become stressed easily, excess production of the stress hormones adrenalin and cortisol can vastly deplete minerals from your bones. Eating too many "acid-forming foods," such as red meat, chocolate, sugar, coffee, alcohol, and pre-packaged foods, can contribute to bone loss, because minerals are withdrawn from your bones to help re-alkalize your blood. The secret, as always, is to find a balance.

Yet, simply increasing calcium intake is not the answer. In fact, without adequate phosphorus and magnesium, an imbalance will occur. This is because calcium, magnesium, and phosphorus levels are kept in a seesawing balance by our body's hormones. Low magnesium levels, for example, will cause calcium to leach out of the bones into the tissues. Vitamin D and boron are also needed for strong bones. Getting calcium into the body is actually easy, because it is abundant in a wide range of foods. The hard part is keeping it in the bones and out of your arteries, where calcium deposits can contribute to hardening.

Like calcium, a problem with phosphorus occurs where, in the absence of other minerals, we ingest too much phosphorus from unnatural sources. Fizzy drinks—a favorite for many—contain phosphoric acid, and sodium phosphate is added to meat, cheese, and other processed foods to extend shelf life and enhance the flavor. It's worth realizing that if you are drinking lots of fizzy drinks, you may be causing considerable damage to your teeth and bones!

High calcium intake is not the answer

In countries like Asia and Africa where calcium intake is much lower than in Western countries, there are far lower rates of osteoporosis. Bantu women in Africa, for example, eat less than 300mg of calcium daily compared to the average Westerner who eats more than 1,000mg. What is also interesting is that the more the calcium intake is reduced, the more it is absorbed. This paradox makes sense when we understand that the overall diet of these people provides the correct ratios of natural phosphorus, magnesium, calcium, and boron. And they have large amounts of exposure to sunshine, which helps the body to manufacture vitamin D, which is vital for healthy bones.

By contrast, the average person in Western countries excretes more sodium and calcium in their urine, while retaining potassium and magnesium. This shows that the excess sodium (in the form of salt) from processed foods, and calcium from dairy products, that is consumed in the absence of other balancing nutrients, such as magnesium, contributes to bone loss and other imbalances in the body.

Other contributory factors are a lack of weight-bearing exercise, a lack of sunlight, premature menopause, anorexia, long-term use of certain drugs, such as steroids, and smoking, as well as the stress mentioned earlier, and consuming too many acid-forming foods and fizzy drinks. Genetic links can also play a part in your chances of developing this condition.

Good diet and lifestyle choices

Phosphorus is part of all living organisms and is therefore found in all our foods in varying amounts. Good natural sources include wheat germ, lentils, fish (particularly salmon and halibut), almonds, Brazil nuts, eggs, chicken, turkey, and goat's milk products. Next to calcium, phosphorus is the second most abundant mineral in the body, with around 85 percent of the body's phosphorus found in the teeth and bones.

To maintain bone density, the tissues need to stay alkaline. The more alkaline our bodies are, the slower the rate of calcium loss will be. Vegetable protein from tofu, beans, peas, and nuts is a better option than animal protein, as has been demonstrated in vegans, who have a much lower incidence of osteoporosis than those who eat meat.

Salt, based only on sodium, encourages the loss of calcium via the kidneys, so try to keep below 2g daily. A better option would be to use powdered kelp, or to take Himalayan crystal salt, sea salt, or a potassium/magnesium-based salt, available in health-food shops.

Green leafy vegetables help to keep your tissues more alkaline. Make sure you eat plenty of kale, broccoli, watercress, collards (spring greens), and bok choy (pak choi), which are good sources of available calcium (although the calcium in spinach may be difficult to assimilate.) These vegetables are also rich in vitamin K, which is necessary for keeping calcium in the bones and not allowing it to migrate to your arteries. In addition, they are excellent sources of magnesium. Other foods rich in both calcium and magnesium include barley, butternut squash, tofu, most types of beans (especially soy), chickpeas, and dried figs. Other good calcium sources include fish oils and fish that you eat with their bones, such as sardines. Sesame seeds (including tahini) and chickpeas are also good sources.

Apart from getting sufficient sunshine, good sources of vitamin D are egg yolks and oily fish, particularly salmon, mackerel, and sardines.

If you consume animal-based dairy products, goat's milk is a better alternative to cow's milk. It has less lactose, smaller fat molecules, and a different protein structure and so is more efficiently assimilated by the body. Goat's yogurt that has been properly cultured will further enhance its bioavailability of calcium.

Other important co-factors in maintaining healthy bones and teeth are the trace minerals boron and silica. Good sources of boron include apples, raisins, cherries, dates, apricots, dried plums (prunes,) almonds, green beans, broccoli, and good-quality honey, such as cold extracted or manuka. Silica, which is particularly important for healthy tooth enamel, is abundant in a wide variety of whole foods, including rye, oats, millet, asparagus, lettuce, cucumber, parsnips, bean sprouts, onions, and beets (beetroot.)

In essence, if we eat a broad range of foods that supply the minerals, trace minerals, and other nutrients mentioned above, together with regular weight-bearing exercise, reducing stress, and watching our hormone levels, we should keep our bones healthy well into old age.

figs with pecan nuts and blue cheese

Food as Medicine

- **Green leafy** vegetables, such as kale, broccoli, arugula (rocket), and bok choy (pak choi), are rich in both calcium and magnesium, and are ideal for maintaining bone density. Other foods rich in these two minerals include barley, butternut squash, fermented soya products, beans, chickpeas, and dried figs.

serves 4, as an appetizer

scant ½ cup/50g pecan nuts

3 tbsp extra-virgin olive oil

2 tbsp lemon juice

1 tsp Dijon mustard

4½ oz/125g arugula (rocket)

6 figs, quartered

generous 1 cup/150g crumbled Roquefort cheese

sea salt and ground black pepper

1 Put the pecan nuts in a nonstick frying pan and toast over a medium heat for 3–5 minutes, turning once, until slightly browned. Remove from the pan and set aside to cool.

2 Pour the olive oil into a small bowl and whisk in the lemon juice, mustard, a pinch of sea salt, and ground pepper until combined.

3 Arrange the arugula on a serving plate with the fig quarters on top. Scatter over the Roquefort and pecan nuts, then pour the dressing evenly over the salad to serve.

health TIP

- **Bones require** minerals to grow and remain strong, and many people drink mineral-rich bottled waters for this purpose; however, minerals such as calcium in water are in an inorganic form and are not easily utilized by the body, so can end up in your arteries and joints contributing to problems such as frozen shoulder or hardening of the arteries. Fruits, plants, and vegetables, on the other hand, combine with sunlight to transform inorganic minerals into an organic (bio-available) form, which we can absorb and utilize far more easily. This is why fresh fruits and vegetables, and their juices, help to quench your thirst more effectively.

summer vegetable and mozzarella platter with herb dressing

Food as Medicine

- **Fruit is ideal** to follow this summer platter. Boron is a trace element that helps to metabolize calcium and magnesium which is needed for strong bones. Although found throughout the body, it is concentrated in the teeth and bones. Apples, raisins, cherries, pears, and avocados are the best sources.

- **Add some nuts!** Around 90 per cent of phosphorus in the body is stored in the teeth, nails and bone, but refined foods will deplete levels. It requires calcium and magnesium for bone mineralization. Good sources include rice bran, almonds, Brazil nuts, lentils, and chickpeas.

serves 4

3 zucchini (courgettes), sliced lengthways

olive oil, for brushing

1 red bell pepper, seeded and sliced lengthways

1 small eggplant (aubergine), sliced into rounds

9oz/250g asparagus, trimmed

1 cup/150g canned chickpeas, rinsed

2 x 4½oz/125g balls buffalo mozzarella, torn into pieces

HERB DRESSING:

2 tbsp lemon juice

6 tbsp extra-virgin olive oil, plus extra for griddling

1 garlic clove, crushed

a handful of fresh basil leaves, roughly chopped

2 long sprigs fresh oregano, leaves roughly chopped

2 tbsp chopped fresh chives

sea salt and ground black pepper

1 Brush the zucchini with the olive oil. Heat a griddle pan over a medium-high heat, then griddle the zucchini for 5–6 minutes, turning once, until tender and charred in places. Remove from the pan and set aside until ready to serve.

2 Repeat with the red bell pepper, eggplant, and asparagus. Arrange the griddled vegetables on a serving platter. Scatter the chickpeas and mozzarella over the top.

3 To make the dressing, stir the lemon juice into the olive oil until combined, then add the garlic and herbs, and season. Spoon the dressing over the salad before serving.

health TIP

- **Vitamin D**—available from sunlight— is vital for healthy bones and teeth, so remember your daily 15 minutes of sunshine, when possible. Expose your skin to sunshine without sunscreen, and away from the midday sun. During the winter months take 1,000iu of vitamin D_3 daily. Eat egg yolks and oily fish, too, as they are rich in vitamin D.

falafel with avocado, tomato, and red onion salsa

serves 4

1¼ cups/225g dried chickpeas, soaked overnight

2 garlic cloves, crushed

1 tsp ground cumin

½ tsp ground coriander

a pinch of chili powder (optional)

½ tsp baking soda (bicarbonate of soda)

2 scallions (spring onions), very finely chopped

3 tbsp chopped fresh flat-leaf parsley

3 tbsp chopped fresh cilantro (coriander)

sea salt and ground black pepper

3–4 tbsp virgin coconut oil, for deep-frying

pita bread, to serve

AVOCADO, TOMATO, AND RED ONION SALSA:

4 ripe tomatoes

1 large ripe avocado

½ red onion, finely chopped

½ small fresh red chili, halved, seeded, and very finely chopped

3 tbsp chopped fresh cilantro (coriander)

finely grated zest and juice of 1 unwaxed lime

2–3 tbsp extra-virgin olive oil

sea salt and ground black pepper

health TIP

- **Ghee** (clarified butter) or organic coconut oil are healthy choices if you are using high heat for cooking/frying. This is because they are higher in saturated fats, therefore more stable when heated. Olive oil is fine for lower heat, but minimize use of refined sunflower, safflower, and corn oils and other poly-unsaturates (found in many margarines,) which become unstable at high temperatures.

1 Drain the chickpeas very well and roll them in kitchen paper to dry. Transfer to a food processor, add the garlic, cumin, coriander, chili powder, and baking soda, and blend to a smooth paste. Taste and season well with salt and ground black pepper. Tip into a bowl, cover, and let rest for 30 minutes.

2 Add the scallions, parsley, and cilantro to the chickpea paste, beat thoroughly, then knead the mixture well to bring it together. Line a tray with plastic wrap (clingfilm). Scoop out small lumps of the mixture and make into flat, round cakes—as small or large as you like—and put them on the tray. Cover and chill for 15 minutes.

3 Meanwhile, to make the salsa, cut the tomatoes in half, seed them, then chop finely and put into a bowl. Chop the avocado and add to the bowl. Add the onion, chili, and cilantro, and stir gently. Put the lime juice, zest, olive oil, salt, and pepper in a small bowl and mix well. Pour over the tomato mixture, fold gently, and set aside.

4 Heat the coconut oil in a large, nonstick frying pan. Cook the falafel, in batches if necessary, for 5 minutes until they are crisp and brown, turning occasionally. Lift out with a slotted spoon and drain on paper towels. Add a little more coconut oil if necessary. Serve the falafel hot or warm, with pita bread and the salsa.

italian lentil salad

serves 4

2 cups/150g cooked or canned brown lentils, rinsed and drained (1 cup/225g raw weight)

4 preserved baby artichokes, preferably broiled (grilled), quartered

1 red onion, halved lengthways and cut into thin slivered wedges

1½ cups/175g diced, or roughly crumbled, feta cheese

a handful of mixed fresh herbs, such as parsley, basil, or marjoram, coarsely chopped, or chopped chives, plus herb sprigs to garnish

ITALIAN DRESSING:

1 tbsp cider vinegar

¼ cup/60ml extra-virgin olive oil

ground black pepper

a pinch of sea salt, if needed

1 Put the lentils in a bowl and add the vinegar, oil, and pepper.

2 Add the artichokes, onion, and feta cheese, then toss together gently. Add salt and pepper to taste—remember that the feta cheese is already salty— then serve, sprinkled with the mixed herbs and garnished with a herb sprig.

Food as **Medicine**

- **Feta cheese** is made from sheep's milk, which, along with goat's milk, is a better source of calcium than cow's milk. Goat's milk is more efficiently assimilated and absorbed by the body because is has less lactose, and its smaller fat molecule and different protein structure make it easier to digest.

quick chickpea salad

serves 4

2 x 14oz/400g cans chickpeas, rinsed and drained

4 marinated artichoke hearts

4 large sun-blushed tomatoes (optional)

9oz/250g very ripe cherry tomatoes, halved

8 scallions (spring onions), sliced diagonally

a handful of fresh basil leaves, torn

a small bunch of chives, finely chopped

1 tbsp chopped fresh flat leaf parsley

2oz (50g) fresh Parmesan, shaved

1 tbsp black pepper, cracked with a mortar and pestle

DIJON DRESSING:

6 tbsp extra-virgin olive oil

1 tbsp lemon juice

1 tsp Dijon mustard

1 small garlic clove, crushed

sea salt

1 Put the dressing ingredients into a small bowl and whisk with a fork.

2 Add the chickpeas, artichoke hearts, and sun-blushed tomatoes, if using, in a serving bowl. Pour in the dressing and turn gently until coated. Cover and chill for 4 hours.

3 When ready to serve, add the cherry tomatoes, scallions, basil, chives, and parsley. Stir gently, then sprinkle with the shaved Parmesan and cracked pepper.

health TIPS

○ **Everything you eat**, after digestion, breaks down into either an acid or an alkaline residue. And if you eat too many acid-forming foods, such as red meat, refined "white" foods, plus coffee or alcohol, or if you are stressed, the more acidic your blood becomes. To help re-alkalize your system, precious minerals are leached from your bones. Maintaining your acid–alkaline balance is crucial to the health of your bones and teeth. In the lentil recipe above, we suggest cider vinegar (organic apple), which has an alkalizing effect after digestion. By adding 1 tbsp apple cider vinegar to warm water and honey, and sipping it throughout the day, you can help to re-alkalize your system and also assimilate more calcium into your bones. See pages 308–309 for more details.

white bean and halloumi pan-fry

serves 4

4 tbsp extra-virgin olive oil

3 large garlic cloves, finely chopped

3 tbsp fresh thyme or oregano leaves

1 long red chili, seeded and finely chopped

2 x 14oz/400g cans lima beans (butter beans), drained and rinsed

scant 2 cups/250g vine-ripened cherry tomatoes

juice of $\frac{1}{2}$ lemon

2 tsp Dijon mustard

$4\frac{1}{2}$oz/125g watercress or arugula (rocket), tough stalks trimmed

9oz/250g halloumi cheese, patted dry with paper towels and cut into 8 slices

sea salt and ground black pepper

basil leaves, to garnish

1 Heat the olive oil in a large frying pan and fry the garlic for 30 seconds before adding the thyme or oregano, chili, lima beans, and tomatoes. Cook over a medium heat, stirring frequently, for 3 minutes or until the tomatoes begin to soften and break down.

2 Stir in the lemon juice, mustard, and watercress or arugula, season with salt and pepper, and heat through, stirring, until the leaves begin to wilt. Cover and keep warm while you cook the halloumi.

3 Heat a griddle pan over a medium-high heat. Griddle the halloumi for 2 minutes on each side or until golden brown in places.

4 Serve the bean mixture topped with slices of halloumi, with basil sprinkled over the top.

health TIP

○ **As well as** eating a good diet to support your bones, men and women over 40 with a fast-paced, highly stressed lifestyle, or those who smoke or have a family history of osteoporosis or anorexia, should have a bone-density test and check their hormone levels every two years. Weight-bearing exercises, such as walking, skipping, jogging and using weights, help bone density.

Food as Medicine

• **Sprinkle some** sesame seeds over your meals. They are an ideal food for bones, especially in their concentrated form as tahini. Rich in calcium, phosphorus, and magnesium they are also a complete vegetable protein. The silica in rye, oats, millet, asparagus, lettuce, cucumber, parsnips, bean sprouts, onions, and beets (beetroot) is also important for healthy bones and tooth enamel. Low levels may lead to arthritic conditions.

big greek salad

Food as Medicine

- **Lettuce** is a good source of the mineral silica needed for healthy bones and teeth. It is also rich in vitamins A, C, and K. The darker the leaves and the more bitter they taste, the higher the antioxidant content.

- **Green leaves**, such as kale, bok choy (pak choi) broccoli, and green cabbage, all contain vitamin K, which is vital for keeping calcium in the bones and out of the arteries.

serves 4

1 iceberg lettuce, quartered and torn apart

2 cups/225g diced, or roughly crumbled, feta cheese

1 cup/175g Kalamata olives

2 red onions, halved, then sliced into thin wedges

2 Kirby (small pickling) cucumbers, halved lengthways, then thinly sliced diagonally

4 large ripe tomatoes, cut into chunks

8 anchovies, or to taste

a few sprigs of fresh oregano, torn

a few sprigs of fresh mint, torn

GREEK DRESSING:

1/3 cup/75ml extra-virgin olive oil, preferably Greek

2 tbsp lemon juice

sea salt and ground black pepper

1 Put the lettuce in a large bowl. Add the cheese, olives, onions, cucumbers, and tomatoes.

2 To make the dressing, put the olive oil, lemon juice, salt, and pepper in a bowl, beat with a fork, then pour over the salad. Or, you can sprinkle the dressing over each salad separately.

3 Top with the anchovies, oregano, and mint, and serve.

homemade sheep's cheese

serves 4–6

2 cups/500ml thick plain (natural) sheep's yogurt

1 tsp sea salt

extra-virgin olive oil, to cover

a handful of mixed fresh herbs, such as oregano, chives, basil, and mint (optional)

1 Put a cheesecloth (muslin) in a sieve, suspended over a medium-sized bowl. Mix the yogurt with the salt and spoon it into the cloth. Pull the cloth up around the yogurt and twist to make a bundle.

2 Leave the yogurt to drain in the refrigerator for 24 hours or so, giving it a gentle squeeze every so often to encourage any liquid to drain away. Remove the yogurt from the cloth—it should now look like a semi-soft ball of cheese.

3 Place the cheese in a bowl and drizzle over some olive oil, then scatter with fresh herbs, if you like. Alternatively, form the cheese into large, walnut-sized balls and put in a sterilized jar. Pour over enough oil to cover and store in the refrigerator for up to one week.

tandoori tempeh kabobs with mint raita

health TIP

○ **Vegetable protein** from fermented soya products, quinoa, oats, lentils, beans, peas, and nuts is a better option than acid-forming, animal-based proteins when it comes to protecting bone loss. These foods are more alkaline-forming, and when combined with leafy greens and fruits, they help to retain calcium in the bones.

Food as Medicine

● **Almonds** make the perfect snack and are great for bones and teeth, since they are highly alkaline and rich in calcium; however, they contain an enzyme-inhibitor in the outer brown covering, which reduces absorbability. To maximize absorption, soak almonds in water overnight at room temperature. Rinse them next morning and they will be ready to eat.

● **Tempeh** is a highly nutritious food because the whole soybean is fermented. It is an excellent source of vegetable protein and a rich source of potassium, plus the bone-strengthening minerals calcium, phosphorus, and magnesium.

serves 4

14oz/400g block of tempeh

scant ⅔ cup/150ml thick plain (natural) sheep's or goat's yogurt

6 tbsp chopped fresh mint

2 tsp lime juice

TANDOORI PASTE:

2 tsp ground coriander

2 tsp ground cumin

2 tsp turmeric

2 tsp garam masala

1 tbsp paprika

½ tsp hot chili powder

2 tbsp sunflower oil

3 garlic cloves, crushed

1 tbsp tamarind paste

3 tbsp plain (natural) yogurt

sea salt

RED ONION AND RADISH SALAD:

1 red onion, thinly sliced into rounds

1 small cucumber, sliced into rounds

8 radishes, sliced

1 tbsp lime juice

a small handful of fresh cilantro (coriander) leaves

1 Pat the tempeh dry with kitchen paper. Steam it for 10 minutes until softened slightly (this also removes any traces of bitterness). Meanwhile, mix together the ingredients for the tandoori paste with 1 tbsp water in a large shallow dish. Remove the tempeh from the steamer and cut into 32 x ¾in/2cm cubes. Add to the dish and turn until coated in the paste; set aside to marinate for at least 1 hour.

2 Preheat the broiler (grill) to high and line the broiler pan with foil. Thread four chunks of tempeh onto a skewer then repeat to make eight kebobs (kebabs) in total. Broil (grill) for 10 minutes, turning occasionally, until deep golden brown in places.

3 Meanwhile, mix together the scant ⅔ cup/150ml yogurt, mint, and lime juice to make the raita dipping sauce.

4 To make the salad, arrange the red onion in a dish and top with the cucumber and radishes. Squeeze over the lime juice, season with salt and scatter over the cilantro.

5 Serve the salad with the tempeh kebabs and a spoonful of the mint raita for dipping.

mozzarella, peach, and chicory salad

serves 4, as an appetizer

3 fresh peaches, cut into thin wedges

4 handfuls of chicory leaves, trimmed

1 large ball of fresh mozzarella, torn into thin shreds

3 tbsp extra-virgin olive oil

1 tbsp white wine vinegar

ground black pepper

1 Put the peach wedges and chicory leaves into a large bowl and gently toss to mix. Arrange on a serving plate. Scatter the mozzarella pieces over the salad.

2 Put the olive oil, vinegar, and black pepper in a bowl, whisk with a fork, and then spoon over the salad to serve.

Food as Medicine

- **Seaweeds** make good additions to salads. They are often overlooked as good foods for bones and teeth, but they are high in magnesium and calcium, and are a natural source of vitamin D. They are also a good source of fluorine. Fluorine-rich foods improve the absorption of calcium and retard the onset of dental cavities.

health TIP

- **Avoid cleaning your teeth** immediately after drinking fruit juice, or eating fresh fruit or a refined-sugary dessert or drink, as you may brush away weakened tooth enamel and cause erosion. Instead, rinse the mouth with water to help neutralize the "acid" effect of the fruit and/or sugar.

- **When making salads**, add a few chopped walnuts, or sunflower or pumpkin seeds for added nutrition, fiber, and essential fats. Boost fruit smoothies by adding finely chopped mineral-rich hazelnuts or soaked flaked almonds to help your bones and teeth.

strawberry and banana smoothie

serves 2

2 bananas

2 cups/225g strawberries, hulled

½ tsp pure vanilla extract (optional)

⅔ cup/150ml thick, plain (natural) sheep's or dairy-free yogurt

1½ cups/350ml rice, oat, almond, or coconut milk

1 Slice the bananas and put them in a blender with the strawberries, vanilla, if using, yogurt, and milk.

2 Blend until the mixture is thick, smooth, and creamy. Pour the smoothie into two glasses.

yogurt and summer fruit swirl

serves 2

3 ripe purple plums

1 cup/150g frozen mixed red berries

a little xylitol, organic maple syrup, or honey, to taste (optional)

6–8 tbsp thick plain (natural) low-fat yogurt

1 Halve the plums and remove the pits (stones), then chop roughly.

2 Put the frozen berries in a pan with the plums and ½ cup/125ml water. Bring to simmering point, then cover the pan and cook gently for 5–7 minutes until they soften and begin to break down.

3 Transfer the fruit and any juice to a blender or food processor and process until smooth, then press through a sieve to remove any seeds. If you like your smoothies sweet, add a little xylitol, maple syrup, or honey.

4 Spoon 3–4 tbsp yogurt into each glass or bowl. Add a few spoonfuls of the fruit purée and swirl it into the yogurt using a spoon handle to give a marbled effect. The swirls also taste good served topped with a few berries, toasted flaked almonds, or your favorite nuts.

Food as Medicine

• **Plums** have a calcium–phosphorus ratio that is well balanced and are one of a number of fruits that provide good calcium sources. Figs, mulberries, dates, and oranges are high in calcium, and most berries and grapes are high in silica. Apples, cherries, and pears are a good source of boron, whereas bananas and dates are rich in magnesium. Fruits tend to be low in phosphorus; however peaches, persimmons, and passion fruit contain relatively high amounts.

chapter 5

a healthy digestive system

The gut is often referred to as the "second brain", because emotional factors, such as stress, anxiety, and depression, can all have a truly dramatic effect on how the digestive system functions, causing problems with short- and long-term health. If your gut is functioning properly, you tend to be healthier. If your gut is not working properly, you can suffer from a host of conditions, ranging from IBS (irritable bowel syndrome), osteoporosis, malnutrition, and eczema, as well as autoimmune conditions, such as rheumatoid arthritis and lupus. Stress also has a huge effect on your gut health, and is mirrored in your digestive system in one form or another, either causing it to slow down (constipation) or to speed up (loose bowels or diarrhea).

We carry around approximately 2lb/1kg of "good" and "bad" bacteria in our intestines. When we are healthy and our bodies are in a state of balance, the good bacteria outnumber the bad and our internal ecosystem fosters a stronger immune system.

In addition to keeping pathogenic (the bad) bacteria in check, our friendly gut flora have other roles to play, such as breaking down food and synthesizing vitamins. When we take antibiotics, we upset the delicate balance, contributing to many of today's common ailments, such as IBS, a condition that affects about 20 percent of the population. Chronic constipation and inflammatory bowel disease

are also more common today. The friendly organisms, or microflora, are fragile creatures and very sensitive to pH changes, temperature, infections, and any form of stress. The typical modern diet—heavily processed with sugar, fat, salt, and refined flour— is not conducive to proper colonization by our good bugs. Neither is chronic stress or excessive alcohol consumption. If we add antibiotics into the mix, this can often be the straw that breaks the camel's back.

Excessive use of laxatives or antibiotics will set up the perfect environment for the wrong type of "gut bugs" to thrive. Stress reduces blood flow to the colon, slowing the action of the bowel, and thereby creating a static environment conducive to over-fermentation. Foods that are not digested properly will also create over-fermentation. This commonly manifests in various gases being produced, which, along with bloating, can cause pain and discomfort.

Nurturing your digestive system

Two criteria are important when considering gut health. The first is to eat foods that are easy to break down, and the second is to eat foods that serve as nutrition for the good bacteria to thrive. Two fibers, fructo-oligosaccharides and inulin, are crucial to this process. These are called prebiotics and include globe artichokes, fennel, celeriac, onions, leeks, chicory, and asparagus. For some people, these oligosaccharides can promote gas and, if that is the case, another option would be to eat foods high in stachyose (another form of prebiotic). This is found in beans (especially soy), peas, and chickpeas, but make sure you soak them (changing the water once) for several hours before cooking to help avoid gas.

There are also many foods that can create excess fermentation in the gut because of their natural sugar content. These include bananas, melons, apples, and pears. Berries and tropical fruit such as mangoes do not ferment as readily.

Beans, nuts, and seeds have other potential problems, so these are best soaked overnight or sprouted. This is because they contain enzyme-inhibitors, and can be difficult to break down in the gut, leading to bloating and discomfort.

The right way to eat the best foods

It's also not simply a question of what we eat but how we eat. It is essential to chew your food thoroughly, and not to eat in a hurry, as you might then ingest lots of air, which can lead to intestinal distress. Food-combining makes digestion easier, and this method has proven very successful for people who tend to have sensitive guts. The idea is to avoid mixing foods that "fight." For example, heavy proteins—meat, eggs, cheese, and fish—should not be eaten with starches, such as rice, bread, pasta, or potatoes.

Eating smaller meals also takes some of the stress off your digestive system. Eliminating hot, spicy foods or very cold foods can also help to reduce gut discomfort. The mild spice turmeric, however, contains curcumins, which have been shown to promote a wide range of benefits, from encouraging better colonization of good bacteria to anti-cancer properties.

A good bio-yogurt (preferably goat's or sheep's, which tend to cause fewer problems than cow's milk products) containing healthy bacteria such as *Lactobacillus acidophilus*, *Lactobacillus bulgaricus,* and *Bifidobacteria bifidum* can help to lower the pH of the large intestine, thus aiding survival of good bacteria.

Certain foods commonly trigger gut problems. These include dairy (from cows), wheat, and foods from the nightshade family—tomatoes, eggplant (aubergines), peppers, and potatoes—because their lectin content is difficult for the gut to break down. Wheat is high in gluten, which can trigger inflammation leading to "leaky gut," where undigested food molecules can enter the bloodstream causing autoimmune conditions, such as lupus or rheumatoid arthritis.

The major problem for many people when it comes to wheat/gluten is inefficient carbohydrate assimilation. Bread always needs to be chewed thoroughly before swallowing, ideally until it tastes sweet. The higher the gluten content, the more chewing will be required. Other kinds of wheat—spelt or kamut, for example—have a lower gluten content, and are easier to digest. Beneficial grains and grasses low in gluten include millet, buckwheat, amaranth, quinoa, and rice (wild or brown).

A slice of pineapple contains the enzyme bromelain and, if eaten prior to a meal, can promote better digestion. Tarragon also helps by stimulating appetite and quelling flatulence.

Fiber is necessary to aid the removal of waste products in the bowel. Soluble fiber—bran derived from rice, soy, or oats—and insoluble fiber from the skins of fruits and vegetables are essential for a healthy digestive system. Wheat bran, oat bran, and rice bran (with their relatively high soluble fiber content) can help to lower cholesterol, although wheat bran can irritate a sensitive gut. A good alternative is to soak 2 tsp of organic linseeds overnight in cold water and eat them with breakfast, as they are high in both soluble and insoluble fiber.

Above all, try to eat your meals sitting down, and take your time. Avoid heavy, rich and/or fried meals, which place a huge burden on your liver, gall bladder, and gut. Put your knife and fork down regularly, and stop eating before you feel very full. It takes 20 minutes from the time you eat anything for the brain to signal a fuller feeling!

soba with chicken and vegetables

serves 2

2 boneless, skinless chicken breasts, sliced into thin strips

sunflower or canola (rapeseed) oil, for brushing

3$\frac{1}{2}$oz/90g soba (buckwheat) noodles

3 cups/750ml hot water

2 tbsp brown rice miso paste

1 tbsp reduced-salt soy sauce

1in/2.5cm fresh root ginger, peeled and cut into thin strips

1 carrot, cut into thin matchsticks

3 scallions (spring onions), diagonally sliced

$\frac{1}{2}$ red bell pepper, seeded and cut into thin strips

2 baby bok choy (pak choi), halved lengthways

$\frac{1}{2}$ tsp toasted sesame oil

a sprinkling of toasted nori (seaweed) flakes

2 tbsp fresh cilantro (coriander) leaves

Food as Medicine

• **Carrots** are the best vegetable source of beta–carotene, which is naturally converted to vitamin A in the body. They are also a good source of chlorine and sulfur—two cleansing minerals that help promote better liver function through detoxification, thereby aiding digestion.

1 Preheat the broiler (grill) to high and line the broiler pan with foil.

2 Arrange the chicken in the pan and brush with oil. Broil (grill) for 5–6 minutes on each side until cooked through with no trace of pink in the center.

3 Meanwhile, cook the soba noodles in plenty of boiling water according to the pack instructions, then drain and refresh under cold running water. Set aside.

4 Put the hot water in a pan, add the miso paste, and stir until dissolved. Add the soy sauce, ginger, carrot, scallions, red bell pepper, and bok choy, and bring up to boiling point. Reduce the heat and simmer for 3 minutes or until the bok choy is just tender. Stir in the sesame oil.

5 Divide the noodles between two shallow bowls and spoon over the vegetables and broth. Slice the chicken breasts and place on top, sprinkle with the nori and the cilantro leaves, then serve.

health TIP

◉ **For healthy digestion** it's crucial to take your time and chew your food thoroughly before swallowing. Chewing helps to encourage saliva and enzyme production, which in turn help to partially pre-digest the food before you swallow it.

char-grilled artichoke and chickpea dip

serves 4

3½ oz/100g char-grilled artichoke hearts in oil, drained

¾ cup/100g canned chickpeas, drained and rinsed

juice of 1 small lemon

2 tbsp extra-virgin olive oil, plus extra to drizzle

1 small garlic clove, crushed

sea salt and ground black pepper

TO SERVE:

toasted slices of spelt or gluten-free bread

vegetable crudités, such as carrots, red bell pepper, baby corn, cucumber, and long-stem broccoli

1 Put the artichoke hearts, chickpeas, lemon juice, olive oil, garlic and 1 tbsp water in a blender and process until smooth and creamy. Add a little extra water if necessary—the dip should be the same consistency as hummus.

2 Spoon into a bowl and season with salt and pepper. Drizzle over some extra olive oil.

3 Serve with toasted bread and/or vegetable crudités.

Food as Medicine

• **Fennel** contains an array of phytonutrients including carotenoids, flavonoids, and phytoestrogens. It has a high fiber content and is a rich source of vitamin C. Some of its compounds act on the smooth muscle of the gut, relieving flatulence and stomach cramps. It also helps to balance stomach acid and freshen the breath.

• **Chickpeas** are a good source of protein and also contain iron, potassium, phosphorus, zinc, and folate. They are one of the best foods for fiber, particularly insoluble fiber, which is beneficial for colon health. Studies have shown it helps to regulate blood sugar.

fennel and mint salad

serves 4

4 small heads of fennel

½ mild red onion

a handful of parsley, chopped

a handful of mint, torn

sea salt and ground black pepper

2 tbsp extra virgin olive oil

2 tsp lemon juice

1 Quarter the fennel lengthways, then finely slice and put into a serving bowl. Finely chop the red onion. Taste the onion, and if it is very strong and peppery, put it in a colander and pour boiling water over, then drain. Add to the salad.

2 Mix together the olive oil and lemon juice and drizzle over the salad, toss well until combined. Sprinkle the parsley and mint over the salad, toss again, then serve.

thai marinated chicken stir-fried in chili oil

serves 4

8 boneless chicken thighs or 4 breasts

3 tsp turmeric

3 whole star anise, crushed

3 garlic cloves, crushed

2in/5cm fresh root ginger, finely sliced

grated zest of I lime or 2 kaffir limes and I tbsp lime juice

2 tbsp Thai fish sauce

I tbsp reduced-salt soy sauce

2 tbsp chili oil

I tbsp peanut (groundnut) oil

10 green beans, cut into 2in/5cm lengths (optional)

2 cups/475ml coconut milk

sliced red chilies, to serve

health TIP

○ **Whenever** possible, sit down when you eat your food, and if you are feeling stressed, avoid eating too much—especially rich, heavy meals. It is especially important to avoid gluten—present in most breads and many cereals—as well as cheese (a concentrated protein.) This is because enzyme production is greatly inhibited when you are stressed, and this will impair your gut's ability to break down your food properly.

I Put the chicken, skin side down, in a shallow non-reactive container. To marinate, rub in the turmeric, star anise, garlic, ginger, and lime zest, then sprinkle with the fish sauce, soy sauce, half the chili oil, and lime juice. Turn the chicken pieces in the mixture to coat well, cover, and leave in the refrigerator to marinate for at least I hour or preferably overnight, turning at least once.

2 When ready to cook, drain and slice the chicken into ½in/I cm strips, reserving the marinade. Heat a wok, add the peanut oil and remaining chili oil, and heat until hot, then add the chicken pieces, skin side down. Cook over a high heat for 1–2 minutes until the skin is crispy, then turn down the heat and continue cooking until browned. Turn the pieces over and brown the other side.

3 Add the beans, if using, the reserved marinade, and the coconut milk. Stir well. Bring to a boil, stirring slowly; reduce the heat and simmer for 10–15 minutes until the chicken is tender. Sprinkle with sliced red chili and serve.

4 Fragrant Thai rice and a vegetable dish would go well with the chicken.

seared chicken with tzatziki

serves 4

4 boneless, skinless chicken breasts

4 tbsp extra virgin olive oil

4 tsp dried thyme

4 tsp ground coriander

1 Bibb (Little Gem) lettuce, leaves separated

3½ oz/100g arugula (rocket) leaves

4½ oz/125g sugar snap peas, sliced diagonally

3 scallions (spring onions), thinly sliced diagonally

1 red bell pepper, seeded and sliced

10 radishes, sliced into rounds

TZATZIKI:

a handful of fresh mint leaves

scant 1 cup/200ml plain (natural) sheep's or goat's yogurt

juice of 1 lime

1 small zucchini (courgette), grated

1 garlic clove, crushed

½ tsp cumin seeds

sea salt and ground black pepper

1 To make the zucchini tzatziki, use a stick blender to blend the mint, yogurt, and lime together, then transfer to a serving bowl. Stir in the zucchini and garlic, season with salt and pepper and sprinkle with the cumin seeds. Set aside until needed.

2 Using a meat pounder or the end of a rolling pin, flatten the chicken until about ½in/1cm thick. Pour the olive oil into a large, shallow bowl and stir in the thyme and coriander. Season to taste, add the chicken, and turn until coated.

3 Heat a griddle pan over high heat. Reduce the heat a little, then griddle the chicken for 6 minutes, turning once, until cooked through and golden.

4 In the meantime, divide the lettuce and arugula among four large, shallow bowls, then top with the sugar snap peas, scallions, red bell pepper, and radishes. Slice each chicken breast diagonally and arrange on top of the salad. Spoon the zucchini tzatziki over before serving.

Food as Medicine

- **Chicken** is a complete protein, containing all the amino acids, and with good amounts of the minerals selenium and zinc, plus B vitamins. Being a white meat it is less acid-forming and is lower in saturated fat than red meats, especially organic or farm fresh (free-range) chicken.

- **Sheep's and goat's** yogurt aid digestion, because, like all fermented foods, they are rich in enzymes. In addition, they provide friendly bacteria (probiotics) in a ready-made, easily absorbable food source and so colonization of the "good" bugs in your gut is made easier.

health TIPS

● **Reduce your intake** of red meats and heavy, rich meals. Concentrated proteins and fats, such as red meat and cheese, are harder to digest, as they require more work as well as oxygen to break them down completely. We need to maintain a high oxygen level in our tissues to keep our bodies healthy. And all junk foods reduce oxygen levels, and accelerate the loss of enzyme reserves in the body.

● **If you add more fiber** to your diet to help with digestion problems, it's important that you also drink plenty of water. Adding additional fiber that you may not be used to without drinking adequate water can actually aggravate digestive problems. You need the water to soften the fiber to help it to move through the bowel.

chicken and papaya noodle box

serves 2

2 boneless, skinless chicken breasts

5oz/150g medium noodles

1 firm papaya, halved, seeded, and peeled

5in/13cm cucumber, peeled

3 large scallions (spring onions), thinly sliced diagonally

3 tbsp chopped fresh mint

3 tbsp chopped fresh cilantro (coriander)

½ red chili, seeded and thinly sliced into rounds (optional)

2 tbsp roughly chopped toasted cashew nuts

DRESSING:

1½ tbsp lime juice

1½ tbsp Thai fish sauce

1 tsp xylitol

1in/2.5cm fresh root ginger, peeled and grated

1 Preheat the broiler (grill) to high and line a broiler pan with foil. Broil (grill) the chicken breasts for 5–6 minutes on each side until cooked through. Slice into strips and let cool.

2 Meanwhile, cook the noodles in plenty of boiling water according to the pack instructions, then drain. Refresh the noodles by running them under cold running water, then leave them in the colander to drain thoroughly and cool completely.

3 To make the dressing, mix the ingredients together in a small bowl.

4 Using a vegetable peeler, shave the papaya lengthways into ribbons. Repeat with the cucumber, peeling from the outside inwards and discarding the seeds.

5 Put the cold noodles into a serving bowl and add the papaya, cucumber, scallions, herbs, and chili, if using.

6 Pour the dressing over and toss gently until combined. Top with the strips of chicken and the toasted cashew nuts.

Food as Medicine

• **Papaya** contains the enzymes papain and chymopapain. These are important for breaking down proteins into amino acids. As we age, we produce less digestive enzymes from the gut and pancreas, so eating a small amount of papaya before a protein meal will encourage proper digestion.

• **Ginger** has long been used in Ayurvedic medicine as an anti-inflammatory, and its warming action encourages blood flow. It has a powerful action in suppressing heartburn and nausea and, owing to its volatile oils, helps break down fats, thus aiding digestion. It is also an anti-flatulent and calms an upset stomach.

Food as Medicine

- **There is a huge variety** of gut conditions—from indigestion or heartburn, gas and bloating, and low or high stomach acid, to more serious problems. These include hiatus hernia (when part of the stomach pushes up through the diaphragm triggering acid reflux, pain, and indigestion, especially when lying down) or "leaky gut syndrome." To help discover a possible root cause for your problem keep an accurate, regular food diary for a month, noting the foods you have eaten and what symptoms occur afterwards. In this way, you can usually discover the culprits. Otherwise, see your doctor!

tarragon chicken with beans

serves 2

4 boneless, skinless chicken thighs, about 11oz/300g, diced

2 large leeks, rinsed and cut into chunks

2 garlic cloves, crushed

²⁄₃ cup/150ml chicken stock

grated zest and juice of ½ unwaxed lemon

1 tbsp chopped fresh tarragon, or 1 tsp dried tarragon

14oz/400g can Great Northern (cannellini) beans, drained and rinsed

6½oz/185g green beans

2 tbsp dairy-free sour cream

sea salt and ground black pepper

1 Season the chicken and dry-fry in a nonstick frying pan for 3 minutes until browned. Transfer to a flameproof Dutch oven (casserole). Add the leeks and garlic to the frying pan with 2 tbsp of the stock, and cook for 2 minutes, then tip into the Dutch oven.

2 Pour the remaining broth into the Dutch oven, and add the lemon zest and juice, tarragon, and Great Northern beans. Bring to a simmer, cover, and cook gently for 15 minutes.

3 Stir in the green beans, cover, and cook for a further 15 minutes or until the beans are tender but still have some bite. Finally, marble in the sour cream just before serving.

health TIP

○ **Tarragon** has a long tradition as an appetite stimulator. Bitters, one of its many compounds, encourage the production of digestive juices and bile, promoting better digestion. It also has natural anaesthetic properties because of its eugenol content. To aid digestion, try to sit down when you eat your meals, and chew your food thoroughly. Remember that digestion begins in your mouth and that your stomach doesn't have teeth! If you eat on the run, your digestion won't work as efficiently and, over time, you can develop what is known as a "leaky gut" which, in turn, can trigger food sensitivities.

cardamom rice pudding

serves 4

1 cup/200g brown rice

1½ cups/350ml rice or oat milk

6 cardamom pods, split

1 tsp ground cinnamon, plus extra to serve

½ tsp freshly grated nutmeg

1 tsp vanilla bean paste

2 tbsp good-quality honey, such as cold extracted or manuka, plus extra to serve

finely grated zest of 1 orange

2 large bananas, sliced

2 tbsp toasted slivered (flaked) almonds

1 Put the rice in a heavy-based pan with the milk, cardamom pods, and 1¾ cups/400ml water. Bring to a boil, then reduce the heat to the lowest setting and simmer, covered, for 25–30 minutes until the rice is tender (there should still be some liquid in the pan).

2 Remove from the heat, then stir in the cinnamon, nutmeg, vanilla, honey, and orange zest.

3 Cover the rice and let sit for 5 minutes to allow the flavors to be absorbed into the rice.

4 Spoon the rice into four serving bowls and top with the banana and slivered almonds. Sprinkle with extra ground cinnamon and drizzle with a little honey before serving.

health TIP

○ **A Chinese** proverb suggests walking 100 paces after each meal, because gentle (not aerobic!) walking after a meal greatly aids digestion. Walking encourages enzyme release and blood flow in the small intestine and thus helps to break food down more efficiently.

Food as Medicine

• **Cardamom** is called a "warm spice" in Ayurvedic medicine and has many health benefits. It contains various compounds with antioxidant properties, in addition to a number of volatile oils that display an array of anti-microbial actions. It is used as a mouth antiseptic, and to neutralize bad breath. One of its most important roles is in balancing digestion. Cardamom enhances the appetite, and its warming action works to alleviate gas, bloating, stomach cramps, and heartburn.

griddled pineapple with pistachio nuts

serves 4

1 small pineapple, unpeeled

2 tbsp virgin coconut oil, melted

1 tsp ground ginger

a handful of pistachio nuts, roughly chopped

GINGER YOGURT:

scant 1 cup/200ml strained plain (Greek) sheep's yogurt

2 balls stem ginger in syrup, drained and finely chopped

1 tsp vanilla extract

1 Cut through the whole, unpeeled pineapple to make four wedges, and cut out the core.

2 To make the ginger yogurt, mix together the yogurt, stem ginger, and vanilla in a bowl.

3 Heat a griddle pan until hot. Brush the pineapple with the coconut oil, then griddle for 2 minutes on each side until golden brown in places.

4 Serve a wedge of pineapple per person with a few spoonfuls of the ginger yogurt. Sprinkle a little ground ginger over the top and scatter with the pistachio nuts.

Food as Medicine

- **Pineapple** is a good fruit to eat prior to a meal because it contains the enzyme bromelain, which helps to break down heavy proteins, such as meats.

- **Fruit** is best eaten either on its own as a snack or before meals. This is because fruit has a fast transit time through the gut and, if mixed with other foods it can ferment, causing gas and bloating.

pineapple crush

serves 4

1 large pineapple, peeled, quartered, cored, and cut into wedges

juice of 1 lemon

TO SERVE:

ice cubes

4 passion fruit

good-quality honey, such as cold extracted or manuka, to taste

Put the pineapple through the juicer, add the lemon juice, and pour into a pitcher (jug) of ice. Stir in the flesh and seeds of 3 passion fruit and top with the remainder. Depending on the sweetness and ripeness of the pineapple, you may like to add a little honey.

chapter 6

a healthy heart

Heart disease and diseases of the arteries kill one in four men and one in six women. Strokes, angina, high blood pressure, arrhythmia, ischaemic heart disease, valvular heart disease, and heart failure all come under this umbrella. Women tend to suffer more from the effects of blood vessel disease whereas men tend to have more problems with the heart muscle itself.

Healthy arteries should have thick, muscular walls, which adapt to the pressure of blood being forced through them. Over time, however, the aging process, inappropriate diet, stress, and lifestyle choices, such as cigarette smoking, can change them to rough, inflexible and narrow "pipes." And as they become "furred up" by fatty deposits and free calcium, the blood is forced through a smaller opening. This is called atherosclerosis.

The danger comes if a piece of the fatty calcified layer, called plaque, detaches itself, or if a clot forms from the reduced blood flow, or from thick, sludgy blood, and causes an obstruction inside the coronary artery, which can lead to a heart attack. Alternatively, if the clot blocks an artery leading to the brain, a stroke can occur.

Low levels of the trace mineral silica have been linked to atherosclerosis. Silica improves the elasticity of blood vessels and may play a part in lowering blood pressure. Good sources of silica include whole grains, such as rye, rice, millet, and oats; also asparagus, lettuce, cucumber,

cabbage, parsnips, and beets (beetroot). Beet has another advantage in lowering blood pressure—it encourages nitric oxide (NO) production in blood vessels, which has a vasodilatory effect, increasing blood flow.

Studies have shown that vitamin K has the ability to help keep the calcium in your bones and not in your arteries. Vitamin K_1 is important for blood coagulation. Good sources are spinach, broccoli, Swiss chard, parsley, avocados, and kiwi fruits. As vitamin K is a fat-soluble vitamin, cooking with a good fat will enhance its absorption. Vitamin K_2 is the important form for heart protection, and is found in animal and fermented products. Good sources are sauerkraut, miso, and natto (fermented soy products) in addition to goat's or sheep's cheese.

The effects of oxidation

Arteries can also become hardened—known as arteriosclerosis—and is one of the triggers for high blood pressure. A slow build up of plaque and consequent narrowing of the artery can lead to angina, whereby less oxygen is available to the heart muscle.

Oxidation is a major problem for the blood vessels, but there are many antioxidants in our foods that can help to slow its progression. An Oxygen Radical Absorbance Capacity (ORAC) score is given to foodstuffs as a measure of their antioxidant capacity. Those with the highest score include raw unprocessed cacao, dried plums (prunes), pinto and red kidney beans, and artichoke hearts—best steamed rather than boiled to preserve their antioxidants. Another high-ORAC group of foods are the anthocyanins, such as blueberries, blackberries, pomegranates, and cranberries. Some studies have shown that this class of flavonoids may help keep veins and arteries more elastic. Vitamin E—in wheat germ, soybeans, avocados, nuts (especially pecan nuts), and seeds—helps prevent oxidation of LDL cholesterol, which partly contributes to hardening of the arteries.

The dangers of high blood pressure

In the UK more than 16 million people suffer from high blood pressure, which can trigger heart attacks and strokes, and according to The American Heart Association, one in three adults over the age of 20 (approximately 65 million people) now have high blood pressure.

An aneurysm can form from long-standing high blood pressure. This is when a weak arterial wall balloons, so blood seeps into surrounding tissues. Foods rich in bioflavonoids, are helpful, including buckwheat, rose hips, and apple peel, as well as foods high in vitamin C, such as kiwi, blueberries, cherries, and bell peppers (capsicum.)

Factors associated with high blood pressure include long-term negative stress, smoking, being overweight, lack of exercise, raised LDL cholesterol levels, HRT, oral contraceptives, diets high in saturated or altered fats, sugar, and salt, and high homocysteine levels. Scallops, oysters, clams, oily fish, mozzarella cheese, and goat's yogurt are high in vitamin B_{12}, necessary for reducing homocysteine levels in the blood. The best formula is to eat more magnesium- and potassium-rich foods (from fruit and vegetables) and less calcium and sodium. Magnesium is a smooth-muscle relaxant and will aid reducing blood pressure. Foods rich in magnesium include leafy greens, kelp, almonds, beans (black, white and soy), and halibut. Potassium-rich foods are celery, asparagus, broccoli, squash, bananas, dried apricots, and figs.

Ginger in food has a warming action on the blood vessels and may improve circulation. Garlic and onions help to thin the blood and improve circulation. Cinnamon has been shown to be effective in reducing blood clots.

Essential fatty acids reduce stickiness in the blood and lower blood pressure. Try to eat oily fish (organic if possible) three times per week. Choose from omega-3-rich salmon, mackerel, and herring. Or sprinkle flax seeds over your cereal. In addition, raw, organic coconut oil is rich in medium-chain fatty acids, which help prevent inflammation in the body—a precursor to plaque formation. Other good fats (mono-unsaturated and omega-6 polyunsaturated) can be found in virgin olive oil (best eaten cold than heated), avocados, olives, nuts, and seeds.

Eliminate table salt, which raises blood volume and attenuates NO production in blood vessels; use powdered kelp instead. Also keep your intake of caffeine, saturated fat, and alcohol to sensible amounts! A glass of red wine is beneficial, as it contains reservatrol, an antioxidant with anti-inflammatory and cholesterol-lowering properties. But drinking to excess will have the opposite effect on blood pressure. The toxic chemicals in cigarette smoke quickly oxidize blood vessels.

Unnatural fats and sugars are major problems, as chemically they do not "fit" our biochemistry. Hydrogenated and trans-fats, in particular, and sugars from high-fructose corn syrup (HFCS), as well as artificial sweeteners, are the "bad" guys.

Fiber is important for helping to control cholesterol. In addition to good vegetable and fruit fiber, eat whole grains (rich in soluble fiber,) such as quinoa, rye, rice, millet, and oats. They are also rich in B vitamins—important for keeping homocysteine levels low.

Taking sufficient and regular exercise is also essential and, together with choosing appropriate foods, will help to keep your heart, arteries, and circulation in better shape.

beet soup with lemon zest

serves 4

5 cooked beets (beetroot)

3 cups/750ml chicken or vegetable stock

sea salt and ground black pepper

TO SERVE (OPTIONAL):

¼ cup/60ml plain (natural) sheep's, goat's, or dairy-free yogurt

grated lemon zest

1 Coarsely chop 4 of the beets, then slice the other beet into matchsticks.

2 Put the chopped beets into a blender, add 2 ladlefuls of stock, and purée until smooth. Add the remaining stock and purée again. Test for thickness, adding extra stock or water if the purée is too thick. Blend again, then season to taste.

3 Serve hot or chilled, topped with a dollop of yogurt, the beet matchsticks, and grated lemon zest.

Food as Medicine

- **Rolled oats,** rich in vitamins B₁ and inositol, contain the highest content of soluble fiber of all grains and are digested slowly, controlling blood sugar and lowering LDL cholesterol. Gluten-free rolled oats are available. Although oats contain avenin, a similar protein to gluten, and may cause intolerances, they are not strictly a gluten-containing food and may be tolerated by some celiacs.

- **Sunflower or pumpkins seeds** make a nourishing and simple alternative topping for oatmeal—just add 1 tbsp. Add ½ cup/50g fresh blueberries, or a finely chopped apple and a few raisins, if you don't have time to make the plum mixture. You can also use a mix of half rice, coconut, or oat milk and half water for this oatmeal, if you prefer.

oatmeal with cinnamon plums

serves 2

¾ cup/65g old-fashioned rolled oats

1⅔ cups/400ml almond milk

a drizzle of organic maple syrup and some chopped pistachio nuts, to serve

CINNAMON PLUMS:

4 slightly firm red plums

½ cup/120ml fresh apple or orange juice

1 cinnamon stick

1 Put the oats in a pan with the milk and 1¼ cups/300ml water. Bring to a boil, then reduce the heat and simmer, part-covered, for 4–5 minutes, stirring frequently.

2 For the cinnamon plums, cut the plums into quarters, then put them into a small pan with the apple or orange juice and the cinnamon stick. Cook, covered, for 4–5 minutes over a medium-low heat until the plums are tender and the juice is reduced and thickened.

3 To serve, divide the oatmeal (porridge) between two bowls, then spoon over the plums and a little of the sauce, discarding the cinnamon. Drizzle with organic maple syrup, and add a sprinkling of pistachio nuts.

mackerel with citrus salsa

serves 2

4 mackerel fillets, about 6oz/175g each

sea salt and ground black pepper

extra-virgin olive oil, for brushing

CITRUS SALSA:

2 oranges

1 shallot, finely diced (optional)

½ mild red chili, seeded and diced (optional)

juice and zest of 1 lime

1 tbsp extra-virgin olive oil

3 tbsp chopped fresh mint

1 To make the salsa, hold an orange with its base on the chopping board. Position a small, sharp knife at the top, and cut off a strip of peel and pith. Remove the remaining peel in the same way. Cut between the segments on both sides of the membranes separating them. Dice the segments. Repeat with the second orange. Preheat the broiler (grill) to high and line a broiler pan with foil.

2 Put the oranges, shallot, chili, if using, lime juice and zest, oil, and mint into a non-metallic bowl. Stir until the ingredients are combined. Set aside to allow the flavors to mingle.

3 Slash the skin of the mackerel in a few places, then brush both sides with oil, and season. Broil (grill) for about 2 minutes on each side. Serve with spoonfuls of the citrus salsa.

Food as Medicine

- **Mackerel** is high in eicosapentaenoic acid (EPA), an omega-3 fatty acid, that helps to lower LDL cholesterol and reduce inflammation in the body. EPA benefits the heart and arteries because it acts like "antifreeze" by keeping blood platelets from sticking together and providing elasticity to blood vessels.

- **Table salt** in the form of chloride (common inorganic sodium) should not be eaten in excess, because it leads to raised blood pressure, hardening of the arteries and kidney damage. Choose a healthier form, such as powdered kelp, unrefined sea salt, or vegetable sources such as celery, parsley, spinach, or artichoke.

health TIP

○ **People with type A** blood generally have "stickier" blood and tend to suffer more circulation-related problems and hardening of the arteries. I have type A blood, and my father—who ate a poor diet, smoked, and was often angry (which thickens the blood)—died at 49 from a heart attack, but by eating more heart-healthy foods as suggested in this section, plus regular exercise, I hope to avoid a similar fate!

char-grilled scallop salad

serves 4

8oz/225g shelled green peas (fresh or frozen) or shelled fava (broad) beans

green and red salad leaves, including arugula (rocket)

8 very finely cut slices pancetta or bacon (optional)

about 20 scallops

¼ cup/60ml extra-virgin olive oil, plus extra for brushing

4 tsp lime juice

sea salt and ground black pepper

1 Microwave the peas or fava beans on hgh for 2 minutes, or boil or steam for 3–6 minutes until tender but still bright; if using frozen peas or beans, follow the pack instructions. Cool under running water, then transfer to a bowl of ice cubes and water. If using fava beans, pop them out of their gray skins, discard the skins, and reserve the beans.

2 Arrange the salad leaves on four plates.

3 Heat a griddle pan or nonstick frying pan, add the pancetta or bacon, if using, and cook until crisp and brown on both sides. Drain on paper towels. Brush the scallops with oil, add to the pan and cook over high heat for 1 minute or until browned on one side. Turn them over and brown the other side—about 1 minute. The scallops should be opaque all the way through. If not, continue cooking for about 1 minute more, or until opaque. Do not overcook or the scallops will shrink and be tough.

4 Meanwhile, divide the peas or beans and the bacon among the plates. As soon as the scallops are cooked, divide them among the plates, on top of the leaves. Pour the oil over the leaves, then sprinkle them with lime juice, salt, and pepper.

Food as Medicine

• **Scallops** are one of the best heart foods. They are high in vitamin B_{12}, necessary for converting toxic homocysteine, and they are a good source of anti-inflammatory omega-3 fatty acids. They also contain good amounts of magnesium and potassium, both of which are important for maintaining a proper heart rhythm.

• **Salads** are a tasty way to include more heart-healthy foods in your diet. Peppers, cucumber, and sea vegetables, such as kelp, contain silica in their skins (as do strawberries and cherries). Silica is important for repairing damaged tissues. Two precursors to arterial disease are oxidation and inflammation and, if left unchecked without adequate nutrients such as silica, they can lead to arterial damage.

health TIP

○ **Generally,** the larger your middle the greater the risk for heart disease—even if you have "normal" cholesterol levels. A good rule to follow is, ladies, don't allow your waist measurement to go above 35in/90cm, and gentlemen, unless you are very tall, keep your waist at no more than 39in/99cm.

fish with a tapenade crust

serves 4

1 tbsp olive oil, plus extra for greasing

1lb 2oz/500g new potatoes, scrubbed and halved, or quartered, if large

4 shallots, halved, or quartered, if large

4 thick skinless white fish fillets

4 fat garlic cloves, unpeeled

1⅓ cups/225g cherry tomatoes

TAPENADE CRUST:

⅓ cup/60g pitted black olives, rinsed

1 garlic clove, crushed

1 tsp extra-virgin olive oil

2 tbsp chopped fresh flat-leaf parsley, plus extra to garnish

1 tbsp lemon juice

sea salt and ground black pepper

1 Preheat the oven to 400°F/200°C/Gas 6. Put the olive oil in a roasting pan, add the potatoes and shallots, and turn until coated in the oil. Season and roast for 30 minutes, turning once.

2 Meanwhile, to make the tapenade crust, put the olives, garlic, and oil in a food processor and blend to a coarse paste. Transfer to a bowl, stir in the chopped parsley and lemon juice, then season to taste. Arrange the fish in a lightly oiled roasting pan and spread the tapenade over the top of each fillet.

3 When the potatoes have cooked for 30 minutes, add the garlic cloves and tomatoes to the roasting pan and put back in the oven. Put the roasting pan with the fish in the oven and roast for 15 minutes or until cooked through. Serve alongside the roasted potatoes, garlic, tomatoes, and shallots, sprinkled with extra parsley.

health TIP

○ **As low vitamin D** levels are linked to heart disease—among other health problems—it's important to expose your skin to sunshine daily for 15–20 minutes without a sunscreen, avoiding the midday sun. Your body can then produce this crucial vitamin. During the winter months take 1,000iu of vitamin D$_3$ daily.

Food as Medicine

• **Selenium and zinc** are both essential for proper growth and function of the body, but are often lacking in the diet because of soil deficiencies or the over-processing of food. They are antioxidants, protecting the body from free radical damage, slowing oxidation of LDL cholesterol and protecting blood vessels. Foods high in selenium include tuna, Brazil nuts, and lentils. Zinc is found in rye, olives, nuts, and chickpeas.

ginger chicken with sautéed spinach

serves 4

3 tbsp olive oil or virgin coconut oil

1lb 5oz/600g boneless, skinless chicken breasts, cut into bite-size pieces

6 vine-ripened tomatoes, seeded and diced

3 large garlic cloves, chopped

1in/2.5cm piece fresh root ginger, peeled and cut into thin strips

2 tsp toasted sesame oil

11oz/300g baby spinach leaves

juice of 1 lime

sea salt and ground black pepper

2 tbsp slivered (flaked) toasted almonds, to serve (optional)

health TIP

- **Meditation** helps to lower blood pressure, decreasing the production of the stress hormones adrenalin and cortisol (high levels of which can trigger heart problems). It also encourages deeper, restful sleep. Numerous research papers have shown that people who meditate regularly are up to 40 per cent less likely to die from heart disease or a stroke.

1 Heat half the olive oil in a large, nonstick sauté pan. Add half of the chicken and fry for 5 minutes until browned on all sides. Using a slotted spoon, remove from the pan and repeat with the remaining chicken.

2 Return the first batch of chicken to the pan and stir in the tomatoes, garlic, and ginger, then cook for 3 minutes, stirring occasionally.

3 Add 5 tbsp water to the pan and cook the chicken and tomatoes for another 5 minutes over medium-low heat, stirring occasionally, until the chicken is cooked through. Stir in the sesame oil and season to taste.

4 In the meantime, heat the remaining olive oil in a wok or large pan over high heat. Stir-fry the spinach for 2 minutes or until wilted, then stir in the lime juice. Heat through and season to taste.

5 Divide the spinach among serving plates and top with the chicken mixture. Scatter over the almonds, if you like.

Food as Medicine

- **Garlic and ginger** both contribute to blood vessel health. Ginger encourages improved circulation, as it has a warming action on the blood vessels, whereas garlic helps thin the blood naturally, preventing the platelets from sticking together. Garlic, with its high sulfur content, promotes liver detoxification, thereby cleansing the blood.

Food as **Medicine**

- **Asparagus** is high in potassium and magnesium as well as vitamin E. In addition, it is a rich source of folate, important for lowering toxic homocysteine levels. The smell often detected in the urine after eating asparagus is from the breakdown of the non-essential amino acid asparagine—this is a natural diuretic, removing excess salts from the body, and reducing the risk of edema.

honey-glazed salmon with asparagus

serves 2–4

2 salmon fillets, about 6oz/175g each, bones removed

10 asparagus spears, trimmed

extra-virgin olive oil, for brushing

2 tsp toasted sesame seeds, to serve

MARINADE:

1 garlic clove, sliced (optional)

2 tbsp reduced-salt soy sauce

2 tbsp good-quality honey, such as cold extracted or manuka

2 tsp toasted sesame oil

1 tsp balsamic vinegar

1 Mix together the ingredients for the marinade in a shallow non-metallic dish. Put the salmon, skin-side up, in the dish and spoon the marinade over. Cover and marinate in the refrigerator for at least 1 hour.

2 Preheat the broiler (grill) to high. Line a broiler pan with foil and put the salmon, skin-side up, on top, reserving the marinade. Broil (grill) for 3–4 minutes, then turn the fish and spoon over some of the marinade. Cook for another 3 minutes until the tops of the fillets are lightly golden and the fish is cooked through.

3 Meanwhile, heat a griddle pan and brush the asparagus with oil. Arrange the asparagus in the pan and cook for 4–5 minutes until tender.

4 Put the remaining marinade in a small pan and bring to boiling point, then reduce the heat and cook until slightly thickened and reduced.

5 Arrange the asparagus spears on two or four plates, then top with the salmon (halved if serving four). Spoon the marinade over the fish and sprinkle with the sesame seeds.

health TIP

○ **"Getting things** off your chest" can literally save your life. People who tend to be more positive, adaptable, and happy are less likely to suffer from heart disease. Whereas, regularly becoming angry—or suppressing strong emotions—can have a major impact on your health.

fish and spicy sauce

serves 4

1 medium mackerel, about
1lb 2oz (500g)

1 onion, finely chopped

5 garlic cloves, peeled and
left whole

4 large fresh red chilies,
coarsely chopped

3 tbsp Thai fish sauce

3 tbsp lemon or lime juice

1 tbsp cilantro (coriander)
leaves, finely chopped

a selection of salad and
vegetables, to serve

1 Preheat the broiler (grill). Wrap the fish in foil, leaving the top open, then put into the broiler pan and broil (grill) until thoroughly cooked through. Remove to a plate and let cool. When cool, break up the fish with your fingers to make small pieces. Discard any bones and set the flesh aside.

2 Wrap the onion, garlic, and chilies in foil, again leaving the top open, and set them under the broiler. Cook until they begin to soften.

3 Using a large mortar and pestle, pound the onion, garlic, and chilies to form a liquid paste. Stir in the fish sauce and lemon juice, then fold in the fish. Spoon into a small bowl and sprinkle with cilantro. Serve surrounded by a selection of salad and vegetables, such as crisp lettuce, radish, celery, carrot, and cucumber.

Food as **Medicine**

- **Oily fish**, such as salmon, mackerel, and sardines, are rich in omega-3 fats, which reduce inflammation. Inflammation of the arteries is the first step towards heart disease, as it creates a suitable environment for calcium and LDL cholesterol to be deposited.

- **Beet** (beetroot) encourages nitric oxide production in the blood vessels. They then dilate, as the inner lining (the endothelium) relaxes. This has the effect of increasing blood flow and lowering blood pressure.

herring with beets on sourdough rye

serves 4

8 herring fillets

extra-virgin olive oil, for brushing and drizzling

juice of 1 lemon

8 slices sourdough rye bread

8 soft lettuce leaves

2in/5cm piece cucumber, thinly sliced into
rounds

3 cooked beets (beetroot) in natural juice, diced

½ small red onion, diced

sea salt and ground black pepper

small sprigs of fresh dill, to garnish

1 Preheat the broiler (grill) to high and line the broiler pan with foil. Lightly brush the foil with oil. Arrange the herring fillets skin-side up in the pan and squeeze over half the lemon juice. Season, then broil (grill) the fish for 3–4 minutes until cooked through.

2 Meanwhile, put 2 slices of bread on each serving plate and top with a lettuce leaf and a few slices of cucumber. Mix together the beets and red onion.

3 Put a herring fillet on each slice of bread. Top with the beets and onion, squeeze over the remaining lemon juice and add a drizzle of olive oil. Serve topped with a few sprigs of dill.

thai salmon fishcakes with dipping sauce

makes about 12/serves 4

4 scallions (spring onions), sliced

½ tsp dried chili flakes (optional)

a handful of chopped fresh cilantro (coriander)

2 kaffir lime leaves, sliced

2 tsp finely chopped lemongrass

2 free-range eggs

14oz/400g canned salmon, drained, and skin and bones removed

virgin coconut oil, for frying

sea salt and ground black pepper

wedges of fresh lime, to serve

DIPPING SAUCE:

3in/7.5cm cucumber, seeded and diced

1in/2.5cm fresh root ginger, peeled and finely chopped

½ tsp xylitol

4 thin round slices of red chili (optional)

1 tbsp Thai fish sauce

juice of ½ lime

1 tbsp reduced-salt soy sauce

Food as Medicine

● **Steamed broccoli** is a perfect accompaniment to this dish. It contains magnesium, a smooth-muscle relaxant, aiding circulation and reducing blood pressure (particularly the diastolic component). Foods rich in magnesium include other vegetables high in chlorophyll, such as leafy greens, as well as kelp, almonds, beans (black, white, and soy), and halibut. Magnesium deficiency is the commonest in the Western world. Anyone who is stressed needs more magnesium-rich foods, because the adrenal glands will use up large amounts, leaving less for other organ systems, such as the heart.

1 Put the scallions, dried chili flakes, if using, cilantro, lime leaves, lemongrass, and eggs in a food processor and blend until the flavorings are finely chopped. Add the salmon, season with salt and pepper, and process briefly until the ingredients are combined; the mixture will be quite loose, but the cakes will hold together when cooked.

2 Heat 2 tbsp coconut oil in a large nonstick frying pan. Make 2 tbsp of the mixture into a fishcake and put into the pan; you will probably be able to cook three or four at a time. Fry the fishcakes for 3 minutes or until the bottom is set and golden, then carefully turn them over and cook for another 2–3 minutes.

3 Drain the fishcakes on paper towels and keep them warm. Repeat to make about 12 fishcakes. Meanwhile, mix together the ingredients for the dipping sauce in a bowl.

4 Serve three fishcakes per person with a small bowl of the dipping sauce and wedges of fresh lime. Steamed broccoli or a salad makes a good accompaniment.

Note: The fishcakes can be frozen for up to one month. Let cool thoroughly, then stack, putting a piece of baking parchment between each cake, and wrap in plastic wrap (clingfilm).

health TIPS

● **Unfortunately,** too many children today get little or no exercise, and many snack on "white" refined, high-fat and sugary foods, which eventually contribute to clogged arteries. Find ways to get children running about or being active, by playing games outside or just joining you for a walk. No matter what your age, start taking exercise every day—even if it's only a gentle walk for 30 minutes. You'll feel the benefit immediately, and children who are active feel more confident and happier about themselves.

mackerel with spiced lentils

serves 4

4 tsp harissa paste

8 mackerel fillets

SPICED LENTILS:

scant 1 1/4 cups/225g Puy or brown lentils, rinsed

3 tbsp olive oil, plus extra for brushing

1 large onion, chopped

3 garlic cloves, chopped

2 tsp cumin seeds

2 carrots, sliced

2 tsp ground coriander

1/2 tsp smoked paprika

14oz/400g can chopped tomatoes

scant 1 cup/200ml vegetable stock

7oz/200g baby spinach leaves

1 tbsp chopped fresh cilantro (coriander) (optional)

sea salt and ground black pepper

Food as Medicine

• **Celery** tastes good as a healthy snack, perhaps with hummus. It has more sodium content than any other vegetable, making it valuable for the blood and lymph. It is also high in potassium and a compound called phthalide, which helps to relax the arteries and dilate the blood vessels by blocking the stress hormones. This lowers blood pressure.

1 Spread the harissa paste over the skin of the mackerel fillets, then set them aside.

2 Put the lentils in a pan, cover with water, and bring to a boil. Turn down the heat, part-cover the pan and simmer for 25 minutes or until tender, then drain.

3 Meanwhile, heat the olive oil in a pan over a medium heat. Fry the onion for 6 minutes, stirring occasionally, until softened. Add the garlic and cumin seeds, and cook for another 1 minute.

4 Steam the carrots for 4–5 minutes until just tender. Set aside.

5 Stir the ground coriander into the onions with the smoked paprika, cooked lentils, chopped tomatoes, and stock. Bring to a boil, then turn down the heat and simmer for 10 minutes until reduced and thickened. Add the spinach to the pan and cook, covered with a lid, for 2 minutes or until wilted, then stir in the carrot. Season to taste.

6 Preheat the broiler (grill) to high and line the broiler pan with foil. Broil (grill) the mackerel, skin-side up, for 3–4 minutes until cooked.

7 Divide the lentil mixture among four serving plates, top with the mackerel, then scatter over the cilantro, if using, before serving.

celery and grape juice

serves 1–2

6 celery sticks, trimmed

about 20 seedless white grapes

1 bunch watercress or arugula (rocket) (optional)

ice cubes, to serve

Push the celery sticks into the juicer, leaf end first. Alternate with the grapes, which are very soft and difficult to push through on their own. Press through the watercress or arugula, if using, and serve plain, in glasses filled with ice, or zapped with ice cubes in a blender to produce a delicious celery-grape froth.

pomegranate squeeze

serves 2

3 pomegranates

2 oranges

ice cubes, to serve

fresh mint leaves, to decorate

Cut the pomegranates in half. Using a lemon squeezer, squeeze the juice from the pomegranates and oranges. Serve over ice and decorate with fresh mint leaves.

beet and orange juice

serves 1

1 medium beet (beetroot), trimmed and peeled, if you like

2–3 oranges

good-quality honey, such as cold extracted or manuka, to taste

Cut the beet into pieces and press through a juicer. Squeeze the oranges. Stir well, then taste, adding honey if necessary.

Note: Beet leaves are also delicious. Either juice them separately or with spinach leaves—or sauté in olive oil and serve as an accompaniment.

Food as Medicine

• **Pomegranate** seeds and juice help to reduce the formation of damaged LDL cholesterol, which clumps together to form arterial plaque and contributes to hardening of the arteries. In studies, people who ingest pomegranate regularly have been found to suffer fewer heart problems. You can buy ready-to-eat pomegranate seeds and the juice in most supermarkets. Add the seeds to fruit salads, cooked rice dishes, and summer salads. They can also be blended into fruit smoothies. Or you can take a pomegranate-concentrate capsule daily with breakfast.

fruity crumble pie

serves 4–6

3 apples, cored, pared, and diced

squeeze of lemon juice

5 dark plums, halved, pitted (stoned), and diced

½ cup/50g raisins

2 tbsp fresh apple juice

1 tsp ground cinnamon

TOPPING:

2 tbsp organic agave syrup

5 tbsp/75g butter

1¼ cups/150g old-fashioned rolled oats (porridge)

3 tbsp chopped hazelnuts

2 tbsp sunflower seeds

1 Preheat the oven to 350°F/180°C/Gas 4. Toss the apples in the lemon juice to prevent them browning and put in a 9in/23cm diameter ovenproof dish with the plums, raisins, apple juice, and cinnamon; stir well to combine.

2 To make the topping, melt the syrup and butter in a medium pan. Remove from the heat and stir in the oats, hazelnuts, and sunflower seeds.

3 Sprinkle the oat mixture over the top of the fruit. Bake for 25–30 minutes until the fruit is tender and the top is golden and beginning to crisp.

Food as Medicine

• **Apples** contain pectin, a soluble fiber that gives the fruit its structure. Pectin binds to bile salts in the small intestine, lowering LDL cholesterol. In addition, pectin keeps the bowel healthy, as it provides an excellent food source for our friendly bacteria.

• **Agave syrup** (nectar) is derived from a succulent plant. It is sweeter than sugar, but contains more fructose and is similar in composition to honey. Raw, organic agave nectar is best, as it has been extracted under a lower temperature, preserving its valuable enzymes and nutrients. See page 23 for more details.

superfood mix

serves 4

3 tbsp sunflower seeds

3 tbsp pumpkin seeds

scant ⅔ cup/75g unsulfured, ready-to-eat dried apricots, roughly chopped

½ cup/50g walnuts, roughly chopped

6 tbsp raw cacao nibs

6 tbsp goji berries

4 tbsp dry unsweetened shredded (desiccated) coconut

1 Roast the sunflower and pumpkin seeds in a dry frying pan, turning them occasionally, for 3 minutes or until starting to turn golden; leave to cool.

2 Put the seeds in a bowl with the dried apricots, walnuts, cacao nibs, goji berries, and coconut, then mix until combined. Store in an airtight container for up to two weeks.

chapter 7

healthy kidneys

Your kidneys are remarkable organs. They may only weigh a few ounces each, but if they stop functioning correctly, they must be replaced by a huge dialysis machine. Your kidneys have a number of important functions, such as filtering blood plasma, regulating salt and water balance, extracting urea, ammonium, and water-soluble toxins, and maintaining the acid–alkaline balance in the body, which is vital to good health.

About one person in nine in the Western world has chronic kidney disease (CKD). Half a million Americans have advanced kidney disease, and approximately ten million have moderate kidney disease. This is not surprising considering that one in four adults in the US have high blood pressure (a leading cause of kidney disease), coupled with increasing levels of diabetes, particularly among the young, in addition to dependence on painkillers and other prescription drugs.

Three-quarters of patients on dialysis have high levels of the toxic compound homocysteine, which is often caused by eating too much junk food without ingesting sufficient B vitamins, especially B_6, B_{12}, and folic acid. High homocysteine levels tend to increase with age and can damage blood vessels throughout the body, especially in the heart, brain, and kidneys. Good levels of vitamin B_6 are found in bell peppers, squashes, watercress, red cabbage, and cauliflower. Vitamin B_{12} can be found in salmon, flounder, sole, trout, and cod; and leafy green vegetables, leeks, lettuce, asparagus, and sunflower seeds are good sources of folic acid.

By the age of 70, the average person's kidney function might be reduced by up to two-thirds, hence why eating a balanced diet can help you to detoxify more efficiently and stay healthier!

Foods to eat or avoid

Phosphorus is a necessary mineral that is fundamental to bone health, but it is a problem in advanced kidney disease, where high levels of phosphate can block the absorption of calcium. Although excess phosphate over and above the amount the body needs is normally excreted by healthy kidneys, anyone with sub-optimal kidney function will benefit from reducing foods high in the phosphates.

Many processed foods have phosphate added to them to extend their shelf life. They may also be found in cakes, processed cheeses and meats, and fizzy (soda and cola) drinks. High levels of phosphorus naturally occur in protein foods such as meat, animal-sourced milks, cheese, eggs, and, to a lesser extent, fish. High amounts are also found in beans, particularly black-eyed peas and lima (butter) beans, nuts, chocolate, sardines, brown rice, and mushrooms, so if you suffer from kidney disease, it is best to avoid these foods, which are otherwise excellent additions to any balanced diet.

Low phosphorus foods include squashes, lemons, cucumber, lettuce, asparagus, cabbage, eggplant (aubergine), cauliflower, carrots, radishes, onions, watermelon, and apples. Potassium can also be a problem in advanced kidney disease, as the ability of the kidneys to remove it adequately may be impaired, resulting in problems with heart rhythm. Foods high in potassium include avocados, kiwi fruit, dried fruits, potatoes, bananas, oranges, animal-based milks, tomatoes, nuts, chocolate, and beans. Low-potassium foods include red bell peppers, onions, apples, cabbage, cauliflower, watermelon, blueberries, and garlic.

The kidneys function better on less animal and more plant-based protein. Consider eating more organic fish instead of red or white meat. Egg whites, quinoa, and fermented soy products, such as tofu, tamari, or miso soup, are good sources of protein. A more vegan-based diet is kidney-friendly; and reducing salt (sodium chloride) found in processed foods, will benefit kidney function.

Alleviating kidney stones

Kidney stones are another common problem. In some cases, abnormal functioning of the glands or problems with uric acid build up (as seen in gout) can be responsible. Other factors, such as dehydration, pH changes, geographical location, and water hardness, are also important.

Foods that are naturally high in purines (an organic compound that breaks down into uric acid in the body) should therefore be avoided. Purines are found in many foods, but the content will be higher in animal-based foods. Major purine foods, which should be avoided by anyone with a tendency to kidney stones, are mackerel, red meats, offal, beer, sardines, anchovies, herring, poultry, game, and scallops. Foods low in purines are celery, pineapple, lettuce, broccoli, strawberries, blueberries, raspberries, leeks, Brussels sprouts, carrots, eggplant (aubergine), and peaches. To clear uric acid build-up in the body eat cherries, cranberries, and other red and purple fruits.

You need to reduce foods high in oxalates if you have kidney stones. These are rhubarb, chocolate, spinach, oranges, black teas, grapefruit, strawberries, beets (beetroot,) peanuts, beans, concord grapes, and sweet potatoes. Foods with a low oxalate rating are flounder, plums, peaches, radishes, onions, zucchini (courgettes), water chestnuts, olive oil, honey, mangoes, grapefruits, papaya, kumquats, and pears.

If you live in a hard water area, look inside your kettle—this is how our kidneys can begin to look over time! It's not exactly limescale in your kidneys but a similar build-up generally made from phosphates, oxalates, and carbonates.

Calcium that is not properly assimilated and absorbed into the bones can be a potential problem. So if you are prone to kidney stones, avoid calcium supplements and cow's milk products, as this calcium is poorly absorbed.

Fizzy drinks are high in phosphates, which increases calcium loss from bones, as do refined carbohydrates, such as white flour and sugar.

To keep calcium in your bones and out of your kidneys, a predominantly alkaline diet is needed, which is why eating more fruit and vegetables is essential. Asparagus is excellent, as it contains an ingredient that helps to break up the stones. Other great kidney cleansers include parsley, lemons, limes, coconut water, samphire grass, kelp, cucumbers, and watermelon.

Some of the worst offenders for kidney health are refined sugars, alcohol, instant coffee, sodium-based salt, dairy (particularly cheese), potatoes, beans, tomatoes, chocolate, wheat and red meat.

Finally, keep in mind that many people suffer from kidney problems because they don't drink sufficient fluids. Increase your water intake to six to eight glasses per day. You'll need more in the summer when the body can become dehydrated. Remember, everything in moderation—it's usually the foods that you crave and eat every day that tend to trigger many of your health problems.

miso and seaweed broth with noodles

serves 4

9oz/250g tofu

1¼ quarts/1.2 liters vegetable stock

1½ cups/250g diced sweet potatoes

3 tbsp miso paste

1 medium red chili, seeded and thinly sliced

2 large handfuls of young spinach

1 tsp dried nori flakes

1 tsp dried wakame flakes

7oz/200g soba noodles

1 tsp toasted sesame seeds

2 scallions (spring onions), sliced diagonally

2 tbsp chopped fresh cilantro (coriander)

1 Pat the tofu dry with kitchen paper, then cut into cubes. Heat the stock in a large pan and, when beginning to boil, add the sweet potatoes. Cook the potatoes for 5 minutes or until beginning to soften.

2 Stir in the miso paste and, when dissolved, add the chili, tofu, spinach, and dried nori and wakame flakes, then cook for another 4–5 minutes.

3 Meanwhile, cook the noodles according to the pack instructions until tender. Drain, then divide among four large, shallow bowls.

4 Pour over the miso soup and serve sprinkled with sesame seeds, scallions, and cilantro.

health TIP

○ **Vegetarians** tend to suffer fewer incidences of kidney stones than those who eat considerable amounts of red meat. This is because meat eaters tend to produce more uric acid, which can trigger kidney stones and conditions such as gout. As always, everything in moderation!

Food as Medicine

• **Kelp** and other seaweeds such as nori are high in organic sodium, which cleanses the blood and lymph, and they are a perfect food for the kidneys. High in potassium and magnesium, plus all the trace elements, this highly alkaline food reduces strain on the kidneys.

quinoa tabbouleh

serves 4

1 cup/200g quinoa

2 zucchini (courgettes), coarsely grated

4 large scallions (spring onions), thinly sliced diagonally

a handful of fresh mint leaves, chopped

a handful of fresh flat-leaf parsley leaves, chopped

a handful of fresh cilantro (coriander) leaves, chopped

2oz/50g sugar snap peas, thinly sliced diagonally

10 walnut halves, chopped

DRESSING:

6 tbsp extra-virgin olive oil

juice of ½ lemon

2 tsp Dijon mustard

1 large garlic clove, crushed

sea salt and ground black pepper

Food as Medicine

- **Tabbouleh** is a very healthy salad, especially when made with quinoa instead of the traditional bulgur wheat, because quinoa is easier to digest. Parsley is a great kidney cleanser whereas scallions (spring onions), mint, garlic, and zucchini (courgettes) add a host of nutrients, particularly vitamin C.

1 Put the quinoa in a pan and pour over 2 cups/475ml water. Bring to a boil, then turn down the heat to its lowest setting. Cover with a lid and simmer for 15 minutes or until the water has been absorbed and the grains are tender. Set aside, covered, for 5 minutes.

2 Transfer the quinoa to a bowl and add the zucchini, scallions, mint, parsley, cilantro, and sugar snap peas.

3 Mix together the ingredients for the dressing, then pour it over the quinoa mixture. Turn gently until combined.

4 Lightly toast the walnuts in a dry frying pan for 3–5 minutes until starting to color. Leave the walnuts to cool, then roughly chop and scatter them over the tabbouleh. Serve at room temperature.

health TIP

- **To keep your kidneys** in good shape and to help avoid developing kidney stones, it's important to drink sufficient fluids each day. Drink six glasses of water daily. Herbal tea is fine, but avoid too many fizzy drinks, as they are high in phosphorus, which can deplete the calcium from your bones!

roasted sweet potatoes with beet and carrot salad

serves 4

2lb/900g sweet potatoes, cut into wedges

1 tbsp virgin coconut oil, melted

8oz/225g spinach

sea salt

COUSCOUS:

1½ cups/250g couscous

2¼ cups/550ml boiling water

2 tbsp fresh chopped cilantro (coriander)

SPICY PEANUT SAUCE:

1 red onion, thinly sliced

1 red bird's eye chili, finely chopped

1in/2.5cm fresh root ginger, peeled and grated

1 garlic clove, crushed

1 tsp paprika

14oz/400g can chopped tomatoes

¾ cup/175ml pineapple juice

¾ cup/175ml vegetable stock or water

2 cups/225g organic peanut butter

1 tbsp tamari

BEET AND CARROT SALAD:

1¾ cups/225g grated carrots

1½ cups/175g grated raw beets (beetroot)

¼ cup/60ml lime juice

1 tbsp tamari

Food as Medicine

● **Sweet potatoes** are higher in dietary fiber than the common potato, promoting better bowel health. They are high in beta-carotene (the more orange the skin, the more beta-carotene the food contains) and vitamin C, which help protect the mucous membranes in the urinary tract against infection.

1 Preheat the oven to 400°F/200°C/Gas 6. Put the sweet potatoes on a baking sheet and sprinkle with the oil and salt. Roast for 30 minutes or until tender.

2 Meanwhile, put the couscous into a heatproof bowl and pour over the boiling water. Leave for 15 minutes in a warm place to allow the grains to absorb the liquid.

3 While the couscous is soaking, make the sauce. Put the onion, chili, ginger, garlic, and paprika in a medium pan. Cook over medium heat for 10 minutes until the onion is soft. Stir in the tomatoes, pineapple juice, stock or water, peanut butter, and tamari, and continue cooking gently for 10–15 minutes until the sauce has thickened.

4 Heat a wok or frying pan and add the spinach. Cook for 1–2 minutes until just wilted, then add the sauce and cooked sweet potatoes. Turn carefully to coat, then keep the pan warm over gentle heat.

5 To make the salad, put the carrots, beets, lime juice, and tamari in a bowl and toss well. Fluff up the couscous grains using a fork, then fork in the chopped cilantro and seasoning. Serve the salad and sweet potatoes with the couscous.

griddled vegetable salad with parmesan

serves 2

1½ tbsp balsamic vinegar

1 tbsp extra-virgin olive oil

1 large red onion, cut into 8 wedges

1 small red bell pepper, seeded and cut into 6 wedges

1 small fennel bulb, trimmed and cut into 6 wedges

10 asparagus spears, trimmed

2 zucchini (courgettes), thinly sliced lengthways

6 walnut halves, dry-toasted in a pan and broken into pieces

1oz/25g Parmesan in a piece

sea salt and ground black pepper

fresh basil leaves, to garnish

whole-wheat spelt rolls or bread, to serve

DIP:

2 tbsp plain (natural) sheep's or goat's yogurt

1 tbsp fresh pesto

1 Mix together the balsamic vinegar and oil in a shallow dish and add the vegetables. Turn the vegetables in the marinade until they are coated, then season with the salt and pepper.

2 Preheat a griddle pan over a medium heat. Arrange the onion, red bell pepper, and fennel in the pan and griddle for 7–8 minutes, turning halfway, until just tender. Remove from the pan and keep warm while you cook the remaining vegetables.

3 Arrange the asparagus and zucchini on the hot pan and griddle for 5–6 minutes, turning halfway.

4 While the vegetables are cooking, mix together the yogurt and pesto for the dip, then set aside.

5 Arrange the vegetables on a serving platter and sprinkle over the walnuts. Using a vegetable peeler, shave the Parmesan thinly, then scatter over the griddled vegetables with the basil leaves. Serve with the pesto dip and a fresh whole-wheat spelt roll or bread.

Food as Medicine

• **Asparagus** is a perfect kidney cleanser, being very alkaline, which reduces the acidity of the urine. Other good kidney cleansers include parsley, lemon, lime, coconut water, samphire, cucumber, watermelon, and seaweeds. Asparagus is also high in the antioxidant glutathione, which protects cells, especially in the liver, from free-radical damage, promoting better detoxification and thereby cleansing the blood. An efficient liver will take the burden off the kidneys—and clean blood means healthier kidneys too.

health TIPS

◉ **Much is written about cholesterol** being an important health marker, but doctors are now realizing that another vital factor is your homocysteine level. Homocysteine is a harmful compound produced in the body which is normally broken down by B vitamins, especially B_6, B_{12}, and folic acid. A high homocysteine level of 12 or above is linked to heart disease, high blood pressure, and kidney problems. As homocysteine levels tend to increase with age, help protect yourself by taking a B complex daily with food. You can use a home test kit to find your homocysteine level, available from www.yorktest.com.

green vegetable salad with hazelnut dressing

serves 4

about 12 small asparagus tips

a handful of thin green beans (untrimmed)

4 baby zucchini (courgettes), cut into thirds lengthways (optional)

4oz/115g sugar snap peas

1 cup/115g shelled green peas

4–6 very thin scallions (spring onions)

¾ cup/75g hazelnuts, dry-toasted in a pan, then lightly crushed

Parmesan cheese shavings, to serve

sea salt and ground black pepper

HAZELNUT OIL DRESSING:

3 tbsp extra-virgin olive oil

1 tbsp lemon juice

½ tsp Dijon mustard

1 tbsp hazelnut oil

Food as Medicine

- **Zucchini** (courgettes) have a high water content, making them ideal for hydrating the kidneys. They are a very alkaline vegetable and a good source of vitamin C and potassium.

1 Steam the asparagus tips, beans, zucchini, sugar snap peas, and green peas individually for 4–5 minutes until just tender, but still al dente. Transfer immediately to a bowl of ice cubes and water. This stops them cooking and sets the color. Alternatively, bring a large pan of water to a boil, then add each vegetable and blanch as above. Keep the peas until the end, and drain well before chilling.

2 To make the dressing, put the olive oil, lemon juice, mustard, hazelnut oil, and pepper in a large bowl and beat well with a fork or small whisk to form an emulsion.

3 Add the drained vegetables, one type at a time, and toss until lightly coated. Arrange the asparagus, beans, zucchini, and scallions on a serving platter or four rectangular salad plates. Add the sugar snap peas and green peas, then sprinkle with the toasted hazelnuts. Shave fresh Parmesan over the top and serve.

health TIP

- **Healthy snacks** should be incorporated into your day. Fruit smoothies are a good choice. You can add 1 tsp of non-GM lecithin granules to each portion, if you like. Lecithin helps to control the growth of gallstones as well as lowering LDL cholesterol and nourishing your brain.

sea bass with pickled japanese vegetables

serves 4

8 sea bass fillets

juice of 1 lime

2 tsp balsamic vinegar

1 garlic clove, crushed

1 long red chili, seeded and finely chopped

sea salt

1 tsp toasted sesame seeds and fresh basil leaves, to garnish

PICKLED VEGETABLES:

2 carrots, cut into ribbons

$\frac{1}{2}$ cucumber, halved and seeds scooped out, cut into ribbons

2 scallions (spring onions), finely shredded

4 tbsp rice vinegar

1 Put the sea bass, skin-side down, in a roasting dish. In a small bowl, mix together the lime juice, balsamic vinegar, garlic, and chili. Pour the mixture over the sea bass and season with salt. Cover and set aside in the refrigerator for 30 minutes.

2 To make the pickled vegetables, put the carrots, cucumber, and scallions into a small bowl. Pour the rice vinegar over the vegetables, then turn gently until combined.

3 Preheat the broiler (grill) to high and line the broiler pan with foil. Put the sea bass, skin-side up, in the broiler pan and brush with the marinade. Grill (broil) for 3–4 minutes until the skin becomes crisp.

4 Drain the pickled vegetables. Serve the sea bass on top of the vegetables, sprinkled with sesame seeds and fresh basil.

Food as Medicine

- **Cucumbers** are one of the best fruits for kidney health. They have a high water content and are rich in alkaline-forming minerals that help to regulate pH in the tissues and blood. This "cooling" food also eliminates excess uric acid, thereby reducing the likelihood of kidney stones.

health TIP

- **Therapies** such as reflexology, manual lymph drainage, skin brushing, and regular massage all encourage toxins to move out of the tissues and into the kidneys ready for excretion. Although these treatments are beneficial to health, they can cause the kidneys to be somewhat overworked for short periods, and this is why it is important to drink fluids if you have received one of these therapies.

watermelon and lime slush

serves 4

red flesh from 1 watermelon

½in/1cm fresh root ginger, peeled and grated

xylitol, to taste (for sorbet)

TO SERVE:

grated lime zest, to decorate

lime wedges (optional)

crushed ice

1 Press the melon and ginger through a juicer, then pour into a pitcher (jug) half-full of crushed ice. Serve immediately in chilled glasses decorated with lime zest and served with lime wedges, if you like, or use to make sorbet.

2 If serving as a sorbet, add xylitol to taste, then churn in an ice cream maker. Alternatively, partially freeze in freezerproof trays, then blend in a food processor and freeze again. Just before serving, crush into an icy slush.

Food as Medicine

- **Watermelons** clean the kidneys and bladder of "gravel"—small amounts of debris—and reduce levels of uric acid in the blood, lowering the risk of kidney stones forming. They are a natural diuretic, consisting of about 92 per cent water, and a good source of beta-carotene and lycopene. In addition, watermelon contains the amino acid citrulline, which relaxes blood vessels, enhancing arterial blood flow.

- **Coconut water** is isotonic, meaning that it resembles our blood plasma, because it is made of similar constituents. It contains all the necessary electrolytes and its high content of distilled water makes hydration easier. This superfood for the kidneys has also been shown to prevent and slow down the formation of stones in the bladder and kidneys.

sea trout with fresh cucumber relish

serves 4

4 large pink sea trout fillets

sea salt and ground black pepper

FRESH CUCUMBER RELISH:

1 small cucumber, very thinly sliced into rounds

2 tbsp white wine vinegar

2 tsp xylitol

2 tbsp chopped fresh dill

1 First make the cucumber relish. Put the cucumber slices in a colander and sprinkle with salt, then set aside for 15 minutes. Rinse the cucumber to remove the salt, then drain well. Mix together the vinegar, xylitol, and 2 tbsp water in a bowl until the xylitol dissolves. Add the cucumber and dill, then turn until mixed together. Season with pepper and set aside.

2 Half-fill a large sauté or frying pan with water and bring to a boil. Put the trout in the pan and return to a boil. Turn off the heat, cover with a lid, and leave the fish to cook in the hot water for 6–8 minutes—you may need to cook the fish in two batches.

3 Using a metal spatula, remove the trout from the pan, drain slightly, then put on a plate with the cucumber relish. Season to taste before serving.

parchment-baked fish with herb dressing

serves 4

4 thick skinless white fish fillets

8 lemon slices

sea salt and ground black pepper

HERB DRESSING:

a large handful of fresh flat-leaf parsley, stems discarded

2 large garlic cloves

6 tbsp extra-virgin olive oil, plus extra for greasing

1 tbsp fresh oregano

1 tsp ground cumin

large pinch of dried chili flakes

health TIP

○ **When your kidneys** are functioning correctly, your urine should be a light, straw color. If it's strong-smelling and a very dark yellow, you need to take in more fluids. Taking vitamin B_2 will turn your urine a yellowy/orange color for a short time, but this is normal.

1 Preheat the oven to 400°F/200°C/Gas 6. Put each fillet of fish in the center of a sheet of baking parchment large enough to make a package. Season and top with the lemon slices.

2 Fold over the edges of the paper to make a package, then put in a large roasting pan. Bake for 15–18 minutes, depending on the thickness of the fillets, until the fish is cooked through.

3 In the meantime, make the herb dressing. Put the parsley, garlic, oil, oregano, cumin, and chili in a cup and blend with a stick blender until the herbs are finely chopped and combined.

4 Remove the fish packages from the oven and open the paper. Remove the lemon slices, and serve the fish topped with the herb sauce.

Food as Medicine

● **Fish** is a healthier choice than meat (particularly red meat—a more concentrated, denser protein) since the kidneys function better on less animal and more plant-based protein, which reduces the breakdown of amino acids to ammonia. In addition to fish, other good sources of protein include egg whites, quinoa, or fermented soy products, such as tempeh. A vegan-based diet will take the load off the kidneys and, by removing processed foods as well, you reduce salt (sodium chloride), which further benefits kidney function.

golden coconut cookies

serves 6

virgin coconut oil, to grease

2 egg whites

4 tbsp dry unsweetened shredded (desiccated) coconut

2 tsp xylitol

poached fruit or fruit salad, to serve

1 Preheat the oven to 300°F/150°C/Gas 2. Lightly grease a baking sheet.

2 In a clean, greasefree bowl, whisk the egg whites until frothy and starting to thicken, but not stiff. Fold in the coconut and xylitol.

3 Put spoonfuls of the mixture in 2in/5cm rounds on the prepared baking sheet—you should have six.

4 Bake for 10 minutes or until starting to brown, then turn off the oven and leave for another 10 minutes to cook through. Remove from the oven and leave to cool on the baking sheet.

5 Serve the coconut cookies with poached fruit or a fruit salad.

Food as **Medicine**

• **Eggplant** (aubergine) is relatively low in phosphorus—as are cauliflower, squash, lemons, cucumber, lettuce, asparagus, cabbage, carrots, radishes, onions, watermelon, and apples. This makes it ideal for people on kidney diets. Eggplant also has a high water content, is low in nitrates, and the skin contains anthocyanins—flavonoids with antioxidant properties.

• **Pineapple** is a good food for the kidneys, as it is low in purines, which are metabolized to create uric acid and can cause kidney stones to form. Concentrations of purine are highest in meat products and lowest in plant-based foods, such as lettuce, broccoli, strawberry, blueberry, raspberry, leek, Brussels sprouts, carrot, eggplant, and peach.

eggplant and walnut dip

serves 4

1 eggplant (aubergine)

1 garlic clove, crushed

½ tsp ground cumin

1 tbsp walnut oil

1–2 tbsp lemon juice, to taste

4 walnut halves, roughly chopped

2 tbsp chopped fresh mint

salt and ground black pepper

1 Heat the broiler (grill) to high. Put the eggplant on the broiler pan and broil (grill), turning occasionally, for 20–25 minutes until the skin is blackened in places and very tender and soft inside. (Alternatively, lay the eggplant on a wire rack and cook, turning occasionally, directly over the gas burner so that the flesh is just touching.) Leave until cool enough to handle.

2 Peel off and discard the eggplant skin then finely chop the flesh. Put in a bowl and stir in the garlic, cumin, walnut oil, lemon juice, walnuts, and mint. Season to taste and serve.

roast cinnamon plums with pecan nuts

serves 4

¾ cup/175ml pineapple juice

1 tsp lemon juice

½ tsp ground cinnamon

2 cloves

1 star anise

1 tbsp pure organic maple syrup or xylitol

12 dark red plums, halved and pitted

a handful of pecan nut halves

1 cup/250ml thick plain (natural) bio yogurt

1 Preheat the oven to 400°F/200°C/Gas 6. Mix together the pineapple and lemon juice, cinnamon, cloves, star anise, and maple syrup or xylitol in a large bowl. Add the plums and turn until coated in the mixture.

2 Lift out the plums and reserve the juice. Arrange the plums, cut-side down, in a roasting pan. Bake for 30 minutes until slightly shrivelled and softened. Put the pecan nuts on a baking sheet and bake for 5 minutes until lightly golden. Remove the plums and pecan nuts from the oven.

3 Just before the plums are ready, put the pineapple juice mixture into a pan and bring to a boil. Turn down the heat and simmer for 5–8 minutes until thickened and syrupy. Remove the whole spices, then add the plums to the pineapple syrup.

4 Divide the plum mixture among four glasses. Top each serving with the yogurt. Roughly chop the pecan nuts and sprinkle over the yogurt before serving warm or cold.

Food as Medicine

• **Pecan nuts,** along with macadamia nuts, contain the highest fat content of all nuts. But these are good fats in the form of oleic acid and other monounsaturated fatty acids known for reducing LDL cholesterol levels. Pecan nuts are also high in plant sterols, calcium, magnesium, zinc, and vitamin A—necessary for protection of the mucous membranes.

• **Plums** help clear uric acid from the blood. Other red or purple fruits, such as cranberries, cherries, and red grapes, have a similar action in mobilizing uric acid, especially from the joints. Plums are also a good source of vitamin C, plus the minerals iron and potassium.

health TIP

o **In the summer,** increase your daily water quota from six to eight glasses. Distilled water works best for preventing kidney stones—this is one of the single most important things you can do to avoid developing stones and/or breaking them down if you already have them.

chapter 8

boost your immunity

Our "internal ecosystem" is the key to the health of our immune function, and so our gut needs to have the correct pH level to create a suitable environment for the "good" bacteria and enzymes that thrive there. Age, pollution, and genetics all have a role to play, but there are other ways we can boost our immunity.

Reducing stress is an important factor in a strong immune system, because negative stress suppresses the production of white blood cells—the very cells needed to keep our immune systems in good shape. A lack of sleep—even one very poor night's sleep—can lower immunity by as much as 60 percent. This is why seven to eight hours' sleep a night is crucial for your long-term health.

The immune system is basically two systems that work in tandem. The first is our innate immune system (the immune system we were born with). The second is our acquired immune system, created through vaccinations and exposure to pathogens such as viruses and bacteria. Killer cells, which form part of our innate system, are always circulating, on the lookout to destroy "foreign invaders," and our T cells respond to antigens by producing antibodies. B cells form part of our acquired immunity and respond to antigens in a similar way. As we age, our killer cells become less abundant, and this is where a healthy diet can make a huge difference.

In addition to keeping our gut flora in balance, our lymphatic system removes toxic debris, and prevents, or deals with, immune onslaughts from viruses, fungi, and bacteria.

Saturated fats thicken the lymph, and stress further constricts lymph through a tightening of our muscles and soft tissues. Sugar also severely undermines our immunity. Highly processed and refined foods full of sugar and "unhealthy" fats putrefy in the intestines, causing the toxic wastes to be absorbed back through the gut wall, ultimately adding to the congestion. Cakes, cookies, and dairy foods therefore need to be greatly reduced, and completely eliminated if your immune system is low.

The lymph system needs exercise to function correctly and depends on your breathing and movement. Research has shown that people who take regular moderate exercise daily (such as walking for 30 minutes) suffer with fewer colds and flu than those who do little or none. In addition, drinking six to eight glasses of pure filtered water daily helps to thin the lymph.

Immune-boosting foods

For a strong immune system, your diet should be high in fruits and vegetables, which are high in antioxidants and immune-boosting nutrients, and which also expel mucous. Ideally, incorporate a broad spectrum of different-colored phyto-nutrients through choosing a rainbow of foods.

Orange-colored vegetables and fruit such as papaya, squash, carrots, sweet potatoes, and mangoes are rich in beta-carotene, which protects mucous membranes. These foods convert naturally within the body to immune-boosting vitamin A.

Blue and purple foods such as blueberries, plums, and purple kale are rich in proantho-cyanidins, a potent antioxidant.

Red foods, such as tomatoes, pink grapefruit, and guava, are rich in lycopene.

Green vegetables, such as kale, broccoli, spinach, bok choy (pak choi), collards (spring greens), and pea shoots are rich in chlorophyll, which acts as a natural cleansing solvent in the lymphatic system. Green plant foods are also full of powerful antioxidants such as lutein and beta-carotene.

Sunshine is also important to our immune system, because it helps the body to manufacture Vitamin D. Research has shown a clear link between vitamin D deficiency, which is very common, and many illnesses. As well as exposing your skin to sun, eat vitamin-D rich foods, such as sardines, mackerel, salmon, herring, eel, sunflower seeds, and egg yolks.

Live yogurt (preferably from goats or sheep) can encourage better immune function in the gut, whereby the friendly bacteria can keep pathogenic bacteria in check.

Protein is also necessary for a strongly functioning immune system: choose from organic fish, turkey, chicken, or tofu. Stir-frying, baking, or steaming foods helps to maximize their nutrient content, but avoid deep-frying or boiling vegetables (unless you want to drink the water).

Zinc is the second most common mineral deficiency in the Western diet after magnesium, and is fundamental for proper immune functioning. It is found in a variety of foods, although poor soil affects the amount. Vegans are often lacking zinc. Good sources are wheat germ, tahini, oysters, pumpkin seeds, chickpeas, lamb, dark chocolate, peanuts, and Brazil nuts.

Avoid the immune suppressants

Refined, processed sugar is the single biggest immune suppressant in your diet, because sugar attaches to proteins in the body through an enzymatic process called glycosylation. This alters the integrity of many of the proteins necessary for immune function. Although glycosylation is a natural process within the body, it needs the proper glyconutrients to work, and only becomes a problem when the modern-day diet of excessive white sugar and man-made sweeteners are consumed. The body has no beneficial use for unnatural sugars and (like trans- and hydrogenated fats) it cannot utilize them correctly. Plant-based low-glycemic sugars such as xylitol and organic agave syrup are preferable.

Alcohol and cigarettes will also lower your immunity. Smokers suffer with far more colds than non-smokers, and an excess of alcohol will compromise the liver's ability to deal with the by-products of viruses and bacteria.

In fighting off colds and flu, good old home-made chicken soup (without any dairy added) can work wonders. It contains the amino acid cysteine, which helps to reduce congestion and the severity of upper respiratory diseases.

Herbs and spices can also be beneficial for the immune system. Cilantro (coriander) has been shown to inhibit the growth of a number of bacteria, and studies on curcumin, the active ingredient in turmeric, have found a reduction in gut inflammation along with anti-bacterial properties, among other benefits.

If you are able to obtain the celery-like vegetable ashitaba ("tomorrow's leaf"), which is grown in parts of China and Japan, it is a powerful antimicrobial. The unique flavonoids found in this food offer a host of immune-boosting benefits.

Finally, remember to laugh a lot, as laughter helps to boost immune function. Eat well, sleep well, keep a sense of humor, and you will be doing whatever you can to give your body a chance to live a younger life—for longer!

Food as Medicine

- **Vine-ripened foods** contain the most vitamins and minerals, because they have been allowed to mature before harvesting and this guarantees the maximum uptake of nutrients. Studies have shown that produce picked before it is ripe, then placed in cold storage or flown thousands of miles to its destination, has much lower nutritional values.

- **Raw foods** are high in enzymes that are destroyed by heat above 104°F/40°C. Many fragile minerals such as zinc are lost in the cooking process along with water-soluble vitamins such as vitamin C and B vitamins. Each day, try to eat a portion of your vegetables in their raw state—try carrots, celery, parsley, and, of course, lettuce. Some vegetables need a low heat to extract the nutrients that are bound in a complex matrix of the plant's fiber, so lightly steaming them will retain many valuable nutrients.

summer gazpacho with crisp croutons

serves 4

1 thick slice of day-old whole-wheat spelt or gluten-free bread, crusts removed

1½lb/675g (about 6) vine-ripened tomatoes

1 cucumber, cut lengthways into quarters, seeded, and cut into chunks

1 large garlic clove, sliced

1 red bell pepper, seeded and roughly chopped

10 radishes, sliced

1 tbsp extra-virgin olive oil

2 tbsp white wine vinegar

2 tbsp lemon juice

2 tsp sun-dried tomato paste

sea salt and ground black pepper

CROUTONS:

1 tbsp olive oil

2 thick slices of day-old whole-wheat spelt or gluten-free bread, crusts removed and cubed

TO SERVE:

4 hard-cooked (hard-boiled) free-range eggs, quartered

16 pitted black olives, chopped

fresh basil leaves

1 Soak the bread in water until ready to use.

2 Make a small cross-shaped cut in the base of each tomato. Put the tomatoes in a heatproof bowl and cover with boiling water. Leave for 30 seconds, then peel, seed, and chop.

3 Tear the soaked bread into pieces and put half of it in a food processor with half the tomatoes, cucumber, garlic, red bell pepper, radishes, olive oil, vinegar, lemon juice, sun-dried tomato paste, and ⅓ cup/75ml cold water. Process until puréed, then pour the soup into a pitcher (jug).

4 Put the remaining vegetables, olive oil, vinegar, lemon juice, sun-dried tomato paste, and ⅓ cup/75ml cold water into the food processor and process until chunky. (Alternatively, if you like your soup smooth, purée all the ingredients together with ⅔ cup/150ml cold water.)

5 Combine the puréed and chunky vegetables and season with salt and pepper to taste. Cover and let chill in the refrigerator for 2–3 hours.

6 Preheat the oven to 350°F/180°C/Gas 4. To make the croutons, put the oil in a small plastic bag and add the bread. Seal the bag and shake until the bread is coated in the oil. Put the bread cubes on a baking sheet and bake for 10–15 minutes until golden and crisp.

7 Pour the soup into four bowls and scatter over the croutons. Top with the quarters of hard-cooked egg and the chopped black olives. Garnish with basil leaves.

health TIP

○ **Eating healthy**, nutrient-dense foods will help your body to fend off invading viruses and bacteria. And by reducing the amount of refined sugars you ingest, you'll be greatly supporting your immune system. Ingesting too many foods containing refined sugar compromises your immune function by lowering the white blood-cell count.

chickpea, lemon, and mint soup

serves 4

3 x 14oz/400g cans chickpeas

2 garlic cloves, crushed

grated zest and juice of
2 unwaxed lemons

3 tbsp sliced fresh mint

2 tbsp extra-virgin olive oil

sea salt and ground black
pepper

1 Drain the liquid from the chickpeas into a pitcher (jug), and make up to 3 cups/750ml with water.

2 Tip 2 cans of the drained chickpeas into a food processor, add the garlic, lemon zest and juice, mint, olive oil, and enough of the chickpea liquid to blend to a purée.

3 Pour into a pan and stir in the remaining whole chickpeas and liquid. Season to taste and heat through for 5 minutes or until gently bubbling. Ladle into bowls and serve immediately.

Food as Medicine

- **Chickpeas** are one of the best sources of zinc, which is necessary for immune function, and especially for wound healing. Other good foods rich in zinc are wheat germ, tahini, oysters, pumpkin seeds, lamb, dark chocolate, and nuts, especially organic peanuts and Brazil nuts.

- **Olive oil**, specifically extra-virgin, is rich in polyphenols (antioxidants with an anti-inflammatory action). It also contains monounsaturated fatty acids, particularly oleic acid, known for its effects in reducing heart disease. Olive oil also promotes bile flow, encouraging better digestion and reducing the potential for gallstones.

spicy red vegetable soup

serves 4

¼ cup/60ml light olive oil

1 tbsp rice syrup or organic agave syrup

1 red bell pepper, chopped

2¼lb/1kg plum tomatoes, quartered

1 red onion, chopped

1 large red chili, seeded and chopped

2 garlic cloves, chopped

1 cup/250ml vegetable or chicken stock

4 slices of rye bread

2oz/50g soft goat's cheese

1 Preheat the oven to 350°F/180°C/Gas 4. Put the olive oil, syrup, bell pepper, tomatoes, onion, chili, and garlic in a roasting pan. Toss everything together and cook in the preheated oven for 2 hours, stirring often, until the vegetables are really soft and starting to turn brown.

2 Remove the vegetables from the oven. Put the stock in a pan and stir in the vegetables. Spoon the mixture, in batches, into a food processor or blender and process until smooth. Return the soup to a clean pan and cook over a low heat for a few minutes until heated through.

3 Toast the rye bread and, while it's still warm, spread the cheese over the top. Float the toast on top of the soup to serve.

health TIPS

○ **Your immune system** is hugely affected by what you eat and drink, as well as your stress levels and how much quality sleep you get. A poor night's sleep followed by a stress-filled day can suppress immune functioning by up to 60 per cent. Stress triggers the release of the stress hormones cortisol and adrenalin, which can affect your thymus gland (where important T cells needed by your immune system mature). Refined sugars and mass-produced "comfort foods" contain few, if any, nutrients, and can send your immune functioning into free fall. Eat well— be well!

white bean hummus with corn crisps

serves 4

400g/14oz can Great Northern (cannellini) beans, rinsed and drained

5 tbsp extra-virgin olive oil, plus extra for drizzling and brushing

1 large clove garlic, crushed

2–3 tsp harissa paste, to taste

1 tbsp light tahini

4 tbsp lemon juice

2 tsp sesame seeds

1 tsp dried thyme

1 tsp ground sumac

sea salt

4 small corn tortillas and vegetable crudités, to serve

Food as Medicine

• **Live yogurt** (preferably made with goat's or sheep's milk) can encourage better immune function in the gut where the friendly bacteria (usually *Lactobacillus* and *Streptococcus thermophilus*) keep pathogenic bacteria in check. So it's worth adding yogurt to dishes. The proteins from goat's and sheep's yogurt are more efficiently digested than from cow's milk products.

1 Put the beans in a food processor with the olive oil, garlic, 2 tsp harissa, the tahini, lemon juice, and 3 tbsp water. Process again until the mixture becomes a coarse purée. Season with sea salt, then taste and add more harissa and/or water, if necessary. Spoon into a bowl and drizzle over a little more oil.

2 Toast the sesame seeds in a dry frying pan for 3–5 minutes, tossing occasionally, until light golden. Combine the sesame seeds with the thyme and sumac, then sprinkle over the hummus.

3 To make the corn crisps, brush a large, nonstick frying pan with olive oil, then heat until hot. Put the tortilla in the pan and cook for 3–5 minutes until golden in places and beginning to crisp. Brush the top with more olive oil, turn the tortilla over and cook for another few minutes until golden and crisp. Remove from the pan and slice into wedges while still warm, then leave to cool and crisp up. Repeat with the remaining tortillas.

4 Serve the hummus with the corn crisps and vegetable crudités.

health TIP

● **A great way** to boost your immune system is to make sure that you are making sufficient vitamin D. As you will have seen, vitamin D is essential for good health, so always make it a priority to expose your skin to 15 minutes' sunshine daily. Avoid the midday sun and don't use a sunscreen, to encourage production of this crucial immune-protecting vitamin. In winter, take 1,000iu of vitamin D$_3$ daily.

herb, red bell pepper, and ricotta dip

Food as Medicine

• **Tender young broccoli** florets make good crudités to go with this dip. Broccoli contains chlorophyll—the "green blood" of plants. In addition to it being rich in magnesium, it is a potent cleanser of the lymphatic system, which is a fundamental part of our immune system. The lymphatic system becomes compromised by processed, denatured, sugary and fatty foods. Green vegetables are rich in chlorophyll, so also eat kale, spinach, bok choy (pak choi), collards (spring greens), pea shoots, and bean sprouts to clean the lymph.

serves 4

2 red bell peppers, seeded and each one sliced into 6 lengthways

extra-virgin olive oil, for drizzling

generous 1 cup/250g ricotta cheese

4 tbsp chopped fresh chives

a handful of fresh basil leaves

2 garlic cloves, crushed

juice of 1 small lemon

sea salt and ground black pepper

slices of whole-wheat spelt or gluten-free bread or crackers, to serve

1 Heat the oven to 400°F/200°C/Gas 6. Put the peppers on a nonstick baking sheet and brush with olive oil. Roast for 30 minutes, turning once, until tender and blackened in places. Leave to cool enough to handle, then peel off the skin and roughly chop.

2 In the meantime, put the ricotta cheese, chives, basil, garlic, and lemon juice in a blender, then process until fairly smooth and creamy. Transfer to a bowl, season with salt and pepper, and stir in the red bell pepper.

3 Drizzle a little olive oil over the top and serve spread over whole-wheat spelt or gluten-free bread or crackers. (You could also serve as a dip with vegetable crudités.)

health TIP

○ **Walking in nature** helps to lift your spirits and this, in turn, boosts your body's immune function. Regular exercise helps you to feel more positive, but if you are feeling under par and, for example, you have a sore throat, then don't exercise to excess as this can put a strain your immune system.

papaya salad with squid

serves 4

1lb/450g squid, cleaned, with tentacles separated

4 garlic cloves, peeled

3–4 small fresh red or green chilies

4 Chinese long beans or 12 green beans, chopped into 2in/5cm lengths

1lb/450g fresh green papaya, peeled, seeded, and cut into fine slivers

2 tomatoes, cut into wedges

3 tbsp Thai fish sauce

1 tbsp xylitol

3 tbsp lime juice

TO SERVE:

a selection of fresh firm raw green vegetables in season, such as iceberg lettuce, cucumber, or white cabbage

lime wedges

1 To prepare the squid tubes, slit along both sides of the tubes and open out. Put on a board soft-side up, then lightly run your knife diagonally in both directions, without cutting all the way through, to make diamond patterns. The squid will then cook evenly and curl up attractively. (Alternatively, just cut the tubes into slices.)

2 Put 2 ¾ cups/680ml water in a pan, then bring to a boil and add the squid. Simmer for 3 minutes, drain and set aside.

3 Using a large mortar and pestle, pound the garlic to a paste, then add the chilies and pound again. Add the beans, breaking them up slightly. Stir in the papaya with a spoon. Lightly pound together, then stir in the tomatoes and lightly pound again. Add the squid and mix well.

4 Add the fish sauce, xylitol, and lime juice, stirring well, then transfer to a serving bowl. Serve with fresh raw vegetables and lime wedges, using any leaves as a scoop for the spicy mixture.

Food as Medicine

- **Garlic and onions** contain allicin, a powerful antibiotic. Although the two important phytonutrients in garlic—allicin and s-allicysteine—are better preserved when eaten raw, enough of these active ingredients remain after cooking. Garlic inhibits growth of the fungus *Candida albicans* and has been shown to be effective against many viruses, fungi, and bacteria, including salmonella and E. coli. When cooking, try to add the garlic during the last 5–10 minutes to retain as much of its health-giving benefits as possible.

health TIP

- **If an infection** becomes serious and you are prescribed antibiotics, as soon as you finish the course begin taking the healthy bacteria *Acidophilus* and *Bifidus* for at least six weeks to replenish healthy bacteria in the gut. This will help immune function.

apricot, berry, and orange juice

serves 1

8 ripe apricots, halved and pitted (stoned), then coarsely chopped

8 strawberries, hulled and halved

juice of 2 oranges

1 Remove the skins from the apricots, if you like. To do this, bring a pan of water to a boil, then blanch the apricots for about 1 minute. Pull off the skins with the back of a knife.

2 Put the apricots, strawberries, and orange juice in a blender. Blend until smooth, adding water if needed. (If the mixture is too thick, add a few ice cubes and blend again.) Pour into a glass.

Food as Medicine

- **Apricots**, papaya, and mango contain an abundance of beta-carotene, an important antioxidant that protects the body's mucous-membrane linings, such as inside the nasal passages and lungs, thereby shoring-up your immune system. This is important because the nose is often the first weak entry point for invasion by microorganisms such as fungi or bacteria.

- **Chopped fresh cilantro** (coriander) can be scattered over the stew below and is beneficial for the immune system. It has been shown to inhibit the growth of a number of bacteria. Sage also has antimicrobial properties. Some spices, too, have health-giving qualities—turmeric contains curcumin, a natural antiseptic and antibiotic.

catalan chickpea stew

serves 4

2 tbsp olive oil

3 large garlic cloves, chopped

1 red bell pepper, seeded and sliced

2 zucchini (courgettes), thickly sliced

1 long red chili, seeded and thinly sliced

1 tsp dried thyme

2 long sprigs fresh rosemary

2 bay leaves

2 x 14oz/400g cans chopped tomatoes

1 tbsp tomato purée (paste)

400g/14oz can chickpeas, rinsed and drained

7oz/200g chargrilled artichokes in oil, drained

a handful of black olives

sea salt and ground black pepper

1 Heat the olive oil in a large, heavy-based pan. Fry the garlic, pepper, and zucchini for 3 minutes until softened. Add the chili, thyme, rosemary, and bay leaves, then pour in the chopped tomatoes.

2 Stir in the tomato purée and bring to a boil. Turn down the heat and simmer for 10 minutes.

3 Add the chickpeas, artichokes, and olives, and continue to simmer for another 10 minutes, stirring occasionally, until the sauce has reduced and thickened.

health TIPS

- **Blueberries, plums,** blackberries, and other purple and red fruits are very high in immune- boosting nutrients. Try blending a banana and a few raisins with the above fruits, plus 1 tbsp pumpkin seeds and a small amount of rice milk for an immune-boosting treat!

- **Learn to laugh** a lot more! Socialize with friends who are fun, and watch movies that make you laugh. Laughter helps to relax muscles and triggers the release of endorphins, the feel-good chemicals, which increase your sense of wellbeing—and that boosts your immune function!

Food as Medicine

- **Oregano** is packed with health-giving phytonutrients, including a number of powerful antioxidants and volatile oils. One of these is thymol, which studies have demonstrated is a potent antibacterial and antifungal agent. Its ORAC (oxygen radical absorbency capacity, or antioxidant capacity) shows that it is one of the highest of all plant foods.

- **Sage** makes a soothing gargle to use if you are suffering with a sore throat. Sage's antiseptic properties help to kill bacteria. Add boiling water to some fresh sage leaves and leave to cool before using. Alternatively, gargle with small amounts of diluted pure tea tree oil, but be careful not to swallow it! Both blends can also be applied topically to the throat area to help ease soreness.

roasted butternut squash risotto

serves 4

1 butternut squash (about 2lb/900g), peeled and cut into small cubes

4 tbsp olive oil

4 tbsp/50g unsalted butter

2 garlic cloves, crushed

a handful of fresh oregano leaves, finely chopped

12 sage leaves

1¼ cups/350g risotto rice, such as arborio

1¼ quarts/1.25 liters hot vegetable stock

1 tsp lemon juice

sea salt and ground black pepper

freshly grated Parmesan, to serve

1 Preheat the oven to 400°F/200°C/Gas 6. Put the squash in a baking pan and sprinkle with salt and 2 tbsp olive oil. Roast for 30 minutes or until tender.

2 Put the butter, the remaining olive oil, and the garlic in a medium pan. Cook gently for 2 minutes, then add the oregano, half the sage, and rice. Let the rice absorb the buttery juices, then stir in a ladleful of the hot stock. Stir until the stock has been absorbed, then add the remaining stock, a ladleful at a time, stirring and making sure it has been completely absorbed before adding the next. This will take 20–25 minutes. The rice should be soft with a slight bite in the center.

3 Stir in the squash and lightly mash with the back of a fork, leaving some pieces whole. Stir in the lemon juice and add salt and pepper to taste. Serve topped with freshly grated Parmesan and remaining sage leaves.

health TIP

○ **If you have** cooked food that you aren't going to eat immediately, cool it as quickly as possible (ideally within 1–2 hours) and then store it in the refrigerator. Never cool it down in the refrigerator, as this can raise the overall temperature, which will enable bacteria to grow on food already stored there.

fig, ginger, and raisin muffins

makes 12

1 cup/125g ground almonds

scant ¼ cup/40g xylitol

½ tsp gluten-free baking powder

½ tsp ground cinnamon

finely grated zest and juice of 1 orange

⅓ cup/40g raisins

generous ⅔ cup/125g ready-to-eat dried figs, stalks removed, chopped

2 balls preserved stem ginger, chopped

3 eggs

1 Preheat the oven to 350°F/180°C/Gas 4. Line a 12-cup muffin pan with paper cases.

2 In a large bowl, mix together the almonds, xylitol, baking powder, cinnamon, orange zest, and raisins until well combined.

3 Put the figs in a blender with the stem ginger, orange juice, and eggs, and blend for a few minutes to make a smooth paste.

4 Using a wooden spoon, beat the fig mixture into the almond mixture until a smooth batter. Divide the mixture among the paper cases and bake for 20–25 minutes until golden. Remove from the oven and test the muffins with a toothpick or skewer, which should come out clean if they are ready.

5 Transfer the muffins to a wire rack and leave to cool. Store in a cake tin—they will stay fresh for three to four days.

Food as Medicine

• **Figs** were one of the first cultivated plants and are a perfect food for the blood. They are alkaline-forming and rich in minerals, particularly iron, potassium, magnesium, and calcium. They are also a good source of copper and manganese, as well as the B vitamins, especially B_6, and vitamins A and C. The natural fructose/glucose in fresh figs makes them a good brain fuel. Also high in the soluble fiber pectin, figs are ideal for lowering LDL cholesterol and, combined with their natural high water content, the fiber makes them a natural, healthy laxative.

health TIP

◉ **During the winter** months, eating more "warming" easy-to-digest foods, such as soups, stews, and fruit compotes, will support your immune system. So will taking 500mg of olive leaf extract daily, which acts like nature's antibiotic, while increasing your vitamin C intake to 1g daily in divided doses—and don't forget the 1000iu of Vitamin D_3.

summer pudding

serves 4

4 cups/450g mixed fresh or frozen berries, such as raspberries, blackberries, blueberries, black currants, or mixed summer berries, thawed, if frozen

2 tbsp good-quality honey, such as cold extracted or manuka

½ cup/125ml orange juice

½ cup/125ml water

1 cinnamon stick, bruised

8–10 slices whole-wheat spelt or gluten-free bread, crusts removed

1 tsp arrowroot (optional)

TO SERVE (OPTIONAL):

¼ cup/60ml strained plain (Greek) sheep's yogurt, to serve

fresh mint sprigs, to decorate

1 If you are using fresh fruit, lightly rinse and let dry. Put the fresh or frozen berries, honey, orange juice, water, and cinnamon stick in a pan and gently simmer over low heat for 5 minutes, until the berries are plump and slightly softened. Remove from the heat and let cool. Discard the cinnamon stick.

2 Cut 6–8 slices of bread into triangles and use them to line the base and sides of a 2-cup/500ml bowl or mold. Overlap the bread so that it completely covers the bowl, leaving no gaps. Reserve the remaining 2 slices of bread to cover the top of the pudding. Spoon a little of the berry juice evenly over the bread in the bowl to moisten it. Fill the bowl with the berries, using a slotted spoon. Pack the fruit down with the back of a spoon, taking care not to squash the fruit too much. Cut the remaining 2 slices of bread into triangles. Put these on top of the fruit to make a lid. Reserve any remaining berry juice.

3 Cover the bowl with plastic wrap (clingfilm), put a small plate or saucer on top, then put weights on the plate to press it down onto the pudding. Leave in the refrigerator overnight.

4 Remove the weights, plate, and plastic wrap. Put a large plate upside down on top of the bowl. Carefully invert the bowl and plate, then gently remove the bowl.

5 Put the reserved juice in a pan and heat gently. If necessary, gently drizzle the sauce over any parts of the pudding that are not a consistent color. Blend the arrowroot, if using, with 1 tbsp water and stir into the hot juice. Keep stirring until the juice thickens and clears. Pour the sauce over the pudding. Serve with some yogurt and mint sprigs, if you like.

Food as Medicine

● **Blue and purple** foods, such as blueberries, plums, and purple kale, are rich in proanthocyanidins—a potent antioxidant that protects the body's cells against oxidation from free radicals. Oxidation and inflammation undermine the body's defenses and are the catalysts for conditions such as heart disease and cancer.

citrus and melon fruit salad with mint

serves 1

1 orange

1 wedge cantaloupe melon

6 fresh mint leaves

1 Cut a slice off the top and base of the orange, then stand it upright and slice off the peel and pith in strips. Thinly slice the orange into rounds. Put the orange slices into a shallow bowl.

2 Remove the skin from the melon and cut the flesh into bite-size chunks. Add to the orange in the bowl.

3 Sprinkle the mint leaves over the top and serve immediately.

Food as **Medicine**

● **Dried plums (prunes)** have one of the highest ORAC scores (a measure of their antioxidant value), which helps to protect cells from damage. Other fruits with high ORAC scores include blueberries, raisins, blackberries, strawberries, and raspberries. Vegetables with a high ORAC score include kale, spinach, Brussels sprouts, broccoli, and beet (beetroot).

● **Fruit** for breakfast is an ideal way to start the day. This is because, after a night's sleep, your body is in a more acidic state, owing to the metabolic "slow-down" overnight, when the body has stopped eliminating. Fruit is very alkaline, so it will kick-start your liver into action, which in turn will get your bowels moving.

prune and chestnut pots

serves 4

½ cup/100g ready-to-eat dried plums (prunes), chopped

generous 1 cup/200g chestnut purée

1 cup/250ml low-fat, thick plain (natural) bio yogurt or sheep's yogurt

1 tsp vanilla extract

2 tbsp date syrup or organic agave syrup

2 free-range egg whites

1 Put the dried plums (prunes) in a small pan and cover with ⅔ cup/150ml water. Bring to boiling point, then turn down the heat, cover with a lid and simmer for 5–7 minutes until very soft. Mash the plums with a fork until smooth, then leave to cool.

2 Blend the chestnut purée, yogurt, vanilla extract, and date syrup or agave syrup in a blender until combined, then transfer to a large bowl.

3 In a clean, grease-free bowl, whisk the egg whites until they form stiff peaks. Using a metal spoon, gently fold the egg whites into the chestnut mixture. Gently stir in the plum purée to give a swirled effect then spoon into four glasses. Chill before serving.

chapter 9

great foods for men

Many men do not take eating well and caring for their bodies seriously. They also tend to be slower in reporting health problems, yet many illnesses, such as prostate problems or bowel cancer, could be averted or alleviated if they were diagnosed earlier.

Males now outnumber women in terms of obesity, putting them at a higher risk for heart disease, late-onset diabetes, and cancers. Around one in four men in the UK is now overweight, and approximately 60 percent of men over the age of 65 are overweight, with just 18 percent of males between the ages of 36 and 50 having a healthy weight.

A great number of men take insufficient exercise, drink excessive amounts of alcohol, and eat far too many calorie-dense, fast foods with low nutrition than ever before in our history. Sadly, around half the average man's energy requirement is eaten as bread, cookies, cakes, dairy, and potatoes. Foods high in saturated and man-made fats (trans- and hydrogenated fats) as well as altered sugars (high-fructose corn syrup) and lashings of salt are exacerbating the health problems. We are now seeing more adolescent men with hardening of the arteries and high LDL cholesterol. And in their thirties and forties they are developing osteoporosis and late-onset diabetes. Liver damage in those who drink alcohol to excess is now commonplace in their twenties and thirties—and beyond.

Another problem today is that although many men take little exercise—so their bodies are not building muscle—they still eat large quantities of animal-based protein. Too much of this kind of protein is not good for health. Vegetable proteins, however, are not such a problem. So, unless you are exercising vigorously to build muscle, don't eat large portions of meat and cheese.

Exercise should be part of any man's daily routine, to keep the circulatory and lymphatic systems healthy and to strengthen the bones, keeping calcium there and not in the arteries where it may contribute to hardening. It will also build muscle, which burns fat, so it keeps you trim, fit, and looking good. It should never be underestimated how important it is to find the time for exercise. Start off by walking for 20 minutes a day and build up the time, then perhaps join an exercise class. Whatever you do, choose something that you enjoy.

The missing fats
Healthy fats, known as omega-3, 6, and 9, are often lacking in men, but our brains are made up of about 60 percent essential fats, so oily fish, rich in omega-3s should be a regular part of the diet—and they also help protect the prostate. Using olive oil in salad dressings and raw, organic coconut butter/oil for stir-frying will help protect the heart and blood vessels. Essential fats are

also needed for healthy seminal fluid. Good sources include mackerel, salmon, herring, sardines, anchovies, green-lipped mussels, flax, and hemp seeds.

Protecting the prostate

Prostate cancer is now the most common form of cancer affecting men in the UK, mostly later in life. Prostatitis is an inflammation of the prostate gland, and tends to affect younger men aged between 20 and 50, and can be acute or chronic, bacterial or nonbacterial.

Prostatic enlargement, or benign prostate hypertrophy (BPH), is common in men over the age of 65. Although there may be a natural enlargement as you age, alterations in hormonal balance linked to the environment play a part. The hormone testosterone changes to a more active form, an excess of which can cause cells in the prostate to multiply. Frequency of urination, urgency, passing urine at night, feeling of incomplete emptying, diminished flow and force of urine, painful urination, lower back pain, pain in the perineum, or discharge or blood in the sperm, are all signs that need investigating.

Lycopene, a type of carotene found in pink or red plants, vegetables, and fruits, has been shown to be effective in shrinking prostate tumors as well as lowering prostate-specific antigen (PSA) levels—a possible marker for prostate problems.

Further protective antioxidants can be found in blue, red and purple-colored fruits and vegetables. Eat acai, goji berries, blueberries, blackberries, cherries, raspberries, strawberries, persimmons, pomegranates, beets (beetroot), purple kale, and red grapes.

For general health of the prostate, certain vitamins and minerals are constantly required. One is vitamin C, found in cherries, kiwi fruit, grapefruit, strawberries, black currants, mangoes, kale, bell peppers, and lemons.

Zinc and selenium are two important minerals. There is more zinc stored in the prostate than in any other organ in the body, but the toxic mineral cadmium lowers levels of zinc in the body. Cadmium is present in the environment, and also in tobacco. Smokers have around five times the amount of cadmium in their blood as non-smokers. As cigarettes also severely deplete vitamin C, it's no wonder that smokers have a higher incidence of both prostate enlargement and prostate cancer, and men with low levels of selenium are five times more likely to develop prostate cancer.

Zinc-rich foods include pumpkin, sunflower, sesame and flax seeds, peanuts, pecan nuts, pine nuts, oysters, crab, and shellfish. Foods for selenium include halibut, cod, salmon, snapper, shrimp (prawns), tuna, lentils, Brazil nuts, sunflower seeds, mushrooms, and barley.

Vitamin E is also necessary for healthy sperm, increasing numbers and potency as well as protecting hormones against oxidation. Good sources are wheat germ, soybeans, avocados, nuts (especially pecan nuts), and seeds.

It makes sense to eat organic foods, if you can, as certain pesticides can raise levels of DHT, a hormone that can cause cells in the prostate to multiply. A number of man-made chemicals— the so-called "gender-benders" such as phthalates (plastics) and brominated flame retardants (BFRs)—mimic estrogens and have been shown to interfere with male hormones, lowering sperm counts, and are also linked to testicular cancer.

These unnatural estrogens can be offset to a degree by eating phytoestrogens, such as tofu, tempeh, miso, natto, soybeans, chickpeas, lentils, beans, and fennel. Fiber also helps to remove estrogens. Eat oats, rice bran, millet, quinoa, spelt pasta, rhubarb, figs, raspberries, avocados, kale, peas, and beans.

As well as the above dietary suggestions, you can better protect your prostate by reducing the amounts of alcohol, caffeine, refined white foods (flour and sugar), and fried foods that you consume, and cutting down on saturated fats especially red meat and cow's milk products. Enjoy some exercise to keep you fit and happy!

Food as Medicine

• **Alfalfa** has been called the "father of all foods" because its small seeds can send roots so far into the ground that they pick up a wide range of minerals. It is highly alkaline and a perfectly balanced ratio—it is made up of two and a half parts calcium (alkalizing) to one part phosphorus (which is acid forming).

• **Sesame seeds** are a good source of vitamin E, which is necessary for a healthy sperm count—increasing numbers, motility, and potency—plus protecting hormones against oxidation. Other good sources of vitamin E are wheatgerm, soybeans, avocados, nuts (especially pecan nuts), and seeds.

vietnamese shrimp rolls

serves 4

2¼oz/60g rice vermicelli noodles

16 dried rice paper wrappers, about 4in/10cm square

32 cooked, peeled jumbo shrimp (king prawns)

4 scallions (spring onions), shredded

3¼in/8cm cucumber, quartered lengthways, seeded and thinly sliced into strips

a handful of alfalfa sprouts

6 tbsp chopped fresh basil

6 tbsp chopped fresh mint

DIPPING SAUCE:

4 tbsp Thai fish sauce

2 tbsp tamari

juice of 1 lime

1 tsp xylitol

½ tsp dried chili flakes

health TIP

● **If you are one** of the tens of millions of people in the US, or 7 million people in the UK, taking statin drugs to help control your cholesterol, be aware that long-term use of these drugs can have negative side effects for many people, including muscle wasting and/or pain, memory loss, low libido, insomnia, and nerve damage. Statins block the enzyme which makes cholesterol, but this same enzyme also makes a vitamin-like substance called co-enzyme Q_{10}, which is needed to support the heart and energy production in the body. If you are taking statins, also take 150mg of CoQ_{10} daily (from most chemists and health stores) with breakfast or lunch.

1 Put the noodles in a bowl and cover with just-boiled water. Stir to separate the noodles, cover with a plate, and leave for 4 minutes or until tender. Drain, then refresh under cold running water; set aside.

2 Fill a large bowl with hot water. Carefully dunk a rice paper wrapper into the water and leave for a few seconds until soft and pliable. Lift out the wrapper and lay flat on a work surface; take care, as they easily tear.

3 Put a heaping tablespoonful of the noodles down the center of the wrapper. Top with 2 shrimp, a few shreds of scallion, some cucumber, alfalfa, basil, and mint.

4 Fold in the sides of the wrapper and roll up to make a spring-roll-shaped package. Repeat, making 16 spring rolls in total, then chill until ready to serve.

5 To make the dipping sauce, mix together all the ingredients, then pour into four small bowls. Serve four spring rolls per person accompanied by the dipping sauce.

shrimp and mango salad

serves 4

20 large, uncooked shrimp (prawns)

1 tbsp sesame seeds

1 tbsp chopped fresh cilantro (coriander)

MARINADE:

1in/2.5cm piece fresh root ginger, peeled and grated

1–2 red chilies, seeded and chopped

¼ cup/60ml lime juice

1 tbsp extra-virgin olive oil

2 tbsp reduced-salt light soy sauce

½ tsp good-quality honey, such as cold extracted or manuka

1–2 garlic cloves, crushed

MANGO SALAD:

3oz/75g bok choy (pak choi), shredded

1 large ripe mango, peeled, pitted (stoned), and chopped

generous 1 cup/65g bean sprouts

½ cucumber, chopped

1 red bell pepper, seeded and thinly sliced

1 bunch scallions (spring onions), trimmed and chopped

extra-virgin olive oil, for drizzling

ground black pepper

1 Peel the shrimp and, if necessary, discard the thin black vein that runs down the back, using a toothpick (cocktail stick). Rinse and pat dry with paper towels. Put the shrimp in a shallow dish.

2 To make the marinade, put the ginger in a bowl with the chilies, lime juice, oil, soy sauce, honey, and garlic. Mix well. Pour the marinade over the shrimp, stir, then cover. Refrigerate and let the shrimp marinate for 15–30 minutes.

3 Meanwhile, prepare the salad. Put the bok choy and mango in a serving bowl. Add the bean sprouts, cucumber, red bell pepper, scallions, and black pepper, to taste. Mix well and set aside.

4 Drain the shrimp, reserving the marinade. Heat a nonstick sauté pan or wok, add the shrimp, and cook, stirring frequently, for 2–3 minutes, or until pink. Add to the mango salad.

5 Pour the marinade into a small pan. Bring to a boil and boil for 2 minutes. Pour the marinade over the salad and toss lightly. Sprinkle with the sesame seeds and cilantro, and serve immediately.

Food as Medicine

• **Seafood is a healthy choice**, and much of it contains omega-3 essential fats, which are needed for healthy seminal fluid. In addition, being anti-inflammatory, essential fats are important for conditions such as prostatitis. Good sources include mackerel, snapper, mullet, salmon, herring, sardines, anchovies, shrimps, prawns, and green-lipped mussels (flax seeds also contain omega-3s). Raw, organic coconut oil is rich in medium-chain fatty acids, which also help prevent inflammation in the body.

flash-fried garlic and ginger shrimp

serves 4

8oz/225g uncooked large shrimp (prawns)

1 tbsp virgin coconut oil

2 garlic cloves, sliced

1 tbsp shredded fresh root ginger

1 green chili, seeded and diced

1½ cups/200g cherry tomatoes, quartered

2 tbsp roughly chopped fresh cilantro (coriander)

juice of ½ lime

sea salt and ground black pepper

1 Peel the shrimp and, if necessary, discard the thin black vein that runs down the back, using a toothpick (cocktail stick). Rinse and pat dry with kitchen towels.

2 Heat the coconut oil in a nonstick frying pan or wok. Add the garlic, ginger, and green chili, and stir-fry for 1 minute. Tip the shrimp into the pan and stir-fry for 1 minute or until they start to turn from gray to pink.

3 Add the tomatoes and seasoning, then stir-fry for a further 2 minutes or until the shrimp are cooked through and the tomatoes are beginning to collapse.

4 Remove from the heat and stir in the chopped cilantro and lime juice. Serve immediately.

Food as Medicine

• **Purple kale**, lightly steamed, would go well with this dish to add some health-giving flavonoids. These nutrients, which offer protective antioxidant benefits for the prostate, are found in blue, red, and purple-colored fruits and vegetables. Studies using pomegranate have shown promising results in reducing prostate tumors. Other foods in this category include bilberries, acai, goji berries, blueberries, blackberries, cherries, raspberries, strawberries, red grapes, persimmon, and beets.

health TIP

○ **Thinning hair** in men is generally triggered by excess dihydrotestosterone, which can be balanced by taking the herb saw palmetto (500mg daily) and 30mg of zinc. You can also buy hormone drops to help slow the thinning process. Details from trichologist Philip Kingsley at www.philipkingsley.co.uk. Rosemary helps to increase the circulation to the scalp—try massaging rosemary oil blended with almond oil firmly into the scalp at night.

roast chicken with sun-blushed tomatoes and goat's cheese

serves 4

extra-virgin olive oil, for brushing

4 boneless, skinless chicken breasts

4½ oz/130g soft goat's cheese

4 garlic cloves, thinly sliced

8 sun-blushed tomatoes in oil, drained and roughly chopped

1 tbsp lemon thyme

sea salt and ground black pepper

arugula (rocket) or watercress salad and new potatoes, to serve

health TIP

- **To discover** if you are a healthy weight, work out your body mass index (BMI). It's the ratio of your weight in kilograms (or pounds x 703) to your height in metres (or inches) squared. The easy way to do this is to use a BMI calculator on the internet. The normal BMI range is 20–25, over 25 is considered overweight, over 30 is moderately obese and over 40 is very obese! For example, a man of 1.83m/6ft weighing 80kg/176lb has a BMI of 24 —which is 80 divided by (1.83 x 1.83 = 3.34).

1 Preheat the oven to 350°F/180°C/Gas 4. Brush a roasting pan with oil. Make a slit along the length of each chicken breast and open out slightly to make a pocket. Cover a chicken breast with plastic wrap (clingfilm) and bash with a meat pounder or the end of a rolling pin to flatten slightly. Repeat with the other breasts.

2 Cut the goat's cheese into slices, then fill the chicken pockets with the garlic, sun-blushed tomatoes, lemon thyme, and goat's cheese. Secure the filling with a skewer. Put the chicken in a roasting pan, brush with olive oil, and season.

3 Roast the chicken for 18–20 minutes until cooked through and there is no trace of pink in the middle. Serve with a rocket or watercress salad and new potatoes.

beef and prune stew

serves 4

2 tbsp olive oil

1lb 14 oz/850kg braising steak, trimmed and cut into large, bite-size pieces

12 shallots, peeled and left whole, or halved if large

2 carrots, thickly sliced on the diagonal

2 large garlic cloves, sliced

1 tsp cumin seeds

2 star anise

1 cinnamon stick

1 tsp ground ginger

2 bay leaves

4 long sprigs fresh thyme

2¾ cups/650ml beef stock

juice of 1 orange

12 ready-to-eat dried plums (prunes)

1 Heat the olive oil in a large pan over high heat. Reduce the heat slightly and brown half the steak for 5 minutes, turning once. Remove from the pan with a slotted spoon, and repeat with the remaining beef.

2 Return the beef to the pan and add the shallots, carrots, and garlic, then cook for 5 minutes, stirring regularly.

3 Stir in the cumin seeds, star anise, cinnamon, ginger, bay leaves, and thyme, then add the stock, orange juice, and prunes. Bring to a boil, then part-cover the pan and simmer for 1½–2 hours, stirring occasionally, until the sauce has reduced and thickened, and the meat is tender.

Food as Medicine

• **Grass-fed organic** lean beef is an excellent source of complete protein and rich in B vitamins, iron, and zinc. Furthermore, grass-fed animals provide additional omega-3 fatty acids. Considering that half the fat content of beef is healthy monounsaturated (oleic), and that grass-fed animals have higher levels of folic acid, B_{12} and B_6, it is a good food for lowering toxic homocysteine levels.

beef and broccolini stir-fry

serves 2

6oz/175g broccolini, stalks diagonally sliced

1 tbsp virgin coconut oil

8oz/225g lean beef sirloin, thinly sliced across the grain

1 yellow bell pepper, seeded and sliced

2 garlic cloves, sliced

1in/2.5cm fresh root ginger, peeled and cut into thin matchsticks

3 tbsp orange juice

1–1½ tbsp reduced-salt soy sauce

1 tsp toasted sesame oil

ground black pepper

1 Steam the broccolini for 2 minutes, then put into a colander and refresh under cold running water.

2 Heat a wok until hot. Add the coconut oil, then, when melted, add the beef and stir-fry for 1–2 minutes until browned. Remove the beef from the wok using a slotted spoon and set aside.

3 Put the broccolini, yellow bell pepper, garlic, and ginger in the wok, and stir-fry for 2 minutes. Return the beef to the pan, stir, then pour in the orange juice, soy sauce, and sesame oil, and stir-fry for another 1 minute.

4 Season with ground black pepper and serve.

Food as Medicine

- **Lima** (butter) beans can be served as a side vegetable or added to dishes, providing protein and carbohydrate. They are an excellent source of soluble fiber, which helps remove unnatural estrogens by binding to bile and preventing re-absorption back from the bowel. This fiber also lowers cholesterol and prevents blood sugar levels rising too quickly. Lima beans are also high in the trace mineral molybdenum, which removes toxins such as sulfites from the liver.

shrimp and bean rice

serves 4

1 tbsp olive oil

1 cup/200g basmati rice

1 large onion, chopped

1 tsp ground turmeric

14oz/400g can chopped tomatoes

1 large red bell pepper, seeded and chopped

1–2 garlic cloves, chopped

2 cups/475ml chicken stock

14oz/400g can lima (butter) beans, drained and rinsed

1–2 red chilies, seeded and finely sliced

1lb/450g cooked peeled shrimp (prawns), thawed if frozen

3 tbsp fresh cilantro (coriander), coarsely chopped

sea salt and ground black pepper

1 Heat the oil in a large nonstick pan. Add the rice, onion, and turmeric, and cook over medium heat, stirring, for 2 minutes. Add the tomatoes, pepper, garlic, stock, and salt and pepper, to taste. Cover the pan with a tight-fitting lid, reduce the heat, and simmer for 15 minutes, until most of the stock has been absorbed by the rice.

2 Add the beans, chilies, and shrimp to the rice mixture and stir through gently. Replace the lid and cook for a further 3 minutes, or until the stock is absorbed and the shrimp are thoroughly warmed through. Stir in the cilantro and serve immediately.

Food as Medicine

• **Tomatoes**, especially when cooked, are high in lycopene, which is a type of carotene, or plant chemical, that gives the plant its pink or red color. Lycopene has been shown to be effective in shrinking prostate tumors as well as lowering prostate-specific antigen (PSA) levels, which are a possible marker for prostate problems. To enhance the absorbability of cooked tomatoes, add some olive oil before or after cooking. Other food sources of lycopene include guava, pink grapefruit, and goji berries.

health TIP

○ **Most men** believe that osteoporosis—brittle bones —is a women's problem, yet doctors are diagnosing brittle bones in increasing numbers of middle-aged men. Far too many men (and women) eat excessive amounts of refined carbohydrates, such as pies, cookies, cakes, and pre-packaged meals, and drink too much alcohol, fizzy drinks, and coffee—all of which are highly "acid forming." Everything we swallow, once metabolized, breaks down into either an acid or alkaline mineral-based residue, and if blood and tissues become too acid, then alkalizing minerals are withdrawn from our bones to keep a balance. The simplest way to re-alkalize your body is to eat less of the above foods while increasing green foods. See Chapters 4 and 15 for more information.

chili and ginger red snapper

serves 4

4 red snapper or mullet fillets, bones removed, skin slashed 3 times

2 tbsp virgin coconut oil

1½in/4cm piece fresh root ginger, peeled and cut into thin matchsticks

3 garlic cloves, sliced

1 long red chili, seeded and cut into long thin strips

5½oz/165g sugar snap peas

9oz/250g asparagus, trimmed

brown basmati rice, to serve

MARINADE:

1 tbsp yellow miso

1 tsp sesame oil

juice of ½ lime

2 tbsp tamari

2 tsp good-quality honey, such as cold extracted or manuka

health TIP

O **As men age**, it is common for the prostate gland to gradually enlarge. After the age of 50 or so, levels of testosterone decrease, whereas other hormones, including estrogen, increase. Older men have had a lifetime of exposure to plastics, petrochemicals, and pesticides, which all have hormone-disrupting (estrogenic-like) effects in the body, linked to hormonal cancers. This is why eating more organic foods can help to support your prostate.

1 Mix together the ingredients for the marinade in a large, shallow dish. Add the red snapper or mullet, and spoon over the marinade until coated; set aside for 1 hour.

2 Preheat the broiler (grill) to high and line the broiler pan with foil. Heat the coconut oil in a wok or nonstick frying pan. Stir-fry the ginger, garlic, and chili for 3 minutes, or until beginning to turn crisp. Using a slotted spoon, transfer the ginger mixture to a plate lined with paper towels to drain.

3 Broil (grill) the fish for 4–6 minutes, turning once and spooning over a little more marinade until opaque. Reserve any remaining marinade.

4 Meanwhile, reheat the wok and stir-fry the sugar snap peas and asparagus for 3–4 minutes or until just tender. Add the marinade and stir until the vegetables are coated.

5 Divide the vegetables among four plates and top with the red snapper. Spoon the ginger mix on top of the fish. Serve with rice.

Food as **Medicine**

• **Broccoli and fennel** are versatile and healthy vegetables to accompany dishes of all kinds. Both are good sources of phyto-estrogens (isoflavones), which block the receptor sites in the body sought by "unnatural estrogens" found in our polluted environment. Other excellent sources of these plant-based estrogens include organic tofu, tempeh, miso, natto, soybeans, chickpeas, lentils, and beans.

thai eggplant salad with seafood

serves 4

6 long, thin Japanese or Chinese eggplants (aubergines) or 3 regular eggplants

peanut (groundnut) oil, for brushing

8oz/225g peeled, cooked shrimp (prawns), or shucked oysters or shelled cooked mussels

1 bunch of fresh cilantro (coriander), chopped

THAI DRESSING:

¼ cup/30g dried shrimp

grated zest and juice of 1 lime

2 tbsp Thai fish sauce

1 lemongrass stalk, finely sliced

1 tbsp organic agave syrup

3 red chilies, seeded and chopped

1 Heat a griddle pan over medium heat until hot. Put the eggplants in a plastic bag, add the oil, then shake until well coated. Remove from the bag and add to the griddle. Cook until charred on all sides. Remove the eggplants from the griddle, then cut in half and scrape the flesh into a serving bowl. Chop it into pieces. Add the shrimp, oysters, or mussels.

2 To make the dressing, put the dried shrimp in a food processor and blend until very fine. Mix the lime zest and juice, fish sauce, lemongrass, agave syrup, chilies, and dried shrimp in a bowl, then pour this mixture over the eggplants and fresh shrimp. Top with the cilantro and serve.

health TIP

- **Men, make** regular exercise a part of your everyday regimen to keep your body weight at a healthy level. It will also protect your heart and arteries, increase your libido, reduce stress-hormone release, and help you to live a younger life for longer. Walking, swimming, weight-bearing exercises, jogging, squash, and martial arts are all great exercises for men—but avoid cycling too much, which puts pressure on the prostate. Long car journeys and too much sitting do the same—take a break and get active!

Food as **Medicine**

• **Cilantro** (coriander) is packed with phytonutrients, including B vitamins and vitamin C. It has powerful volatile oils and antioxidants, protecting cells and tissues against free-radical damage. Apart from being a good anti-inflammatory, studies have shown it to be effective in regulating blood sugar and lowering LDL cholesterol.

• **Shrimp** (prawns) are one of the best sources of the mineral selenium. Research has shown that men who have low levels of selenium are five times more likely to develop prostate cancer. Other high-selenium foods include halibut, cod, salmon, snapper, tuna, lentils, Brazil nuts, sunflower seeds, mushrooms, and barley.

shrimp and crab kedgeree

serves 4

1⅓ cups/275g brown basmati rice, rinsed

3 tbsp virgin coconut oil

1 large onion, sliced

2 large garlic cloves, chopped

1 tsp cumin seeds

2 tsp ground coriander

1 tsp turmeric

1 tsp garam masala

½ tsp dried chili flakes

1 cup/150g frozen petit pois, thawed

9oz/250g cooked peeled shrimp (prawns)

6oz/170g can white crabmeat, drained

juice of ½ lime

3 tbsp chopped fresh cilantro (coriander)

4 hard-cooked (hard-boiled) eggs, shelled and halved (optional)

sea salt and ground black pepper

2 scallions (spring onions), finely chopped, to garnish

health TIP

○ **One of the oldest** remedies to help treat an enlarged prostate is nettle! You can try either a nettle tincture—1 tsp/5ml in water twice daily—or alternatively, make some nettle tea and add a small amount of honey to sweeten it.

1 Put the rice in a medium pan and cover with a scant 2 cups/450ml water. Bring to a boil, then turn the heat down to its lowest setting, cover with a lid, and simmer for 20–25 minutes until the water has been absorbed and the rice is tender. Set aside, covered, for 5 minutes.

2 Heat the coconut oil in a large, deep sauté pan and fry the onion for 6 minutes until softened. Add the garlic and cumin seeds, and fry for a further 1 minute before adding the spices and peas.

3 Stir the rice into the spiced oil until coated, then add the shrimp, crabmeat, lime juice, and cilantro. Fold the seafood gently into the rice mixture and heat through for 2 minutes.

4 Season the rice and divide among four plates. Serve topped with the hard-cooked eggs, if using, and sprinkled with scallions.

Food as Medicine

• **Crab** is high in the mineral zinc, which is necessary for a healthy sperm count. Levels of sperm (both the quantity and quality) have been diminishing over the past two decades. There is more zinc stored in the prostate than in any other organ in the body and, next to magnesium, it is the second most common deficiency in the Western world. Other foods high in zinc include pumpkin seeds, sunflower, sesame and flax seeds, peanuts, pecan nuts, pine nuts, oysters, and shellfish.

crab and lime noodles

serves 4

7oz/200g wheat-free noodles

½ cup/70g frozen soybeans (edamame)

2 tbsp virgin coconut oil

2 red chilies, seeded and chopped

3 large garlic cloves, finely chopped

6 large scallions (spring onions), sliced diagonally

1½ in/4cm piece fresh root ginger, peeled and finely chopped

2 x 6oz/170g cans white crabmeat, drained

finely grated zest and juice of 1 large lime

3 tbsp tamari

4 tbsp chopped fresh cilantro (coriander)

1 Cook the noodles according to the pack instructions, adding the soybeans 2 minutes before the end of the cooking time.

2 Return to a boil and cook until the noodles and beans are tender. Drain, refresh under cold running water, and set aside.

3 Heat the coconut oil in a large wok or nonstick frying pan over high heat and stir-fry the chilies, garlic, scallions, and ginger for 30 seconds.

4 Add the cooked noodles, soybeans, crabmeat, lime juice and zest, tamari, and half the cilantro, then turn until combined and heated through. Serve sprinkled with the remaining cilantro.

health TIP

o **If your waist** measures more than 39in/99cm and you have a large, protruding abdomen, your major organs, such as your heart and liver, will be coated with a thick layer of yellow fat. This places you at a far greater risk for heart disease, type-2 diabetes, high blood pressure, and cholesterol, as well as gout! Even if you have what doctors term a "normal" cholesterol level, you need to greatly reduce the fat around your middle by taking more exercise, and eating sensibly and healthily.

thai-style mussels

serves 4

4½ lb/2kg mussels

1 tbsp virgin coconut oil

4 shallots, chopped

2 lemongrass stalks, peeled and center finely chopped

3 large garlic cloves, chopped

2in/5cm piece fresh root ginger, peeled and finely chopped

4 kaffir lime leaves

2 tbsp Thai fish sauce

1 cup/250ml fresh vegetable stock

4 tbsp Thai tom yam paste

juice of 1 lime

4 tbsp chopped fresh cilantro (coriander)

1 To prepare the mussels, pull off the beards and scrape off any barnacles using a short, sturdy knife, then rinse well under cold running water. Discard any mussels with broken shells or those that remain open when tapped.

2 Heat the coconut oil in a large pan and sauté the shallots, stirring, for 2 minutes. Next, add the lemongrass, garlic, ginger, and kaffir lime leaves, then cook for another 30 seconds.

3 Pour in the fish sauce and stock, and bring to a boil. Reduce the heat, stir in the tom yam paste and simmer for 3 minutes until the liquid has reduced slightly.

4 Add the mussels to the pan, cover with a tight-fitting lid, and simmer over medium heat, shaking the pan occasionally for 4–5 minutes or until the mussels open; discard any that remain closed.

5 Turn the mussels into a large colander placed over a bowl, then cover to keep warm. Carefully pour the cooking liquid back into the pan, leaving behind any sediment in the bottom of the bowl. Stir in the lime juice and cilantro, and heat through. Divide among four bowls, and pour the cooking liquid over before serving.

Food as Medicine

• **Mussels** are an ideal food for men, as they provide good amounts of all the important nutrients necessary for a healthy prostate and sperm count, notably zinc, selenium, vitamin C, and omega-3 fatty acids. In fact, mussels have the highest amount of omega-3 fatty acids of any shellfish, and they are low in omega-6 (which is over-consumed in the Western world) and saturated fats. In addition, they are a good source of protein as well as calcium, magnesium, potassium, phosphorus, and iron.

herbed crab wrap

serves 1

2 tsp plain (natural) thick sheep's yogurt

1 tsp lime juice

1in/2.5cm cucumber

1 large soft corn or wheat-free tortilla

2oz/50g canned white crabmeat, drained

¼ yellow bell pepper, seeded, and cut into thin strips

1½ tbsp chopped fresh cilantro (coriander)

sea salt and ground black pepper

arugula (rocket), to serve

1 Mix together the yogurt and lime juice in a bowl. Cut the cucumber lengthways into quarters, then cut out the seeds. Cut into thin strips.

2 Warm the tortilla in a dry frying pan, then remove from the heat.

3 Spread the lime yogurt over the tortilla, then spoon the crabmeat down the center. Arrange the strips of yellow bell pepper and cucumber over the top of the crab and sprinkle with the cilantro.

4 Season to taste, fold in the ends of the tortilla, then roll to encase the filling. Slice in half crossways and serve with a few rocket leaves.

Food as **Medicine**

- **Bell peppers** are a rich source of vitamin C, which is important for healthy seminal fluid (which mobilizes the sperm). Vitamin C is reduced during times of stress, and by cigarette smoking. Other good food sources include cherries, kiwi fruit, grapefruit, strawberries, blackcurrants, mango, and kale.

- **Mango** is rich in beta-carotene, which converts to vitamin A in the body. This important antioxidant protects delicate membranes and linings, such as the urinary tract, against oxidative damage. Other good sources of beta-carotene include carrots, squash, guava, apricots, sweet potatoes, pumpkin, cantaloupe melon, papaya, and tangerines.

mango and pineapple granita

serves 4

1 large ripe mango, halved, pitted (stoned), and flesh scooped out

1 ripe pineapple, peeled, cored, and cubed

juice of 1 orange

2 tbsp lemon juice

1 Put the mango and pineapple in a blender, then purée. Press the mixture through a sieve into a bowl, then discard any fibers left in the sieve. Stir in the orange and lemon juice.

2 Tip the mixture into a shallow freezer-proof container. Freeze the mixture for 40 minutes, then remove from the freezer and beat with a wooden spoon.

3 Repeat this process at 40-minute intervals over a 4-hour period to break the ice crystals down into small chunks. Leave to soften slightly before serving.

health TIPS

Some men eat too much animal protein, such as meat, eggs, cheese, and dairy. If you are sedentary, your body doesn't require large amounts of protein and, as it cannot be stored, if it is not utilized during exercise, it is excreted. This is more of a problem with animal proteins, rather than vegetable proteins such as beans, tofu, or quinoa. Eating excess animal proteins without adequate exercise places a greater strain on the kidneys. If you take regular exercise, however, extra protein is appropriate for maintaining and building muscles. Sensible levels of protein—choosing lean chicken, turkey, or fish, organic beef or venison, and goat and sheep products—are fine.

chapter 10

great foods for women

For all the stages a woman goes through during her lifetime, correct nutrition is fundamental for balancing hormones, not only to increase fertility, but also to ease the transition through the menopause and beyond.

These milestones in a woman's life can involve a number of hormone-related problems. Functional infertility, for example—infertility not due to any known cause—is quite common; it can be verified by a complete hormone blood screen. Approximately 30 percent of infertility is due to inadequacy in male sperm, so partners need to be checked too. A blockage of the fallopian tubes, thyroid imbalances, diabetes, and endometriosis can all be factors, yet it is worth noting that many women do conceive when they remove the stress of not being able to. Smokers are less likely to conceive, and saturated fats and alcohol interfere with hormone levels generally.

At any time of life a more "alkaline" diet is important (see also Chapter 15), but it is especially useful for any woman who wants to become pregnant. Changing from a very acid-forming diet that includes refined sugars, white flour, and other processed foods, to a more alkaline-rich diet of green leafy vegetables, fruits, almonds, good-quality honey, such as cold extracted or manuka, seeds, and whole grains, such as buckwheat and quinoa, will benefit you greatly. And keep in mind that negative stress, alcohol, and caffeine are also highly acid-forming.

Two important minerals, zinc and magnesium, that help to encourage conception are found in alkaline foods. Good sources of magnesium include halibut, lima (butter) beans, artichokes, green leafy vegetables, almonds, Brazil and cashew nuts, pine nuts, pumpkin seeds, brown rice, avocados, peanuts, dried apricots, barley, buckwheat, and kelp. For better absorption, soak grains overnight before cooking. Foods high in zinc include pumpkin, sunflower, sesame, and flax seeds, peanuts, pecan nuts, pine nuts, oysters, crab, and other shellfish. Folic acid is also essential—found in wheat germ, eggs, leafy greens, almonds, and cauliflower.

If you are feeling stressed, the body produces excess amounts of the stress hormones adrenalin and cortisol, which become toxic to the body. At such times, avoid stimulants, such as tea, coffee, cola, and chocolate, and increase quality protein, such as tofu, turkey, and quinoa.

Supporting hormones with nutrition

Hormonal changes can also be responsible for endometriosis, a condition in which there is inflammation of the lining of the uterus, fragments of which migrate to sites throughout the pelvis such as the ovaries, fallopian tubes, or bladder. The primary symptoms are painful periods and abnormal bleeding.

Since the liver cleans the blood, detoxifying the liver is important in treating most illnesses, including endometriosis. The liver needs vitamin B_6, folic acid, magnesium, and zinc to function properly. Wheat germ is a very good source of B_6 and folic acid as well as zinc—sprinkle some on your breakfast cereal. Seaweeds such as kelp provide excellent sources of magnesium, and unrefined grains such as millet are a good source of zinc. Foods high in B_6 include rabbit, pheasant, turkey, oily fish (mackerel, salmon, trout), cod, hazelnuts, bananas, watercress, and red cabbage.

An alkaline diet means more vegetarian choices, and eliminating or reducing highly acid-forming foods, such as red meat, eggs, processed foods, dairy foods, refined sugars, white flour, and caffeine. However, eat oily fish (high in omega-3 fatty acids)—herring, sardines, anchovies, green-lipped mussels—a couple of times a week. Vegetarian sources are flax and hemp seeds.

Changes later in life

The menopause denotes the cessation of menstruation. As ovarian function declines, there is a reduction in the level of estrogen and a complete cessation of progesterone. This transition usually lasts between two and five years, but it can be noticed for longer.

There has been much research into the Japanese diet where the women have fewer menopausal symptoms than women in the West. It has been shown that the natural estrogen-like plant chemicals (phyto-estrogens), called isoflavones, found in large amounts in the Japanese diet, can reduce some menopausal symptoms. Fermented soya foods such as miso, natto, and tempeh are high in these compounds. Other foods include flax seeds, lentils, chickpeas, fenugreek, sesame seeds, yams, kidney beans, alfalfa, mung beans, carrots, and whole grains.

Reduce saturated fats, sugar, alcohol, and caffeine to aid balancing hormones, because they congest the liver, reducing the quality of the blood, which is important for proper hormone function. The liver also breaks down hormones in the body.

Both soluble and insoluble fiber are particularly important, and good sources include brown rice, millet, oats, whole grains, rice bran, celeriac, beans (all types), lentils, broccoli, rhubarb, raspberries, figs, and dried plums (prunes.) The Brassica family (the leafy greens and turnips) offer protection against estrogen-sensitive cancers, such as breast and endometrial cancers.

Synthetic hormones, some of which mimic estrogen, are often found in the food chain and water supply via pesticides and herbicides. These can affect hormonal balance, so organic foods and pure filtered water are preferable.

Iron levels are commonly low in women, particularly if they have heavy menstrual bleeding. Iron-rich foods include blackstrap molasses, lentils, peas, almonds, venison, partridge, pheasant, dried fruit (especially apricots), dates, and dried plums (prunes.) Vitamin C aids absorption of iron, so eat red bell peppers, strawberries, broccoli, Brussels sprouts, cherries, black currants, kiwi fruits, persimmons, mangoes, grapefruit, and blueberries.

Hormones offer some protection against bone loss, but after the menopause there can be an increase in calcium loss from the bones. To help retain calcium and avoid osteoporosis, you need calcium, magnesium, and vitamin D from green leafy vegetables. Other foods include barley, butternut squash, tofu, most types of beans, and chickpeas, as well as goat's and sheep's milk products, sardines, salmon, sesame seeds, peas, almonds, and rhubarb. (See also Chapter 4.)

Many women now avoid exposure to the sun, and low levels of vitamin D are becoming commonplace. On sunny days, try to expose your skin for 15–30 minutes away from the midday sun without a sunscreen to recharge your reserves of vitamin D. Do not allow your skin to burn, and use a sunscreen for the remainder of the day! Foods that provide vitamin D include oily fish and sunflower seeds.

Finally, laugh a lot and enjoy regular exercise—it will help you produce more of the feel-good hormone serotonin.

baked eggs with spinach and feta

serves 4

1 tbsp olive oil

1 large onion, chopped

2 cups/150g sliced mushrooms

2 garlic cloves, chopped

1¼lb/500g baby spinach

4 large free-range eggs

generous ½ cup/130g crumbled feta cheese

ground black pepper

1 Preheat the broiler (grill) to medium-high.

2 Heat the oil in a large, nonstick frying pan over medium heat. Fry the onion for 5 minutes, stirring occasionally, then add the mushrooms and garlic, and fry for another 4–5 minutes until softened.

3 Meanwhile, steam the spinach for 2–3 minutes until wilted. Leave to drain, then squeeze out any excess water and chop. Divide among four large ramekins, and top with the onion mixture.

4 Make slight hollows in the spinach mixture to accommodate the eggs. Break the eggs into the hollows and broil (grill) for 2–3 minutes until the eggs are just set. Season with pepper and scatter over the feta cheese before serving warm.

Food as Medicine

● **Balsamic vinegar** is made from aged white grapes and has been shown to have an anti-microbial action against many different bacteria and viruses. Its polyphenol content promotes digestion by helping to break down proteins. Many people suffer from the inefficient digestion of proteins, because they have very little stomach acid, so the proteins putrefy in the gut. Balsamic vinegar, taken with meals, helps to ensure better protein absorption.

salmon, spinach, and tomato stack

serves 4

1 tbsp olive oil, plus extra to serve

4 salmon fillets, each about 5oz/150g, trimmed and bones removed

1 beefsteak tomato, thickly sliced

handful fresh basil leaves, chopped

4 handfuls of spinach leaves

1 tbsp balsamic vinegar

1 Lightly brush a griddle pan with the olive oil and then heat until sizzling hot. Add the salmon fillets to the pan, skin side down. Add the tomato slices and sprinkle with half the basil leaves. Cook for 3–4 minutes. Turn over the salmon and the tomato, and cook for a further 2–3 minutes, until the salmon is cooked through but still tender. Remove the pan from the heat.

2 Put the spinach leaves on a serving plate, top with the tomato slices and then the salmon. Drizzle with a few drops of olive oil and some balsamic vinegar, then sprinkle with the remaining chopped basil leaves. Serve immediately.

beef, bean, and radish sprout noodles

serves 4

1 tbsp balsamic vinegar

14oz/400g sirloin steaks, trimmed of any fat

11oz/300g wholewheat noodles

7oz/200g fine green beans, halved

8oz/225g shelled fava (broad) beans

4 vine-ripened tomatoes, seeded and diced

1in/2.5cm piece fresh root ginger, peeled and cut into matchsticks

6 scallions (spring onions), sliced diagonally

1 long red chili, seeded and diced

handful of radish sprouts or 10 radishes, sliced

1 tbsp toasted sesame seeds

a large handful of fresh cilantro (coriander), stems discarded

sea salt and ground black pepper

DRESSING:

4 tbsp tamari

3 tbsp extra-virgin olive oil

3 tbsp sesame oil

1 Mix together the balsamic vinegar with 1 tbsp each of the tamari and olive oil, from the dressing ingredients, in a large, shallow dish. Season with salt and pepper, then add the steaks and turn until coated.

2 Cook the noodles in plenty of boiling water according to the pack instructions, then drain and cover with cold water and set aside.

3 Steam the green beans and fava beans for 4–5 minutes or until just tender. Refresh under cold running water then gently squeeze the beans out of their gray outer shell; set aside.

4 Divide the noodles among four large, shallow bowls then scatter over the fava beans, green beans, tomatoes, ginger, scallions, and chili.

5 Mix together the ingredients for the dressing and spoon three-quarters over the noodle salad. Scatter over the radish sprouts.

6 Heat a large griddle pan over high heat. Griddle the steak for about 2 minutes on each side until the outside is seared or cooked to your liking. Leave to rest for 5 minutes, then slice.

7 Top the noodle salad with the sliced steak, spoon over the remaining dressing, then scatter over the sesame seeds and cilantro.

health TIP

- **Varicose veins** can be unsightly at any age, but by staying "regular" you can greatly avoid having them in later life. Include plenty of high-fiber foods in your diet, such as oats, flax seeds, brown rice, quinoa, prunes, apples, and figs. Drink about six glasses of water daily, and get some exercise. If you suffer with varicose veins, you can take the herbs butcher's broom and horse chestnut, plus vitamin C and the bioflavonoid rutin, daily (but not during pregnancy).

seared duck and pomegranate salad

serves 2

1 tbsp olive oil, plus a little extra for frying

5½oz/165g mini skinless duck fillets

2 tsp good-quality honey, such as cold extracted or manuka

1 tbsp reduced-salt soy sauce

2oz/50g crisp salad leaves, such as Bibb (Little Gem) lettuce, shredded

1½ tbsp lemon juice

½ pomegranate, halved

2 tbsp fresh cilantro (coriander) leaves

sea salt and ground black pepper

1 Lightly brush a large nonstick frying pan with oil. Heat the frying pan, then add the duck fillets and sear for 3 minutes, turning halfway.

2 Mix together the honey and soy sauce, and add to the frying pan. Turn the duck to coat it in the sauce and fry for another 2 minutes until golden and the meat is cooked through. Remove the duck from the frying pan and let cool slightly.

3 Arrange the salad leaves in a shallow serving bowl. Mix together 1 tbsp olive oil and the lemon juice, then pour it over the salad; toss it with your hands until the leaves are coated.

4 Arrange the duck on top of the salad greens. Remove the seeds from the pomegranate and sprinkle them over the salad, along with the cilantro leaves. Season to taste with salt and ground black pepper.

Food as Medicine

• **Duck** is a lean source of protein containing around half the saturated fat of chicken. In fact, only a third of the fat in duck is saturated (and is concentrated in the skin), and 50 per cent of its fat is healthy monounsaturated. Duck also contains higher iron levels than both chicken and turkey, and is a good source of selenium.

nori and crab rolls

serves 4

generous ¾ cup/175g sushi rice

4 tbsp rice vinegar

1 tsp xylitol

¼ tsp sea salt

6 sheets nori

4 tsp wasabi

6oz/170g can white crabmeat, drained

1 small avocado, halved, pit (stone) removed, peeled, and cut into 12 strips

2in/5cm cucumber, seeded and cut into 12 long thin strips

tamari and pickled ginger, to serve

1 Put the rice and 1¼ cups/300ml plus 1 tbsp water in a pan. Bring to a boil then turn the heat down to its lowest setting, cover with a lid, and simmer for 12–15 minutes until the water is absorbed and the rice is tender. Set aside, covered, for 5 minutes.

2 In the meantime, mix together the rice vinegar, xylitol, and sea salt, then gently stir into the rice until it is lightly coated. Spread the rice out over a large baking sheet and leave to cool.

3 Cut the nori sheets into 12 x 4in/10cm squares. Smear each square with a little wasabi and place 2 tsp rice diagonally across the center of each one. On top, lay a heaping teaspoonful of crab, then a piece of avocado and cucumber. Wet one edge of the nori and roll into a cone shape; press the edge to seal.

4 Arrange the nori rolls on a serving platter and serve with small bowls of tamari and pickled ginger.

Food as Medicine

• **Nori** is a protein-rich seaweed that could easily be classed as a super-food for women. Not only is it rich in the minerals calcium, zinc, and selenium, but it also contains vitamin C, iron, and copper. Nori also has good amounts of vitamin A (great for mucosal tissue, such as found in the gut and lungs), vitamins B_1, B_2, B_{12} (good for nerves, hair, and nails), plus the trace mineral iodine needed for healthy thyroid function. (You can also buy nori flakes as a salt replacement for fish, soup, and bean dishes.)

tofu with citrus glaze

serves 4

14oz/400g tofu

3 tbsp virgin coconut oil

cornstarch (cornflour), for coating

2 scallions (spring onions), green part only, sliced diagonally

CITRUS GLAZE:

juice of 2 fresh oranges

1 tbsp good-quality honey, such as cold extracted or manuka

3 tbsp tamari

½ tsp dried chili flakes (optional)

1 To make the glaze, mix together the orange juice, honey, tamari, and chili flakes, if using, and set aside.

2 Pat the tofu dry with paper towels and cut into ½in/1cm slices. Heat the coconut oil in a large, nonstick frying pan.

3 Dip both sides of each slice of tofu into cornstarch until lightly coated. Put in the pan and fry over medium heat for about 6 minutes, turning once, until crisp and light golden. Drain on paper towels.

4 Pour the orange juice mixture into the pan and cook over medium-low heat for 2 minutes until the liquid has reduced and thickened. Add the tofu and spoon over the citrus glaze. Warm through, then serve sprinkled with the scallions.

Food as Medicine

• **Tofu** is made from the curds of soybean milk and is a rich source of calcium, B vitamins and iron. It is a complete protein, providing all the essential amino acids in addition to being a source of isoflavones (an estrogen-like plant chemical) and is known for its beneficial effects against osteoporosis and breast cancer. Buy organic and cook before eating.

japanese tofu with basil

serves 4

14oz/400g firm tofu

4 tbsp tamari

1 tsp xylitol

1 tbsp sesame oil

2 garlic cloves, sliced

2in/5cm piece fresh root ginger, peeled and cut into matchsticks

3 scallions (spring onions), shredded

handful of fresh cilantro (coriander)

small handful of fresh basil

1 tsp sesame seeds

1 Pat the tofu dry with paper towels and cut into ½in/1cm slices. Mix together the tamari, xylitol, sesame oil, and garlic in a large, shallow dish. Add the tofu and spoon the marinade over until the tofu is coated. Leave to marinate in the refrigerator for at least 1 hour.

2 Put the tofu in a steamer lined with baking parchment (you will need a two-tiered one or cook the tofu in two batches). Sprinkle the ginger over the tofu, cover, and steam for 5 minutes until hot.

3 Arrange the tofu and ginger on a serving plate, spoon over the marinade, and sprinkle with the scallions, fresh herbs, and sesame seeds.

steak, arugula, and parmesan pasta

serves 4

4 tbsp extra-virgin olive oil

8 large shallots, halved or quartered

4 bay leaves

8 vine-ripened tomatoes, quartered

6 large garlic cloves, unpeeled

1lb/450g gluten-free spaghetti

1¼lb/500g sirloin steaks, trimmed of fat

2½oz/75g arugula (rocket) leaves

sea salt and ground black pepper

Parmesan shavings, to serve

1 Preheat the oven to 400°F/200°C/Gas 6. Put 1 tbsp the oil in a large roasting pan. Add the shallots, turn until coated in the oil, and roast for 10 minutes. Next, add the bay leaves, tomatoes, and garlic, then return to the oven for 20 minutes or until tender.

2 Meanwhile, cook the pasta in plenty of boiling salted water according to the pack instructions. Drain, reserving 3 tbsp of the cooking water.

3 Heat a large griddle pan over high heat. Brush the steaks with oil and cook in two batches for 1–2 minutes each side until golden brown on the outside but still pink in the center. Leave the meat to rest for 5 minutes before cutting into ½ in/1cm slices.

4 Squeeze the garlic out of its papery skin and chop finely. Add the garlic to the roasting pan along with the remaining oil, the pasta, reserved cooking water, arugula, and steak. Toss until combined, then season. Serve topped with shavings of Parmesan.

health TIP

- **If you are one of the** millions of busy women who have a family and who work, shop, and clean, you will almost certainly be lacking in the mineral magnesium. This is vital for healthy bones, which are 50 per cent magnesium! It is also needed to relax nerves and muscles, reduce high blood pressure, headaches, and palpitations when stressed, and it keeps blood circulating smoothly. Raw pumpkin and sunflower seeds, spinach, collards (kale leaves), salmon, and sesame seeds will all help to increase magnesium levels naturally.

venison with rosemary and apple purée

serves 4

2 tbsp extra-virgin olive oil

1 tbsp reduced-salt light soy sauce

½ tsp paprika

4 venison steaks

1 small winter (Savoy) cabbage, tough outer leaves removed, shredded

sea salt and ground black pepper

APPLE AND ROSEMARY PUREE:

3 apples, peeled, cored, and diced

2 long fresh rosemary sprigs

2 tbsp lemon juice

2 cloves

Food as Medicine

• **Venison** is not only free of antibiotics and synthetic hormones, but it is also a good source of the homocysteine-lowering B vitamins plus iron. It is lower in saturated fats than other red meats, and has been called the complete food because of its overall blend of protein, essential fats, vitamins, and minerals.

1 Mix together the olive oil, soy sauce, and paprika in a large, shallow dish. Season and mix again until combined. Lay the steaks in the dish and turn until coated. Set aside while you make the apple purée.

2 Put the apples, 1 rosemary sprig, the lemon juice, cloves, and 1¼ cups/ 300ml water in a nonstick pan. Simmer, part-covered, for 10 minutes or until the apples are very soft. Remove the rosemary and cloves. Transfer the apples to a bowl and mash them with the back of a fork until almost smooth. Finely chop the leaves of the remaining rosemary sprig and stir into the apples. Set aside until ready to serve.

3 Heat a large, nonstick frying pan and cook the venison for 2–3 minutes each side or until cooked to your liking—you may need to do this in two batches. Remove the venison and leave to rest, covered. Pour any marinade left in the bowl into the pan and heat through until reduced.

4 In the meantime, steam the cabbage for 3 minutes or until just tender but still crisp to the bite.

5 Serve the venison with the cabbage, with the apple purée on the side and any pan juices poured over the meat.

oriental shrimp omelet with sesame beans

serves 4

7oz/200g fine green beans, trimmed

2 tsp sesame oil

1 tsp lime juice

1 tsp toasted sesame seeds

4 bok choy (pak choi), halved lengthways

8 eggs

4 tsp tamari

2 tbsp virgin coconut oil

1in/2.5cm piece fresh root ginger, peeled and grated

10oz/275g cooked small, peeled shrimp

8 sprigs of fresh cilantro (coriander), leaves removed

ground black pepper

Food as Medicine

● **Sesame seeds** are the best plant source of calcium, which is concentrated in the hulls. They also contain mono- and polyunsaturated oils in addition to vitamins E and B₁, plus manganese, magnesium, iron, zinc, and copper. In addition, they are rich in lignans, a type of fiber with similar qualities to other phyto-estrogens in helping to prevent hormonal cancers.

1 Steam the green beans for 4–5 minutes or until tender. Transfer to a serving bowl, then drizzle over the sesame oil and lime juice. Sprinkle with sesame seeds. Lightly steam the bok choy, and keep the vegetables warm until ready to serve.

2 Break 2 of the eggs into a bowl and, with a fork, lightly beat with a quarter of the tamari. Season with pepper.

3 Heat a quarter of the coconut oil in a nonstick frying pan, and swirl it around to coat the base. When the oil is bubbling slightly, pour in the egg mixture and move the pan gently back and forth over the heat to distribute the egg evenly over the base.

4 Once the omelet is half cooked, loosen the base then scatter over a quarter of the ginger, shrimp, and cilantro. Using a metal spatula, fold the omelet in half to encase the filling. Warm the filling through for a minute, then slide the omelet onto a plate. Serve immediately, accompanied by the green beans and bok choy.

5 Cook the three remaining omelets in the same way.

chermoula chicken with tomato pilaff

serves 4

4 boneless, skinless chicken breasts

grated zest and juice of 1 lemon

1 tbsp extra-virgin olive oil

1 tsp ground cumin

1 tsp paprika or smoked paprika

2 garlic cloves, crushed

2 tbsp chopped fresh flat-leaf parsley

2 tbsp chopped fresh cilantro (coriander)

sea salt and ground black pepper

TOMATO PILAFF:

1 large eggplant (aubergine), cut into ½ in/1cm dice

4 ripe tomatoes, chopped

1 tsp cumin seeds

2 garlic cloves, crushed

2 tsp tomato paste (purée)

¾ cup/165g basmati rice

14oz/400g can chickpeas, rinsed and drained

1 cup/250ml boiling water

1 tsp olive oil

Food as Medicine

- **Chicken** is a good protein food, helping to balance blood sugar levels. Fish, eggs, and cooked tofu have similar qualities. If you suffer food cravings at certain times of the month due to hormonal imbalances, make the effort to eat more miso, tempeh, pumpkin, cauliflower, and broccoli. Because low blood sugar is common prior to periods, eating protein-based foods will help to balance your blood sugar for longer, as will oatmeal (porridge). If you cannot resist a sugary snack, eating pumpkin and sunflower seeds with your treat will help to slow the sugar rush, but it's always best to eat healthy snacks. Taking 150mcg of chromium daily can really help to reduce food cravings.

1 Toss the diced eggplant for the pilaf with a pinch of salt and set aside in a colander for 15 minutes to draw out the excess liquid.

2 Lightly slash the chicken breasts so that the marinade will be able to permeate the meat. In a small bowl, mix together the lemon zest and juice with the olive oil, cumin, paprika, garlic, parsley, cilantro, and seasoning. Rub into the chicken, cover, and set aside in a baking dish in a cool place while cooking the pilaff.

3 Preheat the oven to 400°F/200°C/Gas 6. Put the tomatoes, cumin seeds, garlic, tomato paste, and 2 tbsp water into a large pan and simmer rapidly for 5–6 minutes until thick and quite dry. Stir in the rice, the chickpeas, boiling water, and a pinch of salt. Bring back to a boil, stir the rice once, then cover the pan tightly and leave to simmer on the lowest heat for 20 minutes.

4 As soon as the rice is cooking, squeeze the liquid from the eggplant and pat dry on kitchen paper. Toss with the olive oil and spread out on a baking sheet. Put on the highest shelf of the oven with the dish of chicken on the shelf below. Cook for 15–18 minutes, stirring the eggplant halfway through cooking to brown evenly.

5 Stir the roasted eggplant into the tomato pilaf, then serve the chermoula chicken breasts on top. Serve with a green vegetable.

health TIPS

- **Regular weight-bearing exercise** not only helps to raise levels of DHEA, a vital anti-aging hormone, but also reduces stress, which makes symptoms and hormone imbalances worse. Also in midlife our waistlines tend to expand. Remember not to let your waist measurement go above 35in/90cm. Exercise keeps you trim and increases bone density. It also makes you feel positive and cheerful about life, and women who exercise regularly tend to suffer from fewer hot flashes.

tagliatelle with half-dried tomatoes and toasted pine nuts

serves 2

2 tbsp pine nuts

6½oz/185g tagliatelle

2 tbsp olive oil

2 garlic cloves, finely chopped

3½oz/90g half-dried tomatoes in oil (or marinated in oil, garlic, and oregano), roughly chopped

4oz/115g spinach, stalks removed and leaves thinly sliced

10 pitted black olives, halved

sea salt and ground black pepper

Parmesan shavings, to serve

1 Put the pine nuts in a dry frying pan and toast for a few minutes, turning occasionally, until light golden—keep an eye on them, as they burn easily.

2 Bring a large pan of salted water to a boil. Cook the pasta according to the pack instructions until al dente. Drain, reserving ½ cup/125ml of the cooking water.

3 Heat the olive oil in a frying pan and add the garlic, tomatoes, and spinach. Fry, stirring continuously, for 2–3 minutes until the spinach has wilted.

4 Add the olives, pasta, and reserved cooking water. Season well and toss thoroughly over low heat until heated through and combined.

5 Transfer to two plates and serve sprinkled with the Parmesan shavings, and salt and pepper to taste.

Food as **Medicine**

- **Pine nuts** (the seedlings from pine cones) are a rich source of both mono- and polyunsaturated fats, plus the amino acid arginine. This has the effect of lowering LDL cholesterol in addition to relaxing blood vessels—important for vascular health. Because of the high fat content, the seeds can go rancid quickly, so keep them in the refrigerator until ready to use.

- **Cumin** tastes good added to hummus—a healthy appetizer. Its volatile oils kickstart the digestive system into motion, activating the digestive juices. It encourages better liver detoxification, and some studies suggest it may also slow the progression of breast cancer.

oat bars

makes about 9

⅔ cup/85g raisins

3 tbsp orange juice

2½ cups/250g rolled oats (porridge oats)

⅔ cup/85g dry unsweetened shredded (desiccated) coconut

⅔ cup/85g pumpkin seeds

⅔ cup/85g sunflower seeds

⅔ cup/65g toasted pine nuts or toasted sliced (flaked) almonds

½ cup/125ml rice syrup or organic agave syrup

1 tsp vanilla extract

2 tbsp virgin coconut oil, melted

1 tbsp extra-virgin olive oil

1 Preheat the oven to 350°F/180°C/Gas 4.

2 Put the raisins in a small pan with the orange juice and heat gently for about 5 minutes until softened, then cool slightly.

3 Meanwhile, put the oats, coconut, pumpkin seeds, sunflower seeds, and pine nuts in a food processor, and process for a few seconds until roughly chopped. Tip the mixture into a large bowl and add the syrup, vanilla extract, both types of oil, and the raisins and orange juice. Stir well until combined.

4 Press the mixture into a 9in/23cm square baking pan (tin) and smooth the top, pressing down firmly into an even layer.

5 Bake for 20–25 minutes until lightly browned on top and firm to the touch. Cut into squares while still warm. When cool, store in an airtight container in a cool cupboard and eat within one week. Serve them with a fruit smoothie, if you like.

Food as Medicine

• **Oats** are rich in potassium, phosphorus, and magnesium, plus mono- and polyunsaturated fats. They are also high in the amino acid arginine, which helps to relax blood vessels. In addition, oats contain the highest content of soluble fiber of any other grain, lowering LDL cholesterol and balancing blood sugar. This makes them an all-around beneficial food for the heart. Gluten-free rolled oats are now available and, although oats generally do not contain gluten (unless they have been contaminated by other grains), many people find them easier to digest than regular oats.

yogurt, orange, and honey "ice cream"

serves 4–6

1¼lb/500g pot strained plain (Greek) yogurt

4 tbsp good-quality honey, cold extracted or manuka

1 tsp vanilla bean paste

finely grated zest of 1 large orange

1 In a bowl, mix together the yogurt, honey, vanilla, and orange zest until combined. Tip into a 1 quart/1 liter freezer-proof container with a lid.

2 Freeze for 4 hours or until solid. Remove from the freezer about 30 minutes before serving to allow the "ice cream" to soften.

PART 2

FEEL GREAT

Good food—fresh and full of natural nutrients—is essential
if you want to feel in top form. It boosts your brain cells,
energizes your whole body, and helps you to beat stress. You'll
notice the difference when you make the feel-good
foods part of your regular diet.

chapter 11

brain-boosters

Our brain is a dynamic living, evolving organism that needs continual feeding to satisfy its voracious appetite. The brain may only make up 2 percent of your body weight but it uses 25 percent of the energy provided by your food. Two-thirds of your brain is made up from fats, therefore the type of fats you eat throughout your life has a huge impact on how you think and feel.

Your brain needs two types of healthier fats known as essential fatty acids (EFAs). Firstly, omega-6 fats, which are found in evening primrose, starflower, black currant, walnut, and sesame oils, as well as walnuts, Brazil nuts, pecan nuts, almonds, sunflower and pumpkin seeds, and olives. The second and more crucial EFA, omega-3, is found in oily fish, and flax and hemp seeds. Mackerel, salmon, herring, anchovies, and sardines are all perfect sources for omega-3. Both these fats are important for the integrity of the cell membranes and the myelin sheaths (which insulate the nerves) in addition to making and protecting neural pathways. Good fats equal healthier brains!

Today, many of us in the West eat far less fish than we did 60 years ago, so our intake of omega-3s has fallen. On the other hand, consumption of omega-6 fats—which are found in various oil-based spreads, pre-packaged meals, and cooking oils—has risen, leading to many people's diets being now too high in omega-6 but low in omega-3. The imbalance this creates can trigger conditions such as depression and attention deficit disorder (ADD).

Grass-fed animals produce a healthier ratio of omega-3 to omega-6 fatty acids than grain-fed animals. Similarly, chickens fed on grass have higher ratios of omega-3 than those fed a diet of soybeans or corn.

If there is a deficiency in these essential fats, the brain utilizes the unhealthy hydrogenated or trans-fats that have been eaten in their place. These unnatural fats are high in omega-6 and can adversely affect the neurotransmitters.

Nutrients for a healthy brain

Your brain also needs plenty of B vitamins to protect and repair the myelin sheaths, and control levels of the toxic compound homocysteine, which is produced naturally in the body and is linked to arterial damage. High homocysteine levels can be lowered by eating more foods with vitamins B_{12}, folic acid, and B_6.

Oily fish contain good amounts of vitamin B_{12}—also choose from cod, oysters, clams, mussels, crab, lobster, and octopus, as well as mozzarella cheese and yogurt. Green leafy vegetables, spinach, lentils, chickpeas, beans (all types), leeks, lettuce, asparagus, and sunflower seeds are great sources of folic acid.

Foods high in vitamin B_6 include rabbit, pheasant, turkey, oily fish, cod, trout, snapper, hazelnuts, bananas, peppers, squash, watercress, spinach, red cabbage, and cauliflower.

Fat-soluble antioxidants, such as vitamin E, are also important for healthy brain functioning, so include sunflower seeds, almonds, hazelnuts, organic wheat germ, avocados, pine nuts, pecan nuts, peanuts, spinach, turnips, flax seeds, and unrefined sesame oil in your diet.

Brain inflammation is now recognized as one of the triggers for conditions such as Alzheimer's, and foods for reducing inflammation include pineapples, apples, onions (white and red), red grapes, cranberries, and blueberries. Using more of the spice turmeric (which contains the active ingredient curcumin) in curries is a good way to protect your brain against inflammation.

Feed your brain cells

Your brain is made up of trillions of cells, called neurons, and chemicals called neurotransmitters that allow communication between the cells by acting like "spark plugs" to ignite processes in the brain. They are essential for memory, mood, learning, behavior, and feeling pain. The main neurotransmitters are serotonin (which relaxes the brain), dopamine (which controls mood), norepinephrine (noradrenaline), and epinephrine (adrenaline). The essential amino acid phenylalanine is the raw material for the brain cells. It is found chiefly in protein foods, such as fish and other seafood, meats, cottage cheese, eggs, lentils, peanuts, and sesame seeds. Artificial phenylalanine can be found in sugar substitutes, such as the commonly used sweetener, aspartame, but should be avoided at all costs.

Tyrosine (which governs alertness and elevates mood) can be sourced directly from Atlantic cod, haddock, shrimp and prawns, turkey, chicken, avocados, soybeans, lima (butter) beans, pumpkin seeds, Parmesan cheese, yogurt, almonds, mackerel, citrus fruits, chocolate, bananas, and eggs.

The essential amino acid tryptophan governs appetite, mood, sleep, and relaxation. Turkey,

chicken, goat's cheese, cottage cheese, brown rice, bananas, yogurt, cod, soybeans, hazelnuts, peanuts, sesame seeds, and sunflower seeds are good sources.

To help keep your brain working at a good speed, eat more egg yolks and soybeans, wheat germ, cabbage, cauliflower, lecithin granules, lettuce, peanut butter, pine nuts, almonds, cod, salmon, turkey, and chicken.

Lecithin is a potent brain food that also lowers the LDL "bad" cholesterol in the body. Lecithin comes from the Greek for "egg yolk", where it is abundant. Lecithin is able to cross the blood–brain barrier easily, acting as a constant regenerator of the phospholipid-rich membranes in the brain.

Vitamin C is needed for more than 40 functions in the body, including the manufacture of neurotransmitters, and your adrenal glands require large amounts of it, especially if you are stressed. Foods rich in vitamin C include bell peppers (capsicum), guavas, kiwi fruit, kale, broccoli, limes, lemons, and cherries.

Foods that are high in carbohydrate but low in protein and high in tryptophan will tend to relax the brain. These include pastries, desserts, chocolate, bananas, nuts (particularly almonds), and other "comfort foods." Conversely, foods that are high in protein but low in carbohydrate and high in tyrosine tend to increase activity in the brain. Meats, eggs, dairy (especially cheese) soya, and seafood are the food choices here.

Alcohol and other toxins, such as recreational drugs, pesticides, refined sugars (including fructose), and some prescription drugs, can impair memory function, so keep them within sensible limits. Note that fructose in its natural form—that is, in fresh fruits or raw, untreated honey—does not have the same negative effect.

Physical exercise is as essential for your brain as for every other part of your body, and it is crucial to stimulate the brain continually by reading and learning. Like every other part of your body—if you don't use it, you lose it!

chicken salad with mint and toasted sesame seeds

serves 4

about 4in/10cm cucumber

2 boneless, skinless chicken breasts

3 small celery sticks, finely sliced

3 scallions (spring onions), thickly sliced

2 tbsp Thai fish sauce

2 tbsp lime juice

3 small red or green chilies, finely sliced

1 tbsp finely chopped mint leaves

2 tbsp toasted sesame seeds

2 tbsp sesame oil

lime wedges, to serve

1 To prepare the cucumber, cut it in half lengthways and scrape out the seeds with a teaspoon. Cut in half crossways, then cut each piece into matchsticks.

2 Bring a pan of water to a boil, add the chicken breasts, and poach at a gentle simmer until cooked through. Drain and let cool.

3 Shred the meat into small pieces over a bowl, letting any liquid fall into the bowl. Add the cucumber, celery, scallions, fish sauce, lime juice, chilies, mint, sesame seeds, and sesame oil, and stir well. Spoon onto a serving platter and serve with wedges of lime.

Food as **Medicine**

• **Chicken** (preferably skinless, as most of the fat is stored in the skin) is a rich protein source. And, like all proteins, it contains the amino acid tyrosine. The "excitatory" neurotransmitter, dopamine, is made from tyrosine and is involved in alertness—so that means chicken will help to wake up your brain!

• **Turmeric** is a good spice to jazz up savory dishes. In countries where it is eaten regularly, there are fewer incidences of conditions such as Alzheimer's and dementia. This is because turmeric has potent anti-inflammatory properties, and inflammation of the brain is linked to degenerative conditions of the brain, heart, and arteries.

pear and roquefort on rye

serves 4

½ cup/60g walnut halves

4 ripe but firm pears, cored and sliced

juice of 1 small lemon

1 tbsp good-quality honey, such as cold extracted or manuka

8 slices dark rye bread

3¾oz/100g watercress, tough stalks trimmed, or arugula (rocket)

1½ cups/175g crumbled Roquefort cheese

ground black pepper

1 Preheat the oven to 350°F/180°C/Gas 4. Put the walnuts on a baking sheet and toast for 6–8 minutes, turning once, until slightly browned. Set aside to cool, then roughly chop.

2 Meanwhile, mix together the lemon juice and honey in a large bowl, then toss the sliced pears into the mixture until coated.

3 Top the bread with the watercress, or arugula, and the pears. Scatter over the Roquefort cheese, season with pepper, and scatter over the walnuts before serving two slices per person.

Food as Medicine

• **Turkey** contains the essential amino acid tryptophan, which is one of the building blocks of DNA. It is crucial to your brain's ability to produce the hormones serotonin and melatonin, which govern appetite, moods, sleep, and relaxation. Other food sources include chicken (a good whole food for a healthy brain,) goat's cheese, cottage cheese, brown rice, bananas, yogurt, cod, soybeans, hazelnuts, peanuts, sesame seeds, and sunflower seeds.

• **Tomatoes** are a plentiful source of vitamin C, which is needed to make neurotransmitters, particularly norepinephrine, in the brain. When stressed, the brain requires larger amounts of vitamin C, so an adequate intake is needed daily to supply the brain's needs. Other vitamin C-rich foods include capsicum, guavas, kiwi fruit, kale, broccoli, limes, lemons, and cherries.

turkey and bay leaf skewers with potato, olive, and tomato salad

serves 2

1 tbsp olive oil

1 tbsp lemon juice

12 small fresh bay leaves

1 small unwaxed lemon, halved and cut into 12 small wedges

10oz/275g skinless, boneless turkey breast, cut into 12 large bite-size chunks

sea salt and ground black pepper

POTATO, OLIVE, AND TOMATO SALAD:

14oz/400g new potatoes, scrubbed

12 pitted black olives, quartered

2 vine-ripened tomatoes, seeded and cut into chunks

3 tbsp chopped fresh flat-leaf parsley

a handful of fresh basil leaves

1½ tbsp lemon juice

1½ tbsp extra-virgin olive oil

1 If using wooden skewers, soak four in water for 30 minutes to prevent them from burning during cooking. Alternatively, use four metal skewers. Preheat the broiler (grill) to medium-high and line a broiler pan with foil.

2 To make the potato salad, cook the potatoes in boiling water for 12 minutes, or until tender. Drain and let cool slightly. Halve or quarter the potatoes if large, then put them in a salad bowl with the olives, tomatoes, parsley, and basil leaves. Mix together the lemon juice and olive oil, and pour over the salad. Season to taste and toss until everything is combined.

3 To make the skewers, first mix together the olive oil and lemon juice. To assemble the skewers, follow this order of ingredients for each one: bay leaf, lemon wedge, turkey chunk, lemon wedge, turkey chunk, bay leaf, lemon wedge, turkey chunk, bay leaf.

4 Arrange the four skewers in the broiler pan. Brush with the olive oil and lemon juice mixture and broil (grill) for 4 minutes. Turn the skewers, brush with more of the olive oil and lemon juice, and broil for another 3–5 minutes, or until the turkey is cooked through.

5 Serve the turkey skewers with a helping of the potato salad.

health TIP

○ **Because your brain** requires a lot of energy in the form of pure glucose to function properly, this is one of the reasons we often crave sugary treats to lift our mood and aid concentration. Unfortunately, a rapid rise of sugar in your system leads to a rapid fall, leaving you craving another "fix!" Sugar is addictive, and triggers inflammation in the body and brain. Far better to snack on fresh fruits, organic dried apricots or raisins, with some sunflower or pumpkin seeds.

simple fish tagine

serves 4

1lb 5oz/600g thick skinless, boneless white fish fillets

1lb/450g new potatoes, halved if large

2 tbsp olive oil

1 onion, sliced

2.5cm/1in piece fresh root ginger, grated

1 red bell pepper, seeded and sliced lengthways

6 fresh thyme sprigs

1½ cups/200g canned cherry tomatoes

1 cup/250ml fresh fish stock

1 tsp harissa paste

generous ½ cup/100g pitted black olives

2 tbsp chopped fresh cilantro (coriander) leaves

4 lemon wedges

MARINADE:

2 tsp ground cumin

2 tsp ground coriander

2 garlic cloves, crushed

4 tbsp lemon juice

sea salt and ground black pepper

Food as Medicine

• **Fish** (particularly cod) is a good source of choline which, in conjunction with vitamin B_3, folic acid, and the amino acid methionine, forms acetylcholine, the neurotransmitter that allows your nerves to communicate with the muscles in your body. Other good sources of choline include egg yolks (used in egg noodles), soybeans, beef, mushrooms, flax seeds, whey, and lentils.

1 Cut the fish into large bite-size pieces. Mix together the ingredients for the marinade in a shallow dish, add the fish and turn until coated. Leave to marinate, covered, in the refrigerator for about 1 hour.

2 Meanwhile, cook the potatoes in a pan of boiling water for 12 minutes or until tender, then drain.

3 Heat the oil in a large, heavy-based pan over medium heat. Turn down the heat slightly and fry the onion, stirring regularly, for 6 minutes or until softened. Add the ginger, red bell pepper, and thyme, then cook for another 3 minutes.

4 Pour in the canned cherry tomatoes and fish stock, and bring to a boil, then stir in the harissa paste. Turn down the heat and simmer for 10 minutes, part-covered, until the sauce has reduced.

5 Remove the fish from the marinade. Stir the potatoes into the pan with the marinade and olives. Arrange the fish on top, cover and cook for 10–12 minutes until the fish is just cooked through. Scatter over the cilantro and serve accompanied by lemon wedges.

pan-fried salmon with white bean purée

serves 4

2½oz/65g arugula (rocket) leaves

3½oz/90g baby spinach leaves

2oz/50g watercress or more arugula leaves

16 cherry tomatoes, halved

1 tbsp olive oil

4 garlic cloves, halved

4 salmon fillets, about 6½oz/185g each, trimmed and bones removed

balsamic vinegar, for drizzling

extra-virgin olive oil, for drizzling

sea salt and ground black pepper

WHITE BEAN PUREE:

14oz/400g can Great Northern (cannellini) beans, rinsed and drained

1 garlic clove, crushed

1½ tbsp lemon juice

2 tbsp chopped fresh thyme

2 tsp olive oil

Food as Medicine

● **Organic salmon** is a great source of omega-3 fats. Your brain is made up of 60 per cent fat, and for it to function properly, you need to ingest a good ratio of omega-3 and 6 essential fats. Many people are deficient in these essential fats, but omega-3s are also found in mackerel, salmon, herring, anchovies, and sardines. Omega-6 essential fats are found in flax seeds, sunflower, hemp, and pumpkin seeds and their oils, as well as walnuts, pine nuts, and olives. Healthy fats equal a sharper brain!

1 Reserve a few arugula leaves for serving, then put the remaining arugula, spinach, and watercress, if using, in a salad bowl. Add the cherry tomatoes and set aside.

2 To make the white bean purée, put the beans, garlic, lemon juice, thyme, oil, and 2 tbsp water in a food processor or blender. Season with salt and pepper to taste, then process to a smooth, soft purée. Add a little more water, if necessary. Transfer to a pan and heat gently for about 5 minutes, stirring frequently, until piping hot. (Alternatively, put the purée in a microwaveable bowl, cover, and cook on high for about 4 minutes, stirring halfway through, until piping hot. Let stand for 1 minute before serving.)

3 Meanwhile, to cook the salmon fillets, heat the oil in a nonstick sauté pan. Add the garlic and fry gently for 1 minute. Add the salmon and cook for 5–8 minutes, turning once halfway through.

4 Drizzle the salad with a little balsamic vinegar, season to taste with salt and pepper, and toss well. Put a spoonful of white bean purée onto each of four warmed serving plates. Put the reserved arugula leaves on top, followed by the salmon. Drizzle with a little olive oil. Serve immediately with the salad.

baked trout with ginger and orange dressing

serves 2

sunflower or canola (rapeseed) oil, for brushing

2 rainbow trout fillets, about 6oz/175g each

6oz/175g medium egg noodles

fresh cilantro (coriander) leaves, to garnish

2 tsp toasted sesame seeds, to serve

sea salt and ground black pepper

GINGER AND ORANGE DRESSING:

1 tbsp lemon juice

2 tbsp orange juice

1 tbsp good-quality honey, such as cold extracted or manuka

1 tsp sesame oil

1 tbsp reduced-salt soy sauce

1in/2.5cm fresh root ginger, peeled and cut into matchsticks

1 Preheat the oven to 400°F/200°C/Gas 6. Lightly brush a baking pan with oil. Put the trout fillets in the pan, season with salt and pepper, and bake for 10–12 minutes, depending on the thickness of the fillets, or until cooked through.

2 Meanwhile, cook the noodles in plenty of boiling water according to the pack instructions until tender, then drain.

3 To make the dressing, put the lemon and orange juice in a small pan with the honey, sesame oil, soy sauce, and ginger, and bring to a boil. Reduce the heat and simmer, stirring occasionally, for 3 minutes or until reduced and slightly thickened.

4 Divide the noodles between two serving plates, top with the trout fillets, and spoon over the warm dressing. Sprinkle with the cilantro and sesame seeds before serving.

health TIP

o **Many people** tend to feel tired after eating a lunch that is high in carbohydrates, such as bread or pasta, or a pastry-based dessert. This is often called a serotonin dip and happens because the carbohydrates (sugars) encourage more efficient uptake of the amino acid tryptophan. If carbohydrate-rich meals are eaten at night, the tryptophan converts more easily to serotonin to make melatonin, which aids a good night's sleep!

sesame-ginger fish

serves 2

1 tbsp reduced-salt soy sauce

1½ tsp toasted sesame oil

1 zucchini (courgette), cut into ribbons

1 carrot, peeled and cut into ribbons

2 tilapia or other firm white fish fillets, about 6oz/175g each

6 x ½in/1cm slices peeled fresh root ginger

sea salt and ground black pepper

1 Mix together the soy sauce and sesame oil.

2 Put half the zucchini and carrot ribbons in the center of a sheet of baking parchment that is large enough to make a package. Put a tilapia fillet on top of the vegetables, then 3 slices of ginger. Repeat with the remaining ingredients to make a second package.

3 Spoon the soy sauce mixture over the fish. Gather up the paper around the fish and fold over to seal and make two loose packages.

4 Put the fish packages in a steamer, cover, and steam for 10–15 minutes, depending on the thickness of the fillets, until cooked. Open up the packages, then season to taste before serving.

Food as **Medicine**

- **Fish** and other foods that are high protein, low in carbohydrates, and high in the amino acid tyrosine tend to increase activity in the brain. This is why lean organic meats, eggs, dairy (especially cheese), soy, and seafood are best eaten either at breakfast or lunch—as you usually need your brain to be at its most alert during the daytime.

- **Seafood** is a good source of the essential amino acid phenylalanine, which is the raw material for the brain cells and converts to tyrosine. We can source tyrosine directly from foods, as well as manufacturing it in the body. Phenylalanine-rich foods are similar to tyrosine foods, being predominantly protein, such as fish, meats, cottage cheese, eggs, lentils, peanuts, and sesame seeds.

trout with fennel and radish slaw

serves 4

2–3 tsp olive oil

1 bulb fennel, grated

2in/5cm piece cucumber, halved, seeded and diced

8 radishes, sliced into rounds

½ small red onion, diced

scant ½ cup/100ml plain (natural) sheep's yogurt

juice of ½ lemon, plus extra to serve

2 tsp whole grain mustard

4 large trout fillets

sea salt and ground black pepper

1 Preheat the broiler (grill) to high, and line the broiler pan with foil. Lightly oil the foil with 1 tsp oil.

2 Put the fennel, cucumber, radishes, and red onion into a large bowl. Add the yogurt, lemon juice, and mustard. Season, then stir until combined. Set aside.

3 Put the trout onto the foil and brush it lightly with oil. Broil (grill) the trout for 2 minutes on each side or until cooked. Serve the trout with the fennel and radish slaw on the side, and squeeze a little extra lemon juice over the fish.

fish with walnut pesto and balsamic tomatoes

serves 4

3 tbsp extra-virgin olive oil

24 cherry tomatoes

1 tbsp balsamic vinegar

4 thick white fish fillets

sea salt and ground black pepper

WALNUT PESTO:

1 handful of fresh flat-leaf parsley leaves

1 handful of fresh mint leaves

2 handfuls of fresh basil leaves

2 tbsp chopped fresh dill

¾ cup/75g walnuts

1 garlic clove, crushed

⅔ cup/150ml light olive oil

½ cup/90g freshly grated Parmesan

health TIP

○ **Get into the habit** of sprinkling non-genetically modified (non-GM) lecithin granules over breakfast cereals, fruit salads, or into fruit smoothies. Lecithin is high in phosphatidyl serine and choline (which is also found in egg yolks). These are excellent brain nutrients that help to protect the myelin sheath in the brain, improving memory function while also reducing LDL cholesterol levels.

1 To make the walnut pesto, put the herbs, walnuts, garlic, and olive oil in a food processor and process until chunky. Transfer to a bowl and stir in the Parmesan. Season to taste with sea salt and black pepper. Cover and refrigerate until needed.

2 Put 2 tbsp olive oil in a nonstick frying pan over a high heat and add the tomatoes. Cook for 2–3 minutes, shaking the pan. Add the balsamic vinegar to the pan with some sea salt and black pepper, cover with a lid and shake the pan over high heat for 1 minute or until the tomatoes soften and start to split.

3 Remove the tomatoes and wipe the pan clean. Add the remaining oil to the pan and cook the fish fillets for 2–3 minutes on each side, until cooked and light golden.

4 Serve the fish with the balsamic tomatoes and spoon the pesto on the side.

turkey with rosemary and garlic stuffing

serves 4

2½lb/1.2kg turkey breast roast

2 tbsp olive oil

1lb 5oz/600g new potatoes, scrubbed

sea salt and ground black pepper

ROSEMARY AND GARLIC STUFFING:

3 large garlic cloves, finely chopped

1 tbsp chopped fresh rosemary

2 tbsp fresh thyme leaves

grated zest of 1 lemon

½ tsp sea salt

1 Preheat the oven to 400°F/200°C/Gas 6. To make the stuffing, put the garlic, rosemary, thyme, lemon zest, and salt in a mortar and grind with a pestle to make a coarse paste.

2 Put the turkey, skin-side down, on a board and make a vertical cut along the length of the roast and half-way into the breast, then open it out like a book.

3 Using a meat pounder or the end of a rolling pin, bash the turkey to flatten it slightly. Spread the stuffing evenly over the turkey then fold in half to enclose it. Use kitchen string to tie the turkey at 1in/2.5cm intervals.

4 Brush half the olive oil all over the turkey, then season and put it, skin-side up, into a large, roasting pan. Roast for 1 hour, occasionally basting the meat with any pan juices.

5 Put the new potatoes and remaining oil in a baking pan. Season and turn the potatoes until coated in the oil. Roast the potatoes and turkey for another 30–35 minutes until the meat is cooked through and there is no trace of pink in the center.

6 Remove the turkey from the oven. Turn the potatoes and continue to roast them while the turkey is resting, loosely covered with foil, for 15–20 minutes. (Reserve the juices in the pan to make gravy.) Serve the turkey carved into slices with the roasted new potatoes on the side. Green beans make a good accompaniment.

Food as Medicine

● **Rosemary** contains carnosic acid, which shields the cells of the brain from free-radical damage, protecting them from aging. Laboratory studies have shown a reduction in the occurrence of strokes by 40 per cent when carnosic acid was used as a supplement. Another helpful herb is sage, particularly Spanish sage, because of its many phytonutrients, which improve memory.

snapper with leek and white bean purée

serves 4

2–3 tbsp olive oil

4 red snapper fillets, or other similar fish

3 tbsp toasted pine nuts

1 tbsp finely chopped chives

sea salt and ground black pepper

LEEK AND WHITE BEAN PUREE:

2 leeks, finely sliced

14oz/400g can Great Northern (cannellini) beans, drained and rinsed

2 tbsp olive oil

1 large garlic clove, finely chopped

5 tbsp vegetable stock

TOMATO VINAIGRETTE:

4 tbsp extra-virgin olive oil

2 tbsp balsamic vinegar

8 vine-ripened tomatoes, seeded and diced

2 tbsp chopped fresh chives

1 Preheat the oven to 425°F/220°C/Gas 7. To make the white bean purée, steam the leeks for 5–6 minutes until tender. Put the beans in a bowl and mash coarsely with a fork. Heat the olive oil in a pan and fry the garlic for 1 minute. Add the beans, leeks, and stock, and heat through, stirring, until combined. Season with pepper and keep warm.

2 To cook the fish, heat the olive oil in a large, nonstick frying pan. Season the snapper with salt and black paper. Fry the fish, skin-side down, for 1–2 minutes until golden and crisp (you may need to do this in two batches). Turn the fillets over, and transfer to a roasting pan. Put in the oven for 4–5 minutes or until just cooked.

3 To make the vinaigrette, whisk together the extra-virgin olive oil and balsamic vinegar in a bowl. Stir in the tomatoes and chives, then season with salt and pepper. Set aside.

4 Divide the purée among four large, shallow bowls. Top the purée with the snapper and drizzle over the tomato vinaigrette. Garnish with toasted pine nuts and chives.

Food as Medicine

- **Beans** (particularly soybeans) and peas (especially chickpeas), peanuts, and egg yolks are all good sources of lecithin. Lecithin is a collective name for a group of fatty-like substances, such as choline, phospholipids, and other fatty acids that coat the nerves and blood vessels with a sticky covering, preventing "bad" fats, such as LDL cholesterol, or man-made trans- and hydrogenated fats, from sticking to the walls and oxidizing. This preserves the neural pathways in the brain from degeneration.

summer rice salad

serves 4

¼ cup/55g wild rice

scant ⅔ cup/125g long grain brown rice

2 cups/475ml vegetable stock

⅔ cup/75g shelled fava (broad) beans

¾ cup/75g shelled fresh peas

2½oz/65g green beans, trimmed

3¾oz/100g asparagus, trimmed

2 carrots, grated

¼ cup/25g toasted slivered (flaked) almonds

¼ cup/25g raisins

2 tbsp sunflower seeds

a handful of fresh chives, chopped

a large handful of fresh cilantro (coriander), leaves chopped

DRESSING:

3 tbsp extra-virgin olive oil

1 tbsp balsamic vinegar

2 tsp good-quality honey, such as cold extracted or manuka

1 tsp Dijon mustard

sea salt and ground black pepper

health TIP

- **If you decide** to try this wonderful salad, you can interchange the fava (broad) beans for navy (haricot) beans, chopped broccoli, artichokes, or any vegetables that you happen to have around. If you prefer sweeter rice dishes, add a few small chunks of fresh pineapple or mango. For extra color, sprinkle with pomegranate—it's high in antioxidant nutrients that are beneficial for the brain.

1 Put the wild rice and brown rice in a pan. Pour over the stock and bring to a boil. Turn the heat down to the lowest setting, cover with a lid, and simmer for 30–40 minutes until tender and the water is absorbed. Set aside, covered, for 5 minutes, then transfer to a large serving bowl to cool.

2 In the meantime, steam the fava beans and peas for 4 minutes or until tender. Remove from the steamer and refresh under cold running water. Steam the green beans and asparagus for a further 3–4 minutes until tender, then refresh under cold running water.

3 Gently squeeze the beans out of their gray outer shell, and add to the rice with the peas. Slice the cold asparagus and green beans into small pieces, and add to the rice with the carrots, almonds, raisins, and sunflower seeds, then mix together well.

4 Blend together the ingredients for the dressing and season. Pour the dressing over the rice salad and add the chives and cilantro, then stir to mix well. This rice salad is also delicious served warm. Simply toss the whole salad, without cooling, with a small amount of the dressing into some hot olive or coconut oil and heat through. Add a few shakes of tamari for extra seasoning. If you like, top it with a poached egg. It's also delicious as a base for curries (without the tamari.)

oat, coconut, and cacao cookies

makes about 18

unsalted butter, for greasing

1 cup/90g rolled oats (porridge oats)

scant ⅓ cup/50g ground almonds

1 cup/100g dry unsweetened shredded (desiccated) coconut

¼ tsp ground cinnamon

½ tsp baking powder

2 large ripe bananas, peeled

½ tsp vanilla extract

5 tbsp virgin coconut oil, warmed until liquid (or olive oil)

generous ½ cup/100g raw cacao nibs or semisweet chocolate chips

1 Preheat the oven to 350°F/180°C/Gas 4 and lightly grease two large baking sheets.

2 In a large bowl, mix together the oats, ground almonds, coconut, cinnamon, and baking powder.

3 In a second bowl, mash the bananas well, then stir in the vanilla extract and coconut oil. Add the wet ingredients to the dry ingredients and stir until combined; fold in the cacao nibs.

4 Put heaped dessertspoonfuls of the dough onto the prepared baking sheets; flatten the tops slightly to make cookies about 1½in/4cm in diameter. Bake for 15–20 minutes until golden. Leave to cool for a few minutes, then transfer to a wire rack to cool.

Food as **Medicine**

- **Almonds** are rich in the fat-soluble antioxidant vitamin E, which helps to prevent the oxidation of fat cells and the fatty myelin sheaths. Other foods high in vitamin E include avocados, sunflower seeds, hazelnuts, pine nuts, pecan nuts, peanuts, spinach, turnips, flax seeds, and sesame oil.

- **Walnuts** look like brains, and the composition of fatty acids in a walnut is not far different to that of the human brain—roughly 50 per cent each of omega-6 and omega-3 fatty acids. A walnut contains 58 per cent alpha-linoleic acid (omega-3), and 32 per cent omega-6 and monounsaturates. The remaining 10 per cent is saturated fat.

beet and walnut cake

makes about 16 squares

generous 1 cup/125g whole-wheat self-rising (self-raising) spelt flour

generous 1 cup/125g self-rising (self-raising) spelt flour

2 tsp ground cinnamon

2 tsp allspice (mixed spice)

¾ cup/125g xylitol

9½oz/270g beets, cooked until slightly softened, peeled, and grated

½ cup/50g chopped walnuts

scant 1 cup/200ml sunflower oil, plus extra for greasing

4 free-range eggs

1 Preheat the oven to 350°F/180°C/Gas 4. Lightly grease and line the base of an 8in/20cm square cake pan (tin).

2 Sift both types of flour into a mixing bowl, adding any bran left in the sieve. Using a wooden spoon, stir in the cinnamon, allspice, xylitol, and beets until combined. Next, stir in the walnuts.

3 Beat together the oil and eggs in a small bowl, then pour the mixture into the large bowl and stir gently until all the ingredients are combined.

4 Pour the cake mixture into the prepared cake pan and smooth the top with the back of a spoon. Bake the cake for 45 minutes or until risen and golden. Leave the cake in the pan for 10 minutes, then turn it out to cool on a wire rack. Serve cut into squares.

energizers

How often do you find yourself saying, "I'm tired"? Lack of energy is a common problem these days, often triggered by a lack of sleep, overwork, chronic low-grade infections, medications, and of course, stress. If energy demands exceed supply, you will often feel as though you are running on empty like a car that has a low battery *and* it's struggling to keep going on low-grade fuel. Part of the answer often lies in our internal "battery." Our cells act like miniature alkaline batteries with a positive and negative charge, but when we eat too many acid-forming foods, such as meat, refined sugar, white flour, eggs, alcohol, tea, and coffee, plus we use drugs (prescription and recreational), smoke, or are stressed, our bodies become over-acidic. Our battery's ability to create a spark is then reduced—so we just don't fire on all cylinders!

A typical Western diet is 80 percent acidic and only 20 percent alkaline, but to have more energy, and be heaps healthier at every level, these figures need to be reversed.

Fruit and vegetables along with relaxation techniques, such as meditation and qigong, are the secret to being more alkaline, and thus improving your energy levels. This is because fruit and vegetables contain an abundance of the alkaline minerals magnesium, potassium, sodium, calcium, zinc, and to a lesser degree, iron. These bind to the acid-forming minerals, such as sulfur and phosphorus, and neutralize them.

Indeed, many people are deficient in some of these minerals, and particularly magnesium, zinc, and iron. Of course, some of them are present in acid-forming foods too, and are necessary for good health, but not in the amounts that we regularly consume them. If a person's day consists of coffee with processed cereal for breakfast, perhaps a sticky bun with more coffee mid-morning, followed by a ham sandwich, cake, and a fizzy drink for lunch, with sweet treats mid afternoon and meat served with overcooked vegetables (devoid of any minerals) for dinner, followed by ice-cream, coffee, and accompanied by half a bottle of wine, that regimen is deficient in alkalizing minerals. The result is that person's body becomes far too acid. And if a stressful job or lifestyle is part of the picture, the body becomes even more acid. It is easy to see how our internal "battery" can run down with no alkalinity. Basically, no charge, no energy!

The best foods for good performance
To run on top-quality fuel, we need a more alkaline diet and lifestyle to buffer these acids, especially when under stress. It's also important to consider that intense farming methods, combined with shipping foods that are often unripe over great distances, and then storing them for weeks, can hugely reduce mineral and other nutrient levels. For these reasons, try to buy fresh, organic, locally grown foods.

Our ability to absorb our food properly is fundamental to our energy levels, so eating foods that are easier to digest—such as soups or oatmeal (porridge) (soaked and well-cooked)—are helpful, as is keeping the gut in good shape to maximize absorption and assimilation.

Choose foods that provide sufficient calories but have a low-glycemic index (GI), because keeping your blood sugar regulated will help you to avoid reaching for too many poor food choices. Unprocessed foods provide good amounts of potassium, magnesium, essential fats, and amino acids. Good sources include whole grains, salmon, sardines, lentils, goat's yogurt, grapefruit, pears, apples, blueberries, cherries, sprouts, peas, broccoli, asparagus, spinach, and sunflower and pumpkin seeds.

You will also get a better return on your calorie investment by eating more "good" fats, which keep you going longer than protein or carbohydrates. Choose from oily fish, nuts, seeds, avocados, olive oil, and the medium-chain fatty acids from organic, unrefined coconut oil/butter.

Nourishing our bodies

Many people are low in iron and vitamin B_{12} causing tiredness, depression, poor memory, and, if severe, pernicious anemia. Iron-rich foods include blackstrap molasses, lentils, peas, parsley, spinach, almonds, venison, eggs, partridge, pheasant, fish, dried fruit (particularly raisins and unsulfured apricots), dates, dried plums (prunes), cherry juice, and strawberry juice. Food choices for vitamin B_{12} include mackerel, sardines, clams, octopus, venison, rabbit, yogurt, and fermented foods.

The Candida yeast fungal overgrowth is common in people who live on fast foods, high in refined sugars, and who also have a rushed, stressed lifestyle. If left unchecked, Candida can damage the cells of the small intestine, which usually means that iron, calcium and B_{12} may not be absorbed sufficiently. If this is you, a gluten-free diet can be a great help, as it allows the cells to heal, thus increasing absorption. Gluten-free foods include, brown/wild rice, millet, sushi, buckwheat, quinoa, corn, and amaranth, or gluten-free breads and pastas. Spelt or kamut, which have lower levels of gluten, are fine in addition to gluten-free oatmeal (porridge oats). For best results soak grains overnight before cooking.

As we age, the production of enzymes that help us to digest our foods slows down, and digestion can be greatly impaired. The "good" bacteria in our gut is also reduced, as are certain liver enzymes that act as antioxidants. If we don't eat the best fuel for our bodies, our ability both to absorb and detoxify will be significantly reduced, leading to under-performance and lethargy.

The antioxidant, co-enzyme Q_{10}, is responsible for cellular energy, but as the body ages, less is made, so we become more tired. Eating more venison (but not frying it), soya, and canola (rapeseed) and sesame seed oils will help. Other sources include sardines, mackerel, herring, trout, sole, eel, chicken, walnuts, chestnuts, soybeans, broccoli, spinach, black currants, and sweet potato.

Another important nutrient for energy is the amino acid L-carnitine, which is stored in the cardiac and skeletal muscles where there is a high demand for using fatty acids for fuel. The best food sources are meat—in fact, the redder the meat the higher the L-carnitine content. Beef, venison, poultry, and fish (especially cod) are good sources. L-carnitine is also found to a lesser degree in goat's and sheep's yogurt, asparagus, mushrooms, broccoli, and in sesame and sunflower seeds.

The antioxidant, alpha-lipoic acid (lipoic acid), converts glucose to energy, and is absorbed from food sources primarily in the stomach. Good sources include lean steak and green leafy vegetables, such as broccoli, Swiss chard, spinach, and bok choy (pak choi).

Organic food will always offer more potential for nutrients. If you eat good food daily, it will help to recharge your "battery" and keep your "engine" working more efficiently.

kick-start kabobs

makes 4

1 large orange

2 small bananas, sliced

juice of 1 lemon

8 cubes of canned pineapple in fruit juice, drained

8 ready-to eat pitted (stoned) dried plums (prunes)

8 ready-to eat dried apricots

1 tbsp good-qualiy honey, such as cold extracted or manuka

½ tsp apple pie (mixed) spice

low-fat plain (natural) yogurt, to serve

1 Soak four long wooden skewers in water for 10 minutes. Hold the orange with its base on the chopping board. Position a small, sharp knife at the top, and cut off a strip of peel and pith. Remove the remaining peel in the same way. Hold the fruit over a small bowl to catch the juice, and cut between the segments on both sides of the membranes separating them. Squeeze the remaining juice from the membrane into the bowl. Set aside.

2 Preheat the broiler (grill) to medium-hot. Put the banana slices in a shallow bowl, sprinkle with the lemon juice, and toss gently to prevent them from browning. Thread the bananas, pineapple, orange segments, dried plums, and apricots onto the four skewers, dividing the ingredients equally among them.

3 Put 2 tbsp orange juice, the honey, and spice in a small bowl and mix together. Brush this mixture over the fruit skewers. Cook the kabobs under the broiler for 5 minutes, turning frequently. Brush with any remaining orange juice mixture while they are cooking to prevent them from drying out. Serve warm, with some low-fat yogurt.

Food as Medicine

• **Some fruits** are better than others at kick-starting your body into action. The ratio of fructose to glucose in the fruit is important. Basically, if the ratio is higher in favor of glucose (or both are the same), the fruit sugars will be better utilized. Therefore, choose fruits that have a higher glucose to fructose ratio, or are in balance, such as bananas, oranges, apricots, berries, pineapple, plums, and dried plums (prunes).

health TIPS

○ **Staying "regular"** is an ideal way to have more energy naturally! If you mix flour and water it makes a very "gooey" mixture that resembles cement—and flour-based foods, or melted cheese, have a similar effect in the bowel! So, eat more flax seeds, which are rich in omega-3 and 6 fats, as well as fiber. If you buy ready-cracked flax seeds, store them in the refrigerator once opened to keep them fresh. Or use whole flax seeds (about 1 tbsp) soaked overnight in cold water, then drain and add to a smoothie at breakfast time.

shrimp with chili and basil

serves 4

2 tbsp virgin coconut oil

2 garlic cloves, finely chopped

2 small fresh red or green chilies, finely chopped

12 raw jumbo shrimp (tiger prawns), shelled and deveined, tail on

2 onions, halved and thickly sliced

3 tbsp Thai fish sauce

2 tbsp reduced-salt light soy sauce

1 tsp xylitol

30 fresh whole basil leaves

1 Heat the oil in a wok or frying pan, add the garlic and chilies, and stir-fry until the garlic begins to brown. Stir in the shrimp, then add the onions, fish sauce, soy sauce, xylitol, and basil, mixing well.

2 Cook until the shrimp are cooked through. They will take just a few minutes, and will become opaque and pink. Be careful not to overcook them.

3 Transfer to a dish and serve with rice and a salad or other Thai dishes.

Food as **Medicine**

• **A banana** eaten before bedtime aids sleep, because its high tryptophan content is converted into serotonin which, in turn (because of the darkness), makes melatonin. Yet, a banana eaten in the middle of the day for more energy will (because of the daylight) not have the same effect of inducing sleep. Eating carbohydrate foods before bedtime helps make you feel sleepy, *but* they also give you energy during the day. This seems a paradox, but the reason is twofold. Firstly, the type of carbohydrate is important—some are simple, such as white bread and pasta (refined foods) and others are complex, such as quinoa and wholegrains (unrefined foods). Secondly, it is linked to our wake–sleep cycle. This is why many people feel sluggish on dull days and reach for more carbs—they are craving the foods their body thinks it needs.

papaya and banana smoothie

serves 2–4

1 small papaya, peeled, seeded, and cut into chunks

1 banana, peeled and cut into chunks

1 cup/250ml ice

½ cup/125ml plain (natural) sheep's or dairy-free yogurt (optional)

1 tbsp wheat germ (optional)

Put the papaya and banana into a blender with the ice and ½ cup/ 125 ml water or yogurt. Pulse until smooth, then add the wheat germ, if using, and extra water or yogurt to make a pourable consistency.

figs with goat's cheese, pecan nuts, and honey-balsamic dressing

serves 4

2 tbsp pecan nuts, chopped

4 ripe figs

2oz/50g goat's cheese

2 tbsp balsamic vinegar

1 tbsp good-quality honey, such as cold extracted or manuka

1 tsp wholegrain mustard

2½oz/65g baby spinach, rinsed

sea salt and ground black pepper

1 Preheated the broiler (grill) to high. Spread the pecan nuts out on a baking sheet and toast under the broiler for 1–2 minutes. Watch the nuts closely to ensure that they don't burn. Transfer to a bowl.

2 Cut the figs in half through the stalk and put onto the baking sheet. Cut the goat's cheese into eight pieces and put one on each fig half. Season, then put under the broiler for 2 minutes or until the cheese is golden and bubbling.

3 Put the balsamic vinegar in a small bowl and beat in the honey, mustard, and seasoning to make a dressing. Divide the spinach among four plates.

4 Put two fig halves on each plate, scatter the pecan nuts on top, and drizzle with the dressing. Serve immediately.

health TIP

○ **Regular exercise** really does help you to feel altogether more energized. A 30 minute walk— preferably away from main roads and all the pollution—increases circulation in the body and oxygen consumption, thus making you feel more invigorated. On rare days when I feel almost too tired to exercise, once I make the effort to walk, even if only for 20 minutes, I definitely feel better!

insalata dei gonzaga

serves 4

¾ cup/75g pine nuts

4oz/115g Parmesan cheese

8oz/225g cooked boneless chicken, preferably breast, pulled into long shreds

1–2 heads radicchio, leaves separated

1 tbsp lemon juice, or to taste

⅓ cup/75ml extra-virgin olive oil, or to taste

¼ cup/40g raisins, soaked in hot water for 10 minutes

1–2 tbsp balsamic vinegar

sea salt and ground black pepper

1 Put the pine nuts in a dry frying pan and heat gently until lightly golden. Take care—they burn easily. Remove to a plate and let cool.

2 Using a swivel vegetable peeler, shave off sections of the Parmesan, then set aside. Put the chicken and radicchio in a bowl, and toss gently. Sprinkle with sea salt, then with the lemon juice. Toss gently with your hands.

3 Sprinkle with olive oil and toss again. Taste, then add extra salt, lemon juice, or oil, as you wish.

4 Transfer the chicken and radicchio to salad plates, then sprinkle with the raisins and pine nuts. Season with pepper and a few drops of balsamic vinegar, then top with the shavings of Parmesan.

health TIP

○ **Many people** use high-caffeine drinks to give them energy. This is not a good idea, as it is creating an artificial increase in energy that is not sustainable, and over time it becomes counter-productive. Propping up your body by taking caffeine rather than food, or drinking coffee every time you are feeling low, will deplete your body's adrenal function, which will eventually make you feel even more tired.

health TIP

○ **If you are eating sensibly,** taking regular exercise, and yet still find that even after a good night's sleep, your energy levels are low, please go to see your doctor for a thorough check-up. You may, for example, have an underactive thyroid, your iron levels could be low, or you might have adrenal exhaustion or low blood sugar. See pages 280–1 for more details about stress. Also, if you are eating foods to which you have an intolerance, these can also cause lethargy. See pages 22–23 for more about allergies and intolerances.

spaghetti with lemon and green olives

serves 2

1 stick/115g unsalted butter

finely grated zest of 2 lemons

¾ cup/75g green olives, pitted and chopped

1 tbsp chopped fresh lemon thyme (optional)

8oz/225g gluten-free spaghetti

½ cup/90g freshly grated Parmesan or Pecorino cheese, plus extra to serve

sea salt and ground black pepper

1 Melt the butter slowly in a pan and add the grated lemon zest. Turn off the heat and leave to infuse for at least 2 hours (or for as long as you can), remelting if necessary.

2 When ready to eat, strain the melted butter and reheat, then add the chopped olives, lemon thyme, if using, and salt and pepper to taste. Keep warm.

3 Cook the pasta in a large pan of boiling salted water, according to the pack instructions. Drain, reserving 2–3 tbsp of the cooking water.

4 Toss the pasta with the lemon and olive butter, the cheese, and more pepper if you like. Add some of the reserved cooking water if it looks too dry. Serve immediately with extra cheese.

Food as Medicine

• **Spaghetti**, and other foods that are carbohydrate-rich, contain glucose. If eaten in the middle of the day, this will be well utilized by the muscles and brain, since most people are active at that time and therefore less likely to store it as fat around the middle than if they were to "sleep on it."

tuscan salad

serves 4

1 avocado

14oz/400g can Great Northern (cannellini) beans, rinsed and drained

14oz/400g can red kidney beans, rinsed and drained

1 red onion, finely chopped

2 tbsp pitted green olives

4 tomatoes, chopped

12oz/350g canned tuna in spring water, drained and lightly flaked

a few chives or chive flowers, to serve

DRESSING:

1 tsp wholegrain mustard

2 tbsp extra-virgin olive oil

¼ cup/60ml balsamic vinegar

2–3 garlic cloves, crushed

2 tbsp finely chopped chives

2 tbsp chopped fresh tarragon

2 tbsp chopped fresh flat leaf parsley

sea salt and ground black pepper

1 To make the dressing, put the mustard, oil, vinegar, garlic, chives, tarragon, and parsley in a large bowl and mix well. Season with salt and pepper, to taste.

2 Cut the avocado in half, then remove the pit (stone). Peel the halves and cut the flesh into cubes. Add to the bowl with the dressing.

3 Add the beans to the bowl with the onion, olives, tomatoes, and tuna. Mix well to coat with the dressing. Serve in individual bowls, sprinkled with some chives or chive flowers.

Food as Medicine

• **Avocados** are a good source of mono- and polyunsaturated fatty acids. Where energy is concerned, fats burn longer and slower than protein or carbohydrate, keeping your energy levels up, although they are higher in calories. Other foods which have predominantly mono- or polyunsaturates include oily fish, flax seeds, nuts, seeds, olive oil, and coconut oil—all of which are healthy.

health TIP

○ **Have you ever noticed** that when you are doing something you love, time passes incredibly quickly, and you tend to feel more inspired and energized? Conversely, if you are bored, time seems to slow down and you find yourself yawning? If this sounds familiar, list all the things that you love doing, then go about finding ways to do more of them. Nearly all self-made millionaires think of their "work" as their favorite hobby and therefore tend to have more energy.

chicken and white bean summer stew

serves 4

2 tbsp olive oil

1¼lb/500g boneless, skinless chicken breasts, cut into large bite-size pieces

1 large red onion, sliced

3 garlic cloves, sliced

1 red bell pepper, seeded and sliced

2 corn on the cob, kernels removed

3½ cups/800ml chicken stock

2 tbsp plain spelt flour

5oz/150g fine green beans, halved

4 long fresh thyme sprigs

14oz/400g can Great Northern (cannellini) beans, rinsed and drained

7oz/200g baby spinach

4 tbsp fresh pesto

finely grated zest of 1 lemon

a handful of fresh basil leaves

sea salt and ground black pepper

Food as Medicine

- **Chicken** (especially the dark meat) is a good source of iron. Iron deficiency is quite common, especially in women and people who take laxatives. Without adequate iron, the body's ability to transfer oxygen around the body is impaired, resulting in tiredness. Vitamin C helps better absorption of iron, so eating chicken with carrots or broccoli (both rich in vitamin C) would be ideal. Other iron-rich foods include lentils, peas, parsley, and spinach.

1 Heat the oil in a large heavy-based pan. Brown the chicken in two batches for 5 minutes until golden all over. Remove from the pan and add the onion. Fry for 6 minutes, stirring occasionally, until softened.

2 Add the garlic, red bell pepper, and corn, and cook for another minute before pouring in the stock. Bring to a boil, then reduce the heat to low.

3 Mix the flour in a little water to make a paste, then add to the pan. Cook, stirring, for a few minutes until starting to thicken.

4 Add the browned chicken, green beans, thyme, and Great Northern beans, then return to a boil. Reduce the heat to low and simmer for 8 minutes or until the vegetables are tender. Add the spinach and cook, part covered, for a further 2 minutes, or until wilted, and the chicken is cooked through.

5 Divide among four large, shallow bowls. Season to taste and top with a spoonful of pesto. Sprinkle with the lemon zest and basil before serving.

moroccan-style lentils with marinated chicken kabobs

serves 4

4 tbsp olive oil

2 tsp ground cumin

1 tsp dried chili flakes

finely grated zest of 1 lemon

2 tbsp chopped fresh cilantro (coriander)

4 boneless, skinless chicken breasts, cut into 1in/2.5cm cubes

sea salt and ground black pepper

MOROCCAN-STYLE LENTILS:

1 large onion, chopped

1 large carrot, diced

1 large garlic clove, chopped

1 tsp ground cumin

2 tsp ground coriander

1 bay leaf

1 cup/200g Puy lentils

7oz/200g can chopped tomatoes

2½ cups/550ml chicken or vegetable stock

7oz/200g baby spinach, washed

handful fresh cilantro (coriander), roughly chopped

1 Mix half the olive oil with the cumin, chilli flakes, lemon zest, and cilantro in a large, shallow dish, then season with salt and pepper. Add the chicken, stir until coated, then leave to marinate, covered, in the refrigerator for 1 hour.

2 To make the Moroccan lentils, heat the remaining olive oil in a large sauté pan over medium heat. Fry the onion for 5 minutes, then add the carrot and cook for a further 3 minutes, stirring occasionally, until softened. Add the garlic and spices, and cook for another minute.

3 Add the bay leaf, Puy lentils, chopped tomatoes, and stock. Bring to a boil then turn the heat down, part-cover the pan, and simmer for 35–40 minutes until tender.

4 If using wooden skewers, soak eight in water for 10 minutes, otherwise use eight metal skewers. Heat the broiler (grill) to medium-high and line the broiler rack with foil. Thread five cubes of chicken onto each skewer. Broil (grill) for 10 minutes, turning once, and brushing with more marinade, until lightly browned and cooked through.

5 Stir the spinach into the lentils, and continue to cook until wilted, then season with pepper. Stir in half the cilantro.

6 Serve the chicken kabobs with the lentils, sprinkled with the remaining chopped cilantro.

health TIP

- **An excellent** way to start your day is by making a breakfast smoothie packed with high-energy foods. Add ½ cup/2oz blueberries, 1 tbsp pomegranate seeds, 1 tbsp sunflower or pumpkin seeds, some flax seeds, 2 ready-to-eat dried plums (prunes), 1 cored, unpeeled apple, chopped, some chopped mango or papaya—you can experiment to find your favorite blends and quantities. Add 1½ tsp organic "green powder" (made with dried wheatgrass, chlorella, barley grass, and so on,) plus a scoop of hemp seed protein powder and lecithin granules (all available from health-food stores.) Blend with rice milk and drink.

goa shrimp curry

serves 4

1 tbsp ground coriander

½ tbsp paprika

1 tsp ground cumin

½ tsp cayenne or hot chili powder

½ tsp ground turmeric

3 garlic cloves, crushed

2 tsp grated fresh root ginger

8oz/225g green beans, halved

1 tbsp tamarind paste or lemon juice

2 tbsp coconut milk

14oz/400g uncooked jumbo shrimp (tiger prawns), shelled and deveined

3½oz/90g baby spinach

sea salt and ground black pepper

1 In a pan, mix the spices to a paste with a little water. Stir in the garlic, ginger, and 1⅔ cups/400ml cold water, add seasoning and bring to a boil. Simmer for 10 minutes until the sauce has slightly reduced and the flavor of the spices is released.

2 Meanwhile, cook the green beans in a separate pan of lightly salted boiling water for 5 minutes or until tender, then drain.

3 Stir the tamarind paste and coconut milk into the spicy sauce base until smooth. Add the shrimp and cook for about 2 minutes or until they turn pink. Stir in the green beans and spinach, and cook briefly until the spinach has wilted. Ladle the curry into bowls and serve with basmati rice or chapattis.

Food as Medicine

• **Spinach** is an abundant source of alpha lipoic acid (lipoic acid), a fat- and water-soluble antioxidant manufactured in the body that converts glucose to energy and is absorbed from food sources in the stomach. Green foods such as spinach have a high concentration of chloroplasts (the green organelle of the plant) that holds the lipoic acid. Other foods containing lipoic acid include other green leafy vegetables such as broccoli, chard, kale, and bok choy (pak choi), as well as lean steak.

health TIPS

- **Co-enzyme Q_{10}** is a vitamin-like substance found in all cells. When we are young, our bodies produce lots of it, which acts like a "spark plug" within our cells to produce energy. It also supports the heart. As we age (and if we take statins), far less CoQ_{10} is produced, and we become more tired. Food sources include venison, soya and sesame seed oils, sardines, mackerel, herring, trout, sole, chicken, walnuts, chestnuts, soybeans, broccoli, spinach, blackcurrants, and sweet potato. Wild or grass-fed animals have about ten times the levels of CoQ_{10} compared with grain-fed animals, and cooking at high temperatures also destroys CoQ_{10} levels.

lamb steaks with fresh mango chutney

serves 4

2 tbsp olive oil

1 tsp garam masala

1 tsp ground coriander

1 tsp ground turmeric

4 lean lamb steaks, about 6oz/175g each

sea salt and ground black pepper

sprigs of fresh cilantro (coriander), to garnish

FRESH MANGO CHUTNEY:

2 tbsp olive oil

1 tsp black mustard seeds

1 large mango, peeled, pit (stone) removed, diced

1 tbsp xylitol

1 red chili, finely chopped

juice of $\frac{1}{2}$ lime

1 Mix together the olive oil, garam masala, ground coriander, and turmeric in a large, shallow dish. Season the lamb, then add it to the dish and turn to coat in the marinade. Cover and marinate for 1 hour.

2 Meanwhile, make the mango chutney. Heat the olive oil in a small pan, add the mustard seeds and stir until they start to pop. Stir in the mango, xylitol, and chili, and cook over medium heat for 5 minutes or until very soft. Stir in the lime juice and season with a little salt. Set aside.

3 Heat a griddle pan until very hot. Griddle the lamb for 6–8 minutes or until cooked to your liking, turning halfway and brushing with the marinade. Served garnished with cilantro.

Food as Medicine

• **Lamb and chicken** are good sources of vitamin B_{12}, which is commonly low in many people. Without adequate B_{12}, red blood cells don't form properly, resulting in tiredness and a host of other problems. Other good sources of B_{12} include animal-derived foods such as mackerel, sardines, clams, venison, and rabbit, as well as yogurt and fermented foods.

roast lemongrass chicken

serves 4

3 lemongrass stalks, outer layers removed, chopped

4 garlic cloves, peeled

2in/5cm piece fresh root ginger, peeled and chopped

1 onion, halved

1 long red chili, stalk removed

2 tbsp tamari

juice and grated zest of 1 lime

1 tbsp olive oil

1 chicken, about 3¾lb/1.75kg

sea salt and ground black pepper

1 Put the lemongrass, garlic, ginger, onion, chili, tamari, lime juice and zest, and the olive oil in a food processor or blender, and purée to a paste, then season.

2 Gently run your hands under the skin of the chicken over the breast to detach it from the flesh. Make two or three slashes in each leg.

3 Rub the marinade under the skin and all over the top of the chicken then put the chicken in a plastic bag and seal. Put on a plate and marinate in the refrigerator for at least 8 hours or overnight.

4 Preheat the oven to 350°F/180°C/Gas 4. Remove the chicken from the bag and put on a rack in a roasting pan. Spoon any marinade left in the bag over the top.

5 Roast for 1½–1¾ hours, occasionally basting with the juices in the pan, or until cooked through and there is no trace of pink when the thigh is pierced with a skewer. Cover the chicken with foil and leave to rest for 10 minutes before carving. Serve hot or cold.

health TIPS

- **Try to control** your blood sugar levels. Eating small meals regularly is better than eating three large meals per day. Try to eat something at least every four hours—snack on fruit, nuts, or oat biscuits with goat's cheese. Not bingeing on junk food (which causes fluctuations in blood sugar) is important to stave off constant exhaustion.

spiced pear, apricot, and fig compote

serves 2

⅔ cup/150ml unsweetened apple juice

1 cup/225g ready-to-eat dried apricots, halved

½ cup/75g ready-to-eat dried figs, halved

8 cardamom pods, lightly crushed

2 pears, cored and sliced into wedges

TO SERVE:

6 tbsp strained plain (Greek) yogurt or dairy-free equivalent

2 tsp pumpkin seeds

1 Put all the ingredients in a pan, bring to a simmer and cook, covered, for 2–4 minutes, depending on the ripeness of the pears.

2 Transfer to a bowl and let cool. Cover, and chill the compote overnight in the refrigerator.

3 To serve, discard the cardamom pods and divide the compote between two serving bowls. Top each bowlful with half the Greek yogurt and the pumpkin seeds.

If you are unable to eat any animal-based yogurts, pour a small amount of coconut or oat cream over the compote instead.

health TIP

○ **Eating breakfast** is one of the easiest ways to energize yourself for the day ahead. Firstly, see my breakfast smoothie recipe under Health Tips on page 259. Protein helps to wake up your brain, and you also need a small amount of carbohydrates to absorb the protein, so a healthy breakfast could also be eggs (poached, scrambled, or boiled), or kippers or trout with some whole-wheat (wholemeal) bread and butter. If you are intolerant to gluten, then flax seed, buckwheat, and quinoa breads and crackers are available in some health-food stores. Quinoa and cooked tofu also make great healthy-protein breakfasts.

Food as Medicine

• **Apricots, pears, and fresh figs** are fruits that have a relatively low glycemic index (GI) which, in addition to supplying good vitamin and mineral sources, keeps your blood sugar regulated. You are then less likely to reach for cookies and cakes made with white flour! Other fruits with a low GI include cherries, grapefruit, pears, apples, peaches, oranges, and all the berries.

gluten-free chocolate fudge cake

serves 10–12

1 stick plus 2 tablespoons/150g unsalted butter, diced, plus extra for greasing

7oz/200g dark chocolate (at least 70% cocoa solids), broken into squares

scant 1 cup/200ml soy, rice, or coconut milk

4 tbsp organic agave or rice syrup

¼ cup/25g rice flour

2 tbsp unsweetened cocoa powder

1 tsp vanilla extract

4 large eggs, separated

¾ cup/75g ground almonds

½ cup/100g xylitol

1 Preheat the oven to 350°F/180°C/Gas 4. Lightly butter the base and side of an 8in/20cm springform cake pan (tin).

2 Melt the chocolate in a heatproof bowl over a pan of gently simmering water, making sure the base of the bowl doesn't touch the water. Stir once or twice until melted, then remove from the heat and leave to cool slightly.

3 Heat the milk and syrup in a pan until just starting to boil, then stir in the rice flour and cocoa powder. Pour into a large bowl and stir in the melted chocolate and butter. Next, beat in, one at a time, the vanilla extract, egg yolks, ground almonds, and half the xylitol.

4 Put the egg whites into a clean, grease-free bowl and whisk until they form soft peaks. Gradually whisk in the remaining xylitol to make stiff, glossy peaks. Using a large metal spoon, gradually fold the egg white mixture lightly into the chocolate mixture until combined.

5 Pour into the prepared pan and bake for 40 minutes until risen – it will still be quite soft in the center. Leave to cool completely in the tin before cutting into slices.

6 This cakes initially rises—but as it cools it "sinks" slightly—and resembles a chocolate brownie in texture. Delicious served with fresh berries and plain, low-fat yogurt.

Food as Medicine

• **Chocolate** is a good source of magnesium, and its theobromine and caffeine content accounts for its stimulating action on the central nervous system, giving us instant energy. It also stimulates endorphins in the brain to produce "happy chemicals" such as serotonin. Although high in saturated fats, only about one-third of the fat is considered problematic, the remainder being neutral or mono-unsaturated, similar to olive oil. Of course, it is high in calories, so shouldn't be consumed in large amounts unless you are "burning it off" with exercise. Dark chocolate is best, because it is usually made using 65 per cent or higher cocoa solids and is therefore richer in antioxidants.

fig, almond, and raw cacao bars

makes about 12

½ cup/50g hazelnuts

½ cup/50g blanched almonds

½ cup/75g whole rolled oats (porridge oats)

generous 1 cup/100g ready-to-eat dried figs, cut into small pieces

1¼ cups/150g unsulfured ready-to-eat dried apricots, cut into small pieces

2 tbsp raw cacao powder

5 tbsp fresh orange juice

2 tbsp dry unsweetened shredded (desiccated) coconut

1 Heat the oven to 350°F/180°C/Gas 4. Put the hazelnuts and almonds on a baking sheet and roast for 6–8 minutes, turning once, until light golden. While the nuts are roasting, put the oats on a baking sheet and bake for 5 minutes until beginning to change color. Leave the nuts and oats to cool.

2 Put the nuts and oats in a food processor and process until finely chopped, then tip into a large bowl.

3 Put the figs, apricots, cacao powder, and orange juice into the processor and blend to a thick purée. Spoon the puréed fruit and coconut into the bowl with the oat mixture. Stir until combined into a thick paste, adding more cacao powder if too wet.

4 Line a 10 x 7in/25 x 18cm shallow pan (tin) with baking parchment. Tip the fruit mixture into the pan and, using a wet metal spatula, spread into an even layer, about ½in/1cm thick. Chill in the refrigerator for about 1 hour to firm up. Cut into bars and store in an airtight container in the refrigerator for up to one week.

health TIP

⊙ **If you want to discover** which foods are giving you more energy and which may be draining your energy, keep an accurate and honest daily food diary. After a month of noting when you feel the most energized, and when you experience food cravings or energy lows, you can usually find which foods suit your unique needs. Also, have your hormones checked, as they play an important part in energy levels.

Chapter 13

feel-good foods

Since the late 1990s there has been a huge increase in the number of people taking medication for depression and other problems linked to mental distress. Depression and anxiety are characterized by altered mood, and symptoms can vary greatly between individuals. One person may lose their appetite or libido, whereas another may suffer from insomnia, or find themselves not wanting to see friends, laugh, or go to work. Yet what you eat can significantly help to improve your mood.

Many factors contribute to depression, such as mental and physical exhaustion, ongoing negative stress, insomnia, family history, low thyroid function (hypothyroidism), alcohol abuse, recreational drug abuse, loss of a loved one or a job, sunlight deprivation, blood sugar imbalances, hormonal fluctuations, postnatal depression, food intolerances, deficiency of key nutrients, some prescription medication drugs, dehydration, and intestinal toxicity.

Sunlight deprivation alone can trigger Seasonal Affective Disorder (SAD) which affects around half a million people each winter in the UK alone. The majority of sufferers are women, and the condition is worse between September and April when levels of natural sunlight diminish.

SAD is a form of depression, which generally comes and goes depending on the amount of full-spectrum light that your eyes are exposed to. When we are exposed to less sunshine, the body makes more melatonin in the brain, which encourages us to sleep. Scandinavia and Finland have a high incidence of SAD, although Iceland has a low incidence, which may be due to their consumption of oily fish, giving them a higher level of the "sunshine" vitamin D in their diets.

Shorter days slow down the metabolism, or in traditional Chinese medical terms, the *qi* goes deeper into the body. It is a time for recharging, reflecting, nurturing, and preparing for next year.

Signs and symptoms of SAD can include depression, anxiety, fatigue, poor sleep quality, irritability, lack of motivation, increased appetite (especially for sweet, starchy foods), weight gain, and feelings similar to pre-menstrual syndrome.

The feel-good chemicals
When there is insufficient light, the body will naturally crave sugary carbohydrates to increase its serotonin production, which is the "feel good" hormone produced in the body—hence why many people put on weight in winter. The problem with eating too many refined sugary foods is that they affect blood sugar levels and consequently can alter your mood. It is better to break the cycle, and opt for a more complex carbohydrate diet.

Our brains have many neurotransmitters (chemical messengers); one is serotonin, and another important one connected to mood is dopamine. Serotonin tends to relax us whereas dopamine is involved with alertness, excitement, and motivation. If out of balance, low serotonin can present as depression, and the imbalanced dopamine is the opposite, causing risk taking.

Foods that will help your body to make more serotonin include turkey, chicken, fish, goat's cheese, cottage cheese, brown rice, bananas, avocado, yogurt, cod, soybeans, hazelnuts, peanuts, seeds, asparagus, mung beans, tofu, and lentils. These foods contain the amino acid tryptophan from which serotonin is formed. Tryptophan is the least common amino acid found in our foods, and requires vitamin C to manufacture serotonin.

The body needs amino acids to be able to make neurotransmitters, but these are derived from protein sources, and too much protein at the expense of carbohydrate will imbalance the levels of serotonin and dopamine leading to a tendency towards depression. You need to eat adequate amounts of carbohydrate to keep the neurotransmitters in balance.

Good low-glycemic sources of carbohydrate include oats, whole-grain spelt, rice noodle or whole-grain spelt pasta, quinoa, basmati rice, sourdough rye, soya and flax seed bread, bulgur wheat, lentils (dahl), and hummus. Dark chocolate also stimulates the release of serotonin, thereby raising "happy" endorphin levels.

The need for good fats

The brain is made up of 60 percent essential fats, so omega-3 fatty acids are fundamental for good health, and to alleviate any form of depressive illness. The other essential fats are also necessary to maintain a healthy nervous system. Eat oily fish—mackerel, salmon, herring, trout, and sardines—as well as walnuts, hemp and flax seeds for omega-3s.

Good sources of omega-6 fatty acids include safflower and sunflower oil, hemp and pumpkin oil, walnuts, pine nuts, sunflower, pumpkin and flax seeds, and olives. The mono-unsaturated fatty acids are found in avocados, olives, peanut butter, coconuts, macadamia nuts, and cashew nuts.

Oily fish also provides valuable vitamin D, a lack of which is becoming common, especially in the elderly and children. Expose your skin on sunny days for 15–30 minutes away from the midday sun without a sunscreen, so that your body can make sufficient amounts of vitamin D. Also eat sunflower seeds and egg yolks.

Reduce your intake of stimulants, such as alcohol and caffeine, and sugary, refined, processed foods. Alcohol lowers levels of serotonin in addition to depleting valuable B vitamins, which are needed for brain chemical production. The B vitamins, B_{12}, B_6, and folic acid (folate), are necessary for the central nervous system to function properly, and they also keep toxic homocysteine levels low. Insufficient amounts of any one of these B vitamins have been linked to all types of depression. Tri-methyl-glycine (TMG)—a compound found in plants such as quinoa, wheat bran and spinach—works with vitamins B_{12}, B_6, and folic acid to lower homocysteine levels, and some studies have found it to be effective in elevating mood.

Good sources of vitamin B_{12} include oily fish, oysters, clams, mussels, mozzarella cheese, and yogurt. Vitamin B_6 can be found in rabbit, pheasant, turkey, oily fish, hazelnuts, bananas, and squashes. High-folate foods include leafy green vegetables, peas, beans and lentils, lettuce, asparagus, and sunflower seeds.

Selenium levels also tend to be low in anyone suffering depression. There are usually good amounts in pheasant, partridge, scallops, Brazil nuts, cashew nuts, sunflower seeds, and lentils.

To feel good all year around, try to avoid the "comfort foods", and go for foods that contain the slow-releasing carbohydrates, which are unprocessed and higher in fiber and tryptophan, as well as being lower in refined sugars and unnatural fats. A healthy diet, plus adequate vitamin D and plenty of exercise are the secrets to feeling happy and healthy.

overnight oatmeal

serves 8

3 cups steel-cut oats (Irish or pinhead oatmeal)

sea salt

oat milk or other dairy-free milk, organic agave syrup, and fruit, to serve (optional)

1 Just before going to bed, bring 1¾ quarts/1.75 liters cold water to a boil in a large pan. Add 2 tsp salt. Shower in the oatmeal, whisking all the time. Return to a boil and boil for 1 minute.

2 Pour into a Dutch oven (casserole), then cover with the lid, and put in a slow oven at 275°F/140°C/Gas 1, or the Aga. Alternatively, put in the stoneware of a preheated crockpot, cover with the lid, and cook on low.

3 Cook for 8 hours or overnight. The oatmeal will be ready the next day—you will have to remove a skin from the top, and probably add a little boiling water to thin it down. Serve with cold milk, agave syrup, and any fruit you like.

Food as **Medicine**

● **Oats** are high in magnesium and B vitamins, which are beneficial for the nervous system. The slow-releasing sugars, and good protein and fatty acid content makes them ideal to eat for breakfast. Oatmeal (porridge) can also encourage deep sleep, thanks to the relaxing effects of B vitamins, plus the slow "drip-feeding" of glucose, which keeps blood sugar regulated at night. Blood sugar irregularities often wake people up during the night (particularly if they go to bed with a busy head!), because adrenalin is released in response to low blood sugar. If you cannot sleep, try eating a bowl of oatmeal, made with rice milk, then add a chopped banana and a few raisins—you'll hopefully be back to sleep in no time.

asparagus, chive, and pea shoot omelet

serves 4

14oz/400g fava (broad) beans, shelled

9oz/250g asparagus, trimmed

4 tsp sunflower oil

8 eggs

generous 1 cup/125g crumbled soft goat's cheese

3½oz/100g pea shoots

4 tbsp chopped fresh chives

sea salt and ground black pepper

1 Steam the fava beans and asparagus for 4 minutes or until the vegetables are tender. Set the asparagus aside. Gently squeeze the beans out of their gray outer shell. Set aside with the asparagus.

2 Heat the oil in a nonstick frying pan. Lightly beat 2 of the eggs, season with salt and pepper, and pour them into the pan. Tip the pan until the egg mixture coats the base. Cook for 2–3 minutes then slip the flat omelet onto a serving plate.

3 Put a quarter of the goat's cheese in the center of the omelet. Top with a quarter of the fava beans, asparagus, and pea shoots. Sprinkle with some chives before serving. Repeat to make three more omelets.

waldorf salad

serves 4

3–4 green eating apples

juice of 1 lemon

2 celery sticks, thinly sliced

1 cup/115g walnut pieces or pecan nuts, coarsely chopped

½ cup/120ml good-quality mayonnaise

1 Cut a few slices of apple with skin for the garnish, then peel and core the remainder and cut into matchstick strips, using a mandoline.

2 Put the lemon juice into a bowl and add the apple matchsticks, tossing to coat them thoroughly.

3 Put the sliced celery in a large bowl, then add the apples and walnuts or pecan nuts. Spoon the mayonnaise over the top. Garnish with the apple slices.

Food as **Medicine**

• **Apples** are packed with antioxidants such as flavonoids and polyphenols. The flavonoid quercetin is anti-inflammatory, and studies have shown it to be effective in preventing lung diseases as well as reducing tumors. In addition, apples are full of pectin (a soluble fiber), which not only helps to lower LDL cholesterol, but also keeps you feeling fuller, aiding weight loss.

• **Coconut butter/oil** is rich in medium-chain fatty acids, which are assimilated quickly by the body, providing a source of energy. Fatty acids also give a feeling of fullness and thereby reduce cravings. Coconut butter/oil is high in lauric acid—found in breast milk—which helps to boost immunity. It does not go rancid in the same way that mass-produced oils and margarines do when heated. Be sure to only use raw, organic, or unprocessed coconut butter.

spanish eggs with shrimp

serves 4

40g/3 tbsp virgin coconut oil

1 red bell pepper, seeded and diced

1 large garlic clove, sliced

1 long red chili, seeded and thinly sliced

10 eggs, lightly beaten

1 tsp paprika

1½ cups/250g small cooked shrimp or prawns

3½ oz/100g arugula (rocket), roughly chopped

4 corn tortillas

sea salt and ground black pepper

1 Heat the coconut oil in a heavy-based, nonstick pan over medium-low heat until melted and gently bubbling. Add the pepper, garlic, and chili, and cook, stirring, for 1 minute until softened.

2 Add the eggs and paprika and, using a wooden spoon, slowly and smoothly move the eggs around the pan to prevent them sticking.

3 When the eggs start to set into large flakes, fold in the shrimp and arugula and cook for another minute until the eggs set to a soft, creamy consistency and the arugula has just wilted.

4 Meanwhile, warm the tortillas in a low oven. Serve the eggs spooned on top of the tortillas. Season to taste and serve.

chicken noodle soup

serves 4

1 pack fresh banh pho or ho fun rice noodles, or dried rice sticks

1 tbsp peanut (groundnut) oil

2 boneless, skinless chicken breasts, finely sliced

1 tbsp brown sugar

2 tbsp fish sauce

CHICKEN STOCK:

1¼ quarts/1.2 liters chicken stock

4 whole star anise

2in/5cm fresh root ginger, sliced or chopped

2 onions, cut into wedges

1 cinnamon stick

TO SERVE:

your choice of scallions (spring onions), bean sprouts, sprigs of fresh cilantro (coriander), mint, and Asian basil, sliced red chilies, lime wedges, and sliced romaine lettuce (not traditional)

1 Put the stock ingredients into a pan, bring to a boil, and simmer gently for about 30 minutes to extract the flavors (or boil hard for 10 minutes, but don't allow it to evaporate).

2 If using dried rice sticks, soak them in hot water for 15 minutes, then drain thoroughly.

3 Heat the oil in a wok or a large pan, add the chicken, sugar, and fish sauce, and stir-fry for 1–2 minutes until the chicken is cooked.

4 Dip the noodles, whether fresh or dried and soaked, in boiling water for about 1 minute to heat through, then drain and divide among four large bowls. Put the chicken on top, and strain over the stock. Serve with your choice of serving ingredients on a separate serving plate, and add them according to taste.

health TIP

○ **Natural sunlight** helps to suppress production of the hormone melatonin, which is made in the pineal gland at night. Melatonin aids restful sleep and is an important antioxidant, but during the winter, production of melatonin increases and can contribute to feelings of lethargy during the day. So, the more exposed you are to natural sunlight, the more positive you will feel.

mexican turkey burgers with corn salsa

serves 4

1lb 5oz/600g ground (minced) turkey

2 tsp paprika

1 tsp hot chili powder

1 tsp ground cumin

1 tsp dried oregano

juice of 1 lime

3 tbsp sunflower oil

sea salt and ground black pepper

4 gluten-free rolls, to serve

CORN SALSA:

6 vine-ripened tomatoes

7oz/200g can no added sugar or salt corn, drained

1 small red onion, diced

1 green chili, seeded and diced

juice of 1 lime

4 tbsp chopped fresh cilantro (coriander)

1 First make the turkey burgers. Mix all the ingredients together, except the oil, in a bowl. Season, then form the mixture into four burgers about ½in/1cm thick. Chill for 30 minutes to allow the burgers to firm up.

2 Meanwhile, to make the salsa, halve the tomatoes, then scoop out the seeds and dice the flesh. Put the tomatoes into a bowl and add the corn, diced onion and chili, lime juice, and cilantro.

3 Heat the oil in a large, nonstick frying pan over medium heat. Fry the burgers for 3 minutes on each side until golden. Serve the burgers in the rolls, topped with a generous spoonful of the salsa.

Food as Medicine

• **Turkey** contains the amino acid tryptophan, which helps the body to make the hormone serotonin— known as the "happy" hormone. Turkey is a good source of lean protein, which helps to balance your blood-sugar levels for longer, and this can greatly enhance your mood. Turkey breast also contains vitamins B_1, B_2, B_3, B_5, B_6, and B_{12}, which support your nerves, and vitamins D and E plus minerals— including calcium, copper, iron, and zinc—are also present. In all, it's a perfect feel-good food.

date, walnut, and cinnamon soda bread

serves 8–10

2¾ cups/375g whole-wheat spelt flour, plus extra for dusting

1 tbsp xylitol

1 tsp ground cinnamon

1 tsp baking soda (bicarbonate of soda)

1 tsp sea salt

generous ⅔ cup/4½oz ready-to-eat dried dates, roughly chopped

scant 1 cup/100g walnuts, roughly chopped

1 cup plus 2 tbsp/280ml buttermilk

1 egg, lightly beaten

1 Preheat the oven to 400°F/200°C/Gas 6. Lightly dust a baking sheet with flour.

2 Sift the flour, xylitol, cinnamon, baking soda, and salt into a large mixing bowl. Stir in the dates and walnuts until combined, then make a well in the center. Pour in the buttermilk and egg, and stir with a fork, then use your fingers to form the mixture into a soft dough.

3 Tip the dough onto a lightly floured work surface, then knead briefly to form into a round loaf. Transfer to the prepared baking sheet. Dust the top of the loaf with flour then make a deep cross in the dough about three-quarters of the way through.

4 Bake for 30 minutes or until risen and golden. Tap the base of the loaf—it should sound hollow when baked. Leave to cool completely on a wire rack.

Food as Medicine

• **Xylitol** is probably the best natural sweetener to take (other than the herb stevia.) It is not strictly a sugar, but actually a sugar alcohol, and has a low glycaemic index (GI), so it raises blood sugar just slightly, and therefore less insulin is released. It is structurally different from other sugars, such as fructose and glucose, and doesn't promote the same fermentation problems in the gut, which encourage bacteria and fungal overgrowths. From this point of view you are less likely to feel tired and bloated after eating your dessert.

lemon-berry cheesecakes

serves 6

generous 1 cup/250g dairy-free cream cheese

4 tbsp organic agave syrup

1 tsp vanilla extract

finely grated zest of 2 large lemons

2 eggs, lightly beaten

1 tsp cornstarch (cornflour)

1¾ cups/200g frozen dark berries, such as blackberries, black currants, red currants, blueberries, and raspberries

BASE:

1 tbsp virgin coconut oil, melted, plus extra for greasing

½ cup/50g jumbo rolled oats (porridge oats)

2 tbsp sunflower seeds

generous ½ cup/60g toasted slivered (flaked) almonds

2 tbsp organic agave syrup

1 Preheat the oven to 350°F/180°C/Gas 4. Lightly grease six 2½in/6cm food presentation rings, or deep ramekins, and put on a baking sheet.

2 To make the base, lightly toast the oats and sunflower seeds in a large, nonstick frying pan over medium-low heat for 4–5 minutes, turning occasionally, until starting to turn golden.

3 In a food processor, grind the oats, sunflower seeds, and slivered almonds until they are the texture of coarse bread crumbs. Transfer to a bowl and stir in the coconut oil and agave syrup. Spoon the mixture into the rings or ramekins and press down with the back of a teaspoon to make a firm, level base. Set aside while you make the topping.

4 Beat together the cream cheese, 3 tbsp agave syrup, the vanilla extract, lemon zest, eggs, and cornstarch until smooth. Pour the mixture into the rings, then bake for 20 minutes or until risen and firm to the touch. Leave to cool, then chill for 1 hour.

5 Put the frozen fruit, the remaining 1 tbsp agave syrup and 3 tbsp water into a small pan and heat gently for 8–10 minutes until the fruit defrosts and the sauce becomes slightly syrupy.

6 Run a knife around the edge of the presentation rings to loosen, then lift off the rings. (If using ramekins, leave the cheesecakes in the individual dishes.) Spoon the fruit and some of the juice over and around each cheesecake before serving.

health TIP

○ **Foods that help to raise** levels of the "happy hormone" serotonin are fish, eggs, wheat germ, oats, avocados, and bananas. Chocolate also makes you feel good, because it contains the amino acid phenylalaline, which lifts one's mood. But please make it dark and organic when possible! Foods that lower serotonin levels are alcohol, high-protein foods, such as red meats and processed meats, caffeine and, artificial sweeteners.

Food as Medicine

- **Sunflower seeds** are a rich source of selenium in addition to omega-6 fatty acids. The quality of soil will always dictate the selenium levels of the food grown in it, so this is another reason to eat organic produce. Selenium levels are often low in people suffering with depression, and this perhaps emphasizes the importance of eating selenium-rich foods. Other good food sources include pheasant, partridge, scallops, Brazil nuts, cashew nuts, and lentils.

- **Agave nectar** (syrup), even though sweeter than sugar or honey, has a relatively low glycemic index (GI). This means that it will not cause blood sugar levels to rise significantly, in the way that refined sugars do—which ultimately drains energy. Because of its high fructose content, which is processed in the liver, Agave is not suitable for those with fructose intolerance or malabsorption problems. Buy organic agave syrup only.

chapter 14

stress-busting

More than 200 million working days are lost in the USA annually—upwards of 13 million in the UK—through stress-related conditions, which are major contributing factors for a variety of health problems. Not all stress is bad. It can help to keep you sharp and alert, but in the longer term, how your body copes depends on your reaction to the stress.

Eons ago when our ancestors were faced with life-and-death situations, the hormones adrenaline and cortisol were released from the adrenal glands, causing the heart to pump faster, and giving an instant energy boost to the body and brain. Muscles tensed, cholesterol production increased, and enzymes in the blood caused it to thicken, so that if our ancestors were injured, their blood clotted more easily. Blood vessels would constrict, endorphins—the body's own painkillers—would be released, and oxygen consumption increased. Known as "fight or flight," these responses saved many lives back then.

Today, our automatic physical response to stress remains the same but it is more frequent, and does not result in the action of fight or flight. With our 24/7 lifestyles, stress is now triggering an avalanche of conditions from heart attacks, strokes, cancers, stomach ulcers, and even Alzheimer's disease.

The secret to managing stress is to look after your adrenal glands through diet and lifestyle. Common triggers for sub-optimal adrenal function include lack of sleep, constantly driving yourself to work hard, living on sugar and caffeine, juggling many tasks at once, childbirth, trying to be perfect, shift working, alcohol or drug abuse, unrelieved pressure of work, major surgery, or death of a loved one—in fact, any situation that provokes a stressful environment.

Signs that stress is taking its toll

Symptoms of stress and "burn out" vary considerably, and can include chronic fatigue, depression, anxiety, low immunity, thyroid malfunctions, rashes, or insomnia, to name a few. Waking in the night is a common problem, which occurs when adrenalin is released because blood sugar levels have dropped. Some people have difficulty getting out of bed in the morning, and yet they are not ready to sleep until late at night. Others may suffer with low libido, fuzzy thinking, headaches, memory loss, or repeated infections.

Signs of low blood sugar manifest as cravings for stimulants, such as chocolate, coffee, cookies, or even salt-based snacks, because more sodium is excreted in the urine. Blood pressure is commonly low if adrenals become severely exhausted.

This type of burn out occurs because the adrenal glands can no longer function normally. They become exhausted, and so their daily rhythm is out of sync with your lifestyle.

Beating stress through food

If we obtain high-quality fuel from our diets, through eating unprocessed and organic foods, this provides a "buffer" against the physical and emotional stressors put on the body.

Tea, coffee, and cocoa contain caffeine and theobromine, which can cause an increase in anxiety and insomnia. Eating too much refined sugar will also contribute to feeling hyper, because the sugar gives you a quick burst of energy. But as blood sugar plummets again, your body starts demanding more. This vicious cycle should be broken by eating more foods that contain slow-releasing sugars. Oatmeal (porridge) is one example. It contains nervine, a class of herbs that relax the nervous system—ideal for helping to reduce feelings of anxiety.

The body can store only a certain amount of Vitamin C, and the adrenal glands contain high concentrations of it, requiring more at times of stress. To replenish stores of vitamin C, eat red bell peppers, broccoli, Brussels sprouts, cherries, black currants, kiwi fruits, persimmons, mangoes, grapefruit, guava, strawberries, and blueberries.

Magnesium, often referred to as the anti-stress mineral, is also required in large amounts when stress builds up. This smooth muscle relaxant plays a major role in keeping arteries and blood vessels supple. Low levels have been linked to anxiety, insomnia, high blood pressure, and cardiovascular disease. Good sources include halibut, lima beans, spinach (cooked), artichokes, green leafy vegetables (especially kale), almonds, Brazil and cashew nuts, pine nuts, pumpkin seeds, brown rice, avocado, peanuts, dried apricots, barley, buckwheat, and kelp. (Grains are best soaked overnight before cooking.)

Likewise, vitamin B_5 is needed in greater amounts when the body is under stress. Good sources of vitamin B_5 include mushrooms, broccoli, squashes, avocados, sweet potatoes, cauliflower, chicken, turkey, clams, lobster, salmon, mackerel, sunflower seeds, and sushi. The body needs a steady intake of B vitamins, which help to protect the nervous system, and when we are under stress, our demand for them is greatly increased, but they are easily lost through the diuretic action of alcohol and caffeine. Keep stores high by eating fish, cottage cheese, yogurt, nuts, poultry, and whole grains (quinoa, bulgur, brown rice, and millet).

Vitamins B_{12}, B_6, and folic acid are of particular importance during stressful periods. Folic acid is found in wheat germ, eggs, leafy greens, beets (beetroot), sprouted seeds, almonds, cauliflower, potatoes, and broccoli. Vitamin B_6 is present in turkey, oily fish, cod, trout, snapper, hazelnuts, bananas, bell peppers, squashes, watercress, spinach, red cabbage, and cauliflower. B_{12} is found in oily fish, cod, oysters, clams, mussels, crab, lobster, octopus, mozzarella cheese, and yogurt.

When stressed, the body breaks protein down far more quickly, often causing weight loss in people who are under long-term negative stress. Protein helps to balance blood sugar levels for longer than other foods, thus reducing sugar cravings, so make sure you include lean meats, cheese, eggs, tofu, quinoa, fish, beans, peas, and lentils in your diet.

In Traditional Chinese Medicine, the kidney qi, which is akin to the adrenal glands, houses our primordial essence, or life force, and aging is either a slow or rapid burning up of this vital energy source. There is a natural ebb and flow in the kidney/adrenal qi every day when many of us enjoy a cup of tea, coffee, or something sweet. Research has shown that this corresponds with a natural dip in the earth's radioactivity every day at about the same time, so we really are tuned into the cosmos!

To keep stress under control, learn to slow down and smell the roses, eat the right foods—choosing organic if you possibly can—laugh a lot, get some regular exercise to help disperse stress hormones, and you can age more slowly and live a healthier life!

full of beans soup

serves 4

1½lb/675g (about 6) ripe tomatoes, halved

2 tbsp chopped fresh basil leaves

2–3 garlic cloves, crushed

14oz/400g can mixed beans, drained and rinsed

3½oz/90g canned red kidney beans, drained and rinsed

1 vegetable bouillon (stock) cube

sea salt and ground black pepper

TO SERVE:

thick plain (natural) sheep's or goat's yogurt (optional)

freshly shaved Parmesan (optional)

a few fresh basil leaves

1 Preheat the boiler (grill). Put the tomatoes in a large roasting pan, cut sides up. Sprinkle with the basil and garlic, then season well with salt and pepper. Broil (grill) for 5–10 minutes, until the tomatoes have softened.

2 Remove the tomatoes from the pan and let cool slightly. When cool enough to handle, peel them, discarding the skins. Put the tomatoes into a food processor or blender, and process until smooth. Add the mixed beans and kidney beans, and process for a further 30 seconds, until the beans are broken down slightly but the soup still has a chunky texture.

3 Transfer the mixture to a pan. Dissolve the bouillon cube in ¾ cup/ 175ml boiling water. Add the stock to the soup and heat gently over medium heat until piping hot, stirring occasionally.

4 Ladle the soup into warmed soup bowls. Serve immediately, topped with a spoonful of yogurt and a sprinkling of freshly shaved Parmesan, if you like, and some basil leaves.

Food as Medicine

• **Beans** are high in folate, which is essential for a healthy nervous system and, in conjunction with vitamins B_6 and B_{12}, helps to lower homocysteine levels. Low levels of any one of these B vitamins has been linked to depression. Other foods high in folate include leafy green vegetables, spinach, leeks, lettuce, lentils, chickpeas, asparagus, and sunflower seeds.

italian bean and vegetable soup

serves 6

1 onion, chopped

2 garlic cloves, crushed

1¼ quarts/1.2 liters vegetable stock

2 carrots, diced

2 cups/150g chopped mushrooms

2 zucchini (courgettes), diced

3 cups/750ml tomato juice

14oz/400g can Great Northern (cannellini) beans, rinsed and drained

1¼ cups/150g shredded green cabbage

3 tbsp chopped fresh basil

sea salt and ground black pepper

1 In a large flameproof Dutch oven (casserole) or pan, soften the onion and garlic in ¼ cup/60ml of the stock for 5 minutes, with the lid on. Stir in the carrots, mushrooms, and zucchini, then season and cook for 2 minutes.

2 Stir in the tomato juice and the remaining stock and bring to a simmer, then cover and cook for 10 minutes.

3 Mix in the beans and shredded cabbage, re-cover the pan and simmer for a further 10 minutes. Adjust the seasoning and stir in the basil just before serving.

Food as Medicine

• **Beans** are a good source of vitamin B₁ (thiamine), which is utilized in the body when we are stressed. Our body can't store much of it, so we need to obtain a continual supply from our diet. Refined foods are deficient in B₁ and it is depleted by alcohol and strenuous exercise. Other rich sources are rice bran, wheat germ, macadamia and pecan nuts, peas, sunflower seeds, brown rice, and fish.

health TIP

○ **At times of stress**, we tend to breathe in a shallower way. Making time to take regular, deep, slow in- and out-breaths really helps to slow the release of the stress hormones adrenalin and cortisol. Stress makes your blood more acidic, but slow breathing helps to re-alkalize it.

cottage cheese pancakes with caramelized tomatoes

serves 4

1 cup/125g plain spelt flour

1 tsp baking soda (bicarbonate of soda)

generous 1 cup/250g cottage cheese

2 eggs

6 tbsp rice milk or other non-dairy alternative

salt and ground black pepper

CARAMELIZED TOMATOES:

4 tbsp olive oil, plus extra for cooking pancakes

12oz/350g vine-ripened cherry tomatoes, halved

5 long fresh thyme sprigs, leaves removed

2 tbsp balsamic vinegar

health TIP

If you find yourself becoming angry much of the time, especially over small issues, or if tears come for little reason and your sense of humor fails, take action. With the overproduction of the stress hormones adrenalin and cortisol, your adrenal glands are put under severe strain, tissues become more acidic, triggering inflammation, and your blood can thicken. Usually, it's not the stress itself that harms your health, but your reaction to it. If possible, make a space and time between what is stressing you and your reaction to it. Instead of concentrating on the problem, focus on what you can learn from any situation, and if you change your attitude to a more positive outlook, you may find that many negative health effects can be reduced.

1 Put the flour, baking soda, cottage cheese, eggs, and milk in a blender and process to make a smooth batter. Leave to rest, covered, for about 30 minutes.

2 To make the caramelized tomatoes, heat the olive oil in a large, nonstick frying pan over medium heat. Add the tomatoes and half the thyme, and cook for 1 minute, turning once. Pour in the balsamic vinegar, reduce the heat to low, and cook for 2 minutes, turning occasionally, until the tomatoes start to caramelize. Season to taste, sprinkle with the remaining thyme, then remove from the pan and set aside.

3 Wipe the pan clean, then heat enough oil to lightly coat the base. Put 3 tbsp of the batter into the pan (you will probably be able to cook three or four pancakes at a time). Cook for 2 minutes on each side until golden and set. Keep warm while you use the remaining batter to make 12 pancakes in total.

4 Serve three pancakes per person accompanied by the caramelized tomatoes, spooning any pan juices over.

turkey skewers with satay dip

serves 4

1 tsp paprika

1 tsp ground turmeric

2 tbsp olive oil

1¼lb/550g turkey breast, cut into strips

sea salt and ground black pepper

lime wedges, to serve

SATAY DIP:

scant 1 cup/200ml coconut milk

6 tbsp "no added salt or sugar" peanut butter

1 tbsp tamari

1 heaping tsp Thai red curry paste

½ tsp dried chili flakes

Food as Medicine

- **Peanuts** are a source of magnesium—the body's tranquilizer (see Health Tip). Other food sources are halibut, lima (butter) beans, cooked spinach, artichoke, green leafy vegetables (especially kale,) brown rice, avocado, dried apricots, kelp, nuts (see Food as Medicine on page 304), barley, and buckwheat (grains are best soaked overnight before they are cooked.)

1 If using wooden skewers soak 12 for 10 minutes. Otherwise use 12 metal skewers. Preheat the broiler (grill) to high. Mix together the paprika, turmeric, and olive oil in a large, shallow dish. Season and add the turkey. Turn until the turkey is coated in the oil and spices. Thread the turkey onto the skewers.

2 Arrange the skewers on a foil-lined broiler rack and grill (broil) for 5–6 minutes, turning once until cooked through.

3 Meanwhile, put the coconut milk, peanut butter, tamari, curry paste, and chili flakes in a small pan. Heat gently, stirring, until combined—add a little water if the sauce looks too thick. Remove from the heat and pour into four small bowls.

4 Serve the turkey skewers with the satay dip on the side and with wedges of lime for squeezing over.

health TIP

- **Anyone** who is under pressure will be low in nature's tranquilizer—the mineral magnesium. Magnesium is vital for relaxing tight muscles and it also keeps arteries and blood vessels supple. Low levels of magnesium are linked to anxiety, insomnia, high blood pressure, and cardiovascular disease. If you are feeling particularly stressed, take 150mg of magnesium citrate before bedtime, with a small amount of banana and/or an oatcake, to help you to relax.

baked garlic and tomato mushrooms

serves 4

8oz/225g cremini (brown cap) or portabello (field) mushrooms, wiped

2–4 tsp olive oil

1 celery stick, finely chopped

1–2 large garlic cloves, crushed

1 green chili, seeded and finely chopped

½ cup/25g fresh whole-wheat bread crumbs

1 tomato, seeded and chopped

2 tbsp chopped fresh chives, plus extra to garnish

sea salt and ground black pepper

1 Preheat the oven to 350°F/180°C/Gas 4. Choose 4 portabello or 8 cremini mushrooms and remove the stalks. Put the caps stem-side up in an ovenproof dish. Finely chop the remaining mushrooms and all the stalks. Heat a nonstick sauté pan and add 2 tsp oil.

2 Add the chopped mushrooms, celery, garlic, and chili, and sauté, stirring frequently, until soft. Let cool slightly, then transfer to a bowl.

3 Add the bread crumbs, tomato, and chives to the bowl, then season with salt and pepper. Mix well, adding a little oil to moisten, if necessary.

4 Fill the mushrooms with the bread-crumb mixture. Pour about ¼ cup/60ml water into the dish, then bake in the oven for 12–15 minutes until the mushrooms are soft and the topping is crisp.

5 Remove from the oven and serve immediately, sprinkled with some chives and accompanied by mixed salad leaves.

Food as Medicine

• **Mushrooms** are a rich source of vitamin B_5 (pantothenic acid); often called the anti-stress vitamin. It is fundamental as a raw material in the manufacture of the stress hormone cortisol, and is used up in considerable amounts during stress. Other good sources include broccoli, squash, avocado, sweet potatoes, cauliflower, chicken, turkey, clams, lobster, salmon, mackerel, sunflower seeds, and sushi.

herbed tomato and artichoke couscous

serves 2

¼ cup/40g couscous

½ cup/125ml boiling chicken stock or water

6 semi-dried tomatoes or 6 fresh cherry tomatoes, halved

2 marinated artichoke hearts, sliced

3–4 scallions (spring onions), sliced

14oz/400g can chickpeas, rinsed and drained

HARISSA DRESSING:

⅓ cup/75ml extra-virgin olive oil

1 tbsp sherry vinegar or cider vinegar

1 tbsp harissa paste

sea salt and ground black pepper

TO SERVE:

a handful of fresh flat-leaf parsley, coarsely chopped

watercress sprigs or arugula (rocket)

fresh mint sprigs

fresh cilantro (coriander) sprigs

fresh chopped chives

health TIP

- **Drinking** green tea can help to reduce stress, as it contains an amino acid called L. theanine, which helps your brain to produce more alpha waves—the same brainwaves that you produce during relaxation. Stroking a pet is also relaxing and produces more alpha waves!

1 Put the couscous in a heatproof bowl and cover with the stock or water. Leave for 15 minutes or until the water has been absorbed. For a fluffier texture, put the soaked couscous in a strainer and steam over simmering water for another 10 minutes, or microwave in a pitcher (jug) or bowl on medium for about 5 minutes. Drain if necessary, pressing the liquid through the strainer with a spoon, then fluff up with a fork. Let cool.

2 When ready to make up the salad, put the couscous in a bowl, add the tomatoes, artichoke hearts, scallions, and chickpeas. Keep the watercress or arugula and herbs in a separate container until just before serving.

3 To make the dressing, put the olive oil, vinegar, and harissa paste into a bowl and beat with a fork. Add salt and pepper to taste. Sprinkle half the dressing over the couscous mixture and toss with a fork. Add the watercress and herbs, and serve. Serve the extra dressing separately for people to help themselves.

Food as **Medicine**

● **Whole grains** are one of the best sources of the B vitamins (apart from B_{12}), which are fundamental to a healthy nervous system. B vitamins are water-soluble and easily lost in cooking or because of the effects of alcohol and caffeine consumption, or cigarette smoking. We should never underestimate how much diet can help us to cope better during times of stress. At such times we need to increase the quality of our fuel to meet the demands. Whole grains, such as brown rice and quinoa, or the pasta-like couscous (if made using coarse-ground durum wheat) will provide most of these essential B vitamins.

Food as **Medicine**

- **Salmon** is a rich source of vitamin B_6, which is essential for the health of the nervous system, but is often lacking where there is adrenal exhaustion. Other good sources include all oily fish, cod, trout, snapper, hazelnuts, bananas, peppers, squash, watercress, spinach, red cabbage, and cauliflower.

- **Chickpeas and lentils** are two of the best blood sugar regulators. High in fiber and with quite high protein ratios, both foods will help with energy and mood by slowly "drip-feeding" their glucose into our bloodstreams over a longer period. Maintaining normal blood sugar is important in times of stress, as cortisol levels fluctuate.

spiced salmon with chickpea dhal

serves 4

½ tbsp grated fresh root ginger

2 tbsp chopped fresh cilantro (coriander)

1 tsp ground cumin

1 tsp ground coriander

1 tbsp lemon juice

4 skinless salmon fillets, about 4oz/115g each

1 tsp safflower oil

sea salt and ground black pepper

DHAL:

1 cup/225g red lentils

1 onion, finely chopped

1 tbsp grated fresh root ginger

½ tsp ground turmeric

2 garlic cloves, sliced

1 tsp cumin seeds

½ tsp black mustard seeds

2 tsp safflower oil

14oz/400g can chickpeas, rinsed and drained

3 tomatoes, seeded and chopped

3¾oz/100g baby spinach, rinsed

1 tbsp lemon juice

health TIP

○ **Stress** breaks down protein very quickly, hence the reason why highly stressed people tend to lose weight more quickly. Make sure that you include a portion of quality protein with your breakfast and lunch to help your body cope with the affects of stress. Tofu, quinoa, eggs, fish, lean meats, lentils, beans, and other pulses will all help to support you.

1 Start by making the spice paste for the salmon. In a bowl, mix the ginger with the cilantro, spices, lemon juice, and seasoning, then rub into the salmon fillets. Cover and set aside at room temperature to allow the flavors to develop while making the dhal.

2 Put the lentils in a pan with the onion, ginger, turmeric, and 2 cups/ 475ml water and cook, covered, for 15 minutes or until the lentils start to break up.

3 Heat the 2 tsp safflower oil in a frying pan and fry the garlic, cumin seeds, and black mustard seeds until the garlic is golden and the seeds begin to pop. Quickly stir into the lentils, followed by the chickpeas. Simmer for 3 minutes.

4 Heat a nonstick frying pan and drizzle the 1 tsp safflower oil over the salmon fillets. Pan-fry the salmon for 3 minutes on each side, until the spice crust is golden and the salmon is just cooked through, but still moist.

5 Stir the tomatoes, spinach, and lemon juice into the dhal until the spinach has just wilted. Add seasoning to taste, then ladle the dhal into deep plates. Place the salmon on top of the dhal to serve.

tabbouleh with chickpeas and spring salad

serves 4

½ cup/50g fine bulgur wheat

2 tbsp lemon juice

¼ cup/60ml extra-virgin olive oil

1 small bunch of fresh flat-leaf parsley, leaves finely chopped

1 large handful of mint leaves, finely chopped

2 tbsp finely chopped fresh dill

1 small basket of cherry tomatoes, halved

14oz/400g can chickpeas, rinsed and drained

4–5 oz/115–150g spring salad mix

sea salt and ground black pepper

corn or wheat-free tortillas or flatbread, and lemon wedges, to serve (optional)

1 Put the bulgur wheat in a heatproof bowl and pour over ½ cup/125ml boiling water. Stir once, cover tightly with plastic wrap (clingfilm) and set aside for 8–10 minutes. Put the lemon juice and olive oil in a small bowl, and whisk. Pour this over the bulgur wheat and stir well with a fork, fluffing up the bulgur and separating the grains.

2 Put the bulgur in a large bowl with the parsley, mint, dill, tomatoes, chickpeas, and salad greens. Use your hands to toss everything together. Season well with sea salt and black pepper. Transfer to a serving plate and serve with tortillas or flatbread and lemon wedges, if you like.

Food as Medicine

• **Bulgur wheat** is cracked and partially cooked, retaining its nutrient status. It is a good source of iron, potassium, zinc, selenium, manganese, and phosphorus, and is high in the anti-stress mineral magnesium. In addition, it supplies good amounts of nerve-calming vitamins B_1, B_2, B_3, and B_6. Owing to its high fiber content, it is a slow-burning fuel that helps to maintain blood sugar levels.

Food as Medicine

- **Brown rice** is known for its calming ability, and this is because it is a rich source of thiamine (vitamin B_1), found in the outer shell, or bran. All whole-grain rice varieties are good sources of the B vitamins, particularly B_1, B_2, and B_3, making it a better choice than plain white rice, particularly with respect to thiamine. Choose brown rice in preference for the stroganoff recipe.

- **Rices** are available in many different types—red, brown, wild, and so on. The long-grain rices, such as basmati and jasmine, tend to be less sticky than short-grain varieties. All rices are a good source of energy, although their glycemic index (GI) varies considerably, depending on type of rice, how it is cooked, and what it is cooked with. One thing in common with all rice is that it is gluten-free and therefore easy to digest.

mustardy mushroom stroganoff

serves 1

½ small onion, sliced

⅔ cup/150ml vegetable stock

5oz/150g mixed mushrooms, chopped if large

1 garlic clove, crushed

1 tsp whole-grain mustard

½ tsp tomato paste (purée)

1 tbsp dairy-free sour cream

sea salt and ground black pepper

chopped fresh flat-leaf parsley, to garnish

1 Cook the onion in a covered pan with 3 tbsp stock for 4 minutes, or until softened and the liquid has evaporated.

2 Stir in the mushrooms, garlic, and seasoning, then add the remaining stock, mustard, and tomato paste.

3 Cook, covered, for 2 minutes, then remove the lid and cook rapidly for 2 minutes to reduce the liquid to a syrup.

4 Remove the pan from the heat, stir in the sour cream, and serve immediately, garnished with parsley, on a bed of rice or couscous. Steamed cabbage or spring greens make a good accompaniment.

health TIP

● **People who meditate** regularly are better able to cope with stress. This is because, over time, regular meditation greatly reduces the "fight or flight" stress response by reducing the amount of toxic stress hormones cortisol and adrenalin that are released. It also helps to balance the thyroid, which can become underactive with prolonged stress. Similar affects are seen in those who practice yoga or t'ai chi.

tonno e fagioli

serves 4

12oz/350g thin green beans

14oz/400g can small navy beans (flageolet) or white kidney beans, rinsed and drained

14oz/400g canned Great Northern (cannellini) beans, rinsed and drained

¼ cup/15g mixed chopped fresh herbs (such as parsley, basil, and chives)

6½oz/185g can tuna steak in spring water, drained and flaked

sea salt

DRESSING:

1 tbsp Dijon mustard

1 tbsp lemon juice

2 tbsp extra-virgin olive oil

1 shallot, finely chopped

4 anchovy fillets, finely chopped

1 Cook the green beans in a pan of lightly salted boiling water for 4–5 minutes until tender. Drain and refresh under cold water. Meanwhile, mix the canned beans together with the herbs in a large bowl. Beat the dressing ingredients together with 1 tbsp water in a separate bowl, then mix two-thirds into the canned beans.

2 To serve, arrange the green beans on a serving platter and drizzle over the remaining dressing. Spoon the dressed canned beans in a mound on top of the green beans, then top with the flaked tuna.

sesame chicken with stir-fried vegetables

serves 4

⅔ cup/100g sesame seeds

6 tbsp spelt flour

2 eggs, lightly beaten

550g/1¼lb boneless, skinless chicken breast, cut into 1in/2.5cm strips

ground kelp or sea salt and ground black pepper

STIR-FRIED VEGETABLES:

2 tbsp sunflower oil, plus extra for greasing

3 garlic cloves, sliced

1in/2.5cm piece fresh root ginger, peeled and cut into matchsticks

1 long red chili, seeded and thinly sliced (optional)

7oz/200g broccolini, trimmed

4 bok choy (pak choi), sliced

3¾oz/100g Chinese leaves, sliced

1 tsp sesame oil

2 tbsp tamari

1 tsp togarashi (Japanese chili pepper seasoning)

2 chopped scallions (spring onions) and fresh cilantro (coriander) leaves, to garnish

Food as Medicine

- **Sesame seeds** are an excellent source of calcium, which is important for proper heart muscle function. Whole (unprocessed) foods contain minerals such as phosphorus, sodium, magnesium, and potassium, which balance calcium in the body. Other good calcium sources include goat's and sheep's milk, sardines, salmon, peas, and almonds.

1 Preheat the oven to 350°F/180°C/Gas 4. Lightly grease two nonstick baking sheets.

2 Put the sesame seeds and flour in separate shallow bowls and season the latter with kelp or sea salt and pepper. Dust the chicken in the flour, then dip into the egg, followed by the sesame seeds until coated. Put onto the baking sheets, then bake for 12–15 minutes, turning once, until the chicken is cooked through.

3 Meanwhile, heat a large wok over high heat. Add the sunflower oil and stir-fry the garlic, ginger, and chili for 30 seconds, then add the broccolini, bok choy, and Chinese leaves. Stir-fry for 3 minutes, then add the sesame oil, tamari, togarashi, and a splash of water. Heat through, then divide among four large, shallow bowls.

4 Top with the sesame chicken, and scatter over the scallions and coriander before serving.

health TIP

- **When feeling tense and tired**, make time to go for a walk, preferably somewhere peaceful. Exercise helps to disperse the stress hormones adrenalin and cortisol, which become toxic to every major organ in the body if not "burned up" during exercise. Walking will help to release tensed muscles which, in turn, helps to relax jangled nerves. It also gives you time to calm down!

cajun chicken with roasted vegetable quinoa

serves 4

1 heaping tbsp Cajun spices

4 tbsp olive oil

4 boneless, skinless chicken breasts, cut into large bite-size pieces

2 fennel bulbs, quartered

4 carrots, quartered

½ butternut squash, cut into bite-size pieces

4 cooked beets (beetroot), halved or quartered

⅔ cup/125g quinoa

2 ½ cups/600ml hot chicken stock

1 large orange, peeled and cut into bite-size pieces

small bunch of cilantro (coriander), chopped

sea salt and ground black pepper

1 Preheat the oven to 400°F/200°C/Gas 6. Mix the Cajun spices with half the olive oil in a large, shallow dish. Season, add the chicken, and turn it until it's coated in the spice mixture. Set aside to marinate.

2 Put the fennel, carrots, squash, and beets into a large bowl and pour in the remaining olive oil, then turn the vegetables until coated. Arrange the vegetables, with the exception of the beets, in an even layer on two baking sheets. Season with salt and pepper, then roast for 20 minutes or until almost cooked.

3 Arrange the chicken in a single layer in a roasting pan and roast for 15 minutes. Turn the vegetables and add the beets, then return to the oven for a further 15 minutes.

4 Meanwhile, put the quinoa in a pan. Add the chicken stock and bring to a boil. Turn down the heat, then cover with a lid and simmer for 10–15 minutes until tender. Drain the quinoa and put into a bowl with the orange and half the cilantro; stir until combined, then divide among four serving plates.

5 Top the quinoa with the vegetables and chicken, pouring over any juices, and scatter over the remaining cilantro.

health TIP

Food as Medicine

• **Steamed broccoli** or a salad goes well with this dish, providing vitamin C. At times of stress, far more vitamin C is needed, but the body can only store a certain amount. Eating fruits, such as cherries, strawberries, kiwi fruits, black currants, mangos, persimmons, blueberries, and grapefruit, will help you to cope more effectively.

○ **Digestive enzyme** production can be greatly inhibited during times of stress, and this can trigger "leaky gut" syndrome, which can then contribute to the onset of multiple food sensitivities, especially to gluten, soya, animal dairy, and corn (maize). (You will find more information on "leaky gut" and digestion in Chapter 5.) When stressed, eat foods that are easier to digest, such as soups, smoothies, and fresh juices, and avoid large, rich, or fried food meals.

caraway and goat's cheese pasta bake

serves 4

8oz/225g wheat-free penne

2 potatoes, diced

2½ cups/275g shredded Swiss chard

3 tbsp olive oil

1 onion, chopped

1 leek, sliced

2 large garlic cloves, chopped

1 tsp caraway seeds

1 tsp dried thyme

2½ cups/175g sliced chestnut mushrooms

⅔ cup/150ml vegetable stock

¾ cup/150g crumbled soft goat's cheese

¼ cup/25g walnuts, roughly chopped

sea salt and ground black pepper

health TIP

○ **As the body's** need for nutrients is far greater when you are stressed, taking extra supplements can be useful along with eating a healthy diet. A good regimen to help support the body would be 250mg of vitamin C, three times daily with meals, plus a high-strength multivitamin–mineral complex that contains a full spectrum of B vitamins to support your nervous system—take with breakfast or lunch. Additionally, take 400mg of calcium with 600mg of magnesium, in divided doses throughout the day, with the last dose just before bedtime. Finally, take 1g of pure fish oil containing EPA and DHA to help thin the blood naturally.

1 Preheat the oven to 375°F/190°C/Gas 5. Lightly grease a large baking dish. Cook the pasta according to the pack instructions until only just cooked and still very al dente. Drain and refresh the pasta under cold running water.

2 Cook the potatoes for 8 minutes or until tender, drain and set aside. Steam the Swiss chard for 3 minutes or until wilted.

3 Meanwhile, heat the olive oil in a large, heavy-based pan and fry the onion and leek for 5 minutes until softened. Add the garlic, caraway seeds, thyme, and mushrooms, and cook for a further 3 minutes, stirring occasionally, until tender.

4 Remove the pan from the heat and add the pasta, potatoes, Swiss chard, and stock. Season, then turn until combined. Transfer to the baking dish, scatter over the cheese and walnuts, and bake for 10–15 minutes until heated through.

orange and almond cake

serves 4

6 eggs, separated

½ cup/100g xylitol

grated zest of 3 oranges

juice of ½ orange

generous 1 cup/150g ground almonds

orange zest, to garnish, (optional)

orange slices, to serve (optional)

TOPPING:

juice of 2 oranges

2 tbsp good-quality honey, such as cold extracted or manuka

1 Preheat the oven to 350°F/180°C/Gas 4. Line and lightly grease an 8in/20cm springform cake pan (tin). Beat together the egg yolks, xylitol, orange zest and juice, and ground almonds in a large bowl.

2 Put the egg whites into a clean, grease-free bowl and whisk until they form stiff peaks. Fold a spoonful into the almond mixture to loosen it, then fold in the remaining egg whites. Carefully pour the mixture into the prepared cake pan. Bake for 45–50 minutes until a toothpick inserted into the center of the cake comes out clean. Leave to cool in the pan.

3 To make the topping, put the orange juice and honey into a small pan and bring to a boil, stir once, then cook undisturbed for 6–8 minutes until reduced, thickened, and syrupy.

4 Using a fork, prick the top of the cake, then pour the syrup over the top, and leave to soak in before serving. (The cake is best left for a few hours before eating.) Garnish with orange zest and serve with orange slices, if you like.

Food as Medicine

- **Almonds** are the most alkaline of all nuts, being rich in magnesium, potassium, and calcium. Their high magnesium content makes them an ideal anti-stress food, because magnesium is used up in huge amounts by the adrenal glands during tense times, and is necessary for proper nerve functioning. Other magnesium-rich nuts include Brazil nuts, cashew nuts, pine nuts, hazelnuts, pumpkin seeds, and peanuts.

- **Raw honey** is honey that hasn't been heated and preferably not filtered, so it has some pollen, propolis, comb, and perhaps royal jelly in its content—it's basically straight from the hive. In this state it is a very alkaline food, full of vitamins and minerals, particularly stress-calming magnesium and vitamins B_5 and B_6. Manuka honey (which is generally cold extracted) will also preserve most of its nutrients.

hot bananas

serves 4

4 just-ripe bananas in their skins

½ cup/50g walnut halves

2 tbsp good-quality honey, such as cold extracted or manuka

½ tsp ground cinnamon

scant 1 cup/200ml thick plain (natural) sheep's or goat's yogurt, to serve

1 Preheat the oven to 375°F/190°C/Gas 5. Put the bananas on a baking sheet and bake for 18–20 minutes until the skin has blackened and the fruit inside is tender.

2 Meanwhile, toast the walnut halves in a dry, nonstick frying pan for 4–5 minutes, turning once, until slightly golden. Leave to cool, then roughly chop.

3 To serve, put a banana on each plate. Make a slit along the curve of the skin and open it out slightly. Scatter the walnuts over the top then drizzle with the honey and cinnamon. Serve with spoonfuls of yogurt.

PART 3

LOOK GOOD

Pamper yourself with good nutrition, because your hair, nails,

and skin show how much you care about your body. And, by

eating well and exercising, you can keep the years at bay,

and keep looking good. Living healthily

has never been so tempting!

chapter 15

eat to stay young

Disease, aging, and illness are basically about two things—deficiency and toxicity—and the bottom line of this equation is based upon your pH, or acid–alkaline, levels. Everything we eat, once metabolized, breaks down into an alkaline or acid mineral-based "ash" or residue.

The problem today, and the basis for practically every major disease associated with aging, is that our bodies have become too acid due to stress, and our over-consumption of acid-forming processed and refined foods.

As we age, we don't eliminate these acids as efficiently as we did in our youth, and they consequently accumulate in our tissues. Normally, our body has the necessary buffering agents (minerals) to sustain a healthy pH, but they usually become inadequate after eating over-processed foods for a period of time. Acidic tissues with a low oxygen status make the perfect environment for aging, because oxidation and inflammation can develop. It is common to see premature hair loss and graying, early osteoporosis, and poor skin elasticity, caused by vital minerals, such as calcium and magnesium, being withdrawn from the nails and bones to buffer an over-acidic condition.

The secret to anti-aging is to eat more green superfoods. Alfalfa, sprouted beans (such as mung and aduki), wheat and barley grass, and sea vegetables, such as kelp, dulse, and samphire, are very alkaline and rich in minerals to balance the body's pH. In addition, green leafy vegetables, parsley, celery, spinach, and bok choy (pak choi) offer similar protection. Avocados are a rich source of mono-saturated fatty acids and are also high in the alkaline mineral potassium.

Take plenty of exercise, drink pure water, eat organic fruit and vegetables—rich in calcium, magnesium, potassium, and sodium—and reduce stress to slow down aging.

The main offenders are alcohol, caffeine, too much red meat, and animal-sourced dairy, unnatural sugars and fats, white flour, and any processed foods—plus our old friend, stress—as they compromise your tissues, preventing you from attaining a healthy pH balance. Yet, not all acid-forming foods are bad. Dried plums (prunes), for example, are very acid-forming, but they are incredibly anti-aging. It's all about balance.

Oxidation causes aging

Another crucial factor in the process of aging is free-radical damage. If you cut an apple and leave it open to the air, it turns brown—it oxidizes. This is basically what happens to our cells as we age. Antioxidants, such as vitamins A, C, and E, as well as minerals such as zinc and selenium, help protect our cells from the oxidation processes by "mopping up" the free radicals that are produced when we eat burnt foods, acid-forming foods, or when we are exposed to pollution and stress. Not all free radicals are "bad", because they are needed for various functions in the body, but problems arise when the "bad guy" free radicals outnumber the "good guy" antioxidants.

Vitamin E protects against fat oxidation, such as LDL (the "bad") cholesterol. Eat sesame seeds, millet, cucumbers, avocados, sunflower seeds, almonds, hazelnuts, wheat germ, mangoes, olives, broccoli, and oils with a high oleic content, such as sesame, and unrefined olive and walnut oils.

Water-soluble Vitamin C (which includes the bioflavonoids) helps prevent oxidation to the blood vessels, and it is also needed for the manufacture of collagen, the main component of your skin. Good sources include cherries, kiwi fruit, grapefruit, strawberries, black currants, mangoes, kale, bell peppers, and tomatoes.

Beta-carotene also acts as an antioxidant and converts to vitamin A in the body. A main function is to protect the mucous membranes (the linings in your lungs and gut), which are often the first line of defense against toxins and microorganisms. Eat pumpkin, carrots, sweet potatoes, mangoes, and apricots.

Anti-aging essential fats and nutrients

The omega-3 essential fatty acids (from oily fish, walnuts, and flax seeds) are vital to reduce inflammation—a major condition of aging and linked to heart and arterial disease, and Alzheimer's. They also help your skin to stay younger for longer. Rosemary, turmeric, garlic, and ginger protect against inflammation.

Both zinc and selenium are considered antioxidants, and although we don't need large amounts, they are commonly deficient because foods grown in soil that is over-farmed tends to be low in nutrients. Zinc-rich foods include seeds, peanuts, pecan nuts, pine nuts, and shellfish. For selenium, eat halibut, cod, salmon, shrimp and prawns, tuna, lentils, sunflower seeds, and barley.

Another antioxidant, called pangamic acid, may help to reduce the effects of pollution, specifically carbon monoxide. Sources include brown rice, pumpkin seeds, and sunflower seeds.

Other powerful antioxidants are found in blueberries, pomegranates, green tea, red wine, dark chocolate, cherries, figs, artichokes, leeks, and apples. Organically grown foods generally contain higher levels of anti-aging nutrients.

The antioxidant amino acid L-carnosine keeps your skin younger for longer and has been found in far higher concentrations in long-lived people such as those on the island of Okinawa. Levels reduce with age, and in people with low-stomach acid, which is a huge majority of the Western population! L-carnosine is found in all protein foods. Good sources are lean beef and chicken.

The cultured or fermented foods are beneficial for helping us to "age gracefully," by providing "soil" for our good intestinal bacteria to grow in. These include goat's and sheep's yogurt, sauerkraut, tempeh, tamari, natto, and tofu.

The cruciferous vegetables—such as broccoli, cabbage, and cauliflower—help to detoxify the liver, which is critical to the healthy aging process.

Sunshine is fundamental to our health and necessary for vitamin D synthesis. Low levels of vitamin D lead to softening of the bones (rickets), peripheral vascular disease, late onset diabetes, multiple sclerosis, and many cancers, plus other age-related illnesses. But you must not allow your skin to burn, as it will age you much faster. Expose your skin for just 15–30 minutes away from the midday sun, then apply sunscreen. Also, eat oily fish and sunflower seeds.

As we age, our cells' ability to absorb water decreases, and we can become dehydrated. This can cause cells to shrivel and die. Drink plenty of pure filtered water, and reduce or eliminate chlorinated or fluoridated waters. Eat fruit, such as melon, which has a high water content in a form that the body can easily utilize and absorb.

Exercise regularly and keep stress to a minimum. Occasionally, breathe deeply to re-alkalize your body. In this way you should age more gracefully, and live a healthier life for longer. It's worth the investment.

blueberry and apple bircher muesli

serves 2–3

2½ cups/225g rolled oats (porridge oats)

1 cup/250ml apple juice

⅓ cup/75ml rice, almond, oat, or coconut milk

½ cup/125ml thick, plain (natural) low-fat dairy-free yogurt

1 apple, cored and grated

blueberries and toasted sunflower seeds, to serve

1 Put the oats in a large bowl and pour the apple juice over. Cover the bowl with plastic wrap (clingfilm) and leave in the refrigerator overnight.

2 Just before serving, stir in the milk, yogurt, and grated apple. Spoon into bowls and top with blueberries and toasted sunflower seeds.

health TIP

● **During different phases** of your life, your lifestyle, diet, and thoughts all contribute to your health. As we age, or when we become stressed, the enzymes needed for digestion and absorption are reduced, and food intolerances can arise. Intolerances trigger inflammation in the body, which is hugely aging! One person may develop a sensitivity to gluten, another a problem with corn (maize), soya, or animal dairy, and so on. Keeping an accurate and regular food diary, and noting when symptoms, such as a runny nose, bloating, or skin problems arise, can fairly quickly lead you to the culprit or culprits. More details in Chapter 1.

coconut power juice

serves 2

4 apples, quartered and cored

2 carrots

1¼in/3cm piece fresh root ginger, grated

1⅔ cups/400ml coconut water

1 Put the apples and carrots through a juicer. Pour the juice into a pitcher (jug).

2 Squeeze the ginger in one hand to extract the juice, then discard the fibrous part. Add the ginger juice to the apple and carrot mixture, then stir in the coconut water until combined. Serve immediately.

Food as Medicine

- **Animal-based dairy foods** can be a problem for some people, but if you are not intolerant to them, eating live, low-fat (preferably organic,) yogurts are fine for health, although you may find that sheep's and goat's milks and yogurts are easier to digest.

- **Coconut water** has the same electrolyte profile as our blood, being rich in potassium, chloride, and sodium, and is therefore what is called isotonic. Its lauric acid content makes it a good antiviral, and its isotonic action means it quickly hydrates the body—and this becomes more important as we age.

yellow gazpacho

serves 4–6

4 yellow or orange bell peppers

1 basket yellow cherry tomatoes, halved

2 garlic cloves, crushed with salt

3 cups/750ml cold chicken or vegetable stock

1 cup/250ml crushed ice, plus extra ice to serve (optional)

1 mini cucumber

6 radishes

4 scallions (spring onions), sliced

4 red cherry tomatoes, quartered

a few fresh flat-leaf parsley, and mint or basil sprigs, leaves chopped

a handful of chives, chopped

salt and ground black pepper

1 Peel the peppers with a vegetable peeler, seed them and chop the flesh. Put the flesh into a blender with the yellow tomatoes and garlic, and blend to a purée.

2 Add the stock and crushed ice, then blend again. Add salt and pepper, then chill until very cold.

3 Halve the mini cucumber lengthways and scoop out the seeds. Using a mandoline or a very sharp knife, cut the cucumber and radishes into paper-thin slices.

4 Pour the purée into a glass soup tureen or separate bowls or glasses, adding extra ice if you like. Top with the cucumber and radish slices, scallions, and red cherry tomatoes. Serve, sprinkled with the herbs, salt, and black pepper.

Food as Medicine

• **Vegetables and fruit** as a regular part of your diet will help to slow aging. Our diets should consist of about 75 per cent alkaline-forming foods and 25 per cent acid-forming foods. In the Western world our diets are far too acid-forming. Alcohol, caffeine, too much red meat and animal dairy, unnatural sugars and fats, white flour, and stress are the main offenders. You can stay younger for longer by eating more alkaline-forming foods—chiefly fruits and vegetables, particularly the green (chlorophyll-rich) vegetables.

roasted red bell pepper soup

serves 4

2 tbsp olive oil

2 onions, halved and finely sliced

2 garlic cloves, crushed

8 long red bell peppers (or yellow or orange)

1 quart/1 liter chicken or vegetable stock

sea salt and ground black pepper

1 bunch wild arugula (rocket), or fresh thyme or oregano sprigs, to garnish

1 Heat the oil in a frying pan, add the onions and sauté gently until soft and golden. Push to the side of the pan, add the garlic and sauté for about 1 minute.

2 Meanwhile, halve and seed the peppers, put on a sheet of foil or a baking sheet under a hot broiler (grill), and cook until the skin is black and charred. Transfer to a bowl or pan and cover tightly with plastic wrap (clingfilm) or a lid. Leave for about 10 minutes to steam, then transfer to a sieve set over the same bowl or pan. Scrape off and discard the skins, putting the flesh back into the bowl or pan (catch as many of the toasted juices as possible).

3 Transfer to a blender, add the onions and garlic, and work to a purée, adding a little stock if necessary. Add the remaining stock and purée again, then transfer to a pan and heat to boiling point. Remove from the heat, season, then serve in heated soup bowls.

4 Garnish with some wild arugula or fresh thyme leaves, or small sprigs of oregano.

Note: If you like, a couple of medium-hot red chilies, such as Fresno or Serrano may be broiled at the same time as the peppers and treated in the same way.

health TIP

○ **How often** have you heard a person say, "It's all in my genes"? Although our genes play a major role in our lives, they can be repaired and altered, depending on our diet and lifestyle. Your parents may have suffered from a specific illness, such as heart disease or arthritis, and you may have a predisposition to that condition, but if you live a healthy lifestyle, you can change which genes are expressed!

sardines and fresh salsa on toast

serves 4

8 slices rye bread

4 vine-ripened tomatoes, seeded and diced

½ small red onion, diced

1½in/4cm piece cucumber, seeded and diced

3 tbsp chopped fresh flat-leaf parsley

juice of ½ lemon

a large pinch of dried chili flakes

3 x 4oz/120g cans boneless, skinless sardines in olive oil

ground black pepper

1 Lightly toast the rye bread.

2 Meanwhile, mix together the tomatoes, red onion, cucumber, parsley, lemon juice, and chili flakes. Season with pepper to taste.

3 Divide the sardines among the pieces of toast. Top with the tomato salsa just before serving.

Food as Medicine

- **Sardines,** salmon, mackerel, and herring are some of the best sources of omega-3 essential fatty acids. As we age, we are more prone to free-radical damage to our cells. Essential fatty acids protect the nerves from oxidative damage as well as reducing stickiness in the blood and lowering blood pressure.

- **Duck** is a good source of selenium, which acts as an antioxidant, helping to repair DNA and promoting better liver function, as well as slowing degenerative conditions. Low levels are linked to a weakened immune system and improper thyroid function. Alcohol and smoking reduce selenium in the body.

duck with juniper red cabbage

serves 4

4 duck breasts

sea salt and ground black pepper

JUNIPER RED CABBAGE:

1 tbsp virgin coconut oil

4½ cups/500g shredded red cabbage

10 juniper berries, lightly crushed

½ tsp ground ginger

2 cloves

1 tbsp good-quality honey (cold extracted or manuka)

zest and juice of 1 orange

1 Preheat the oven to 400°F/200°C/Gas 6. Score the duck skin with a sharp knife and season.

2 Put the duck breasts, skin-side down, in a dry nonstick frying pan over medium heat. Brown the skin for 10–15 minutes, then pour off any excess fat. Put the duck in a roasting pan and roast in the oven for 10–12 minutes until medium-rare.

3 Meanwhile, heat the coconut oil in a large pan and stir-fry the red cabbage for 3 minutes until beginning to soften.

4 Add the juniper berries, spices, and orange juice, and simmer, part-covered, for 15 minutes or until softened. Remove the lid, stir in the honey and orange zest, and cook for another 5–10 minutes until the sauce has reduced and thickened. Season to taste, and remove the cloves.

5 Allow the duck to rest for 10 minutes then serve with the red cabbage.

sesame and mint couscous with vegetables

serves 6

2 tbsp unsalted butter

2 garlic cloves, finely crushed

1 tbsp sweet paprika

2 tsp ground cumin

½ tsp ground ginger

1 tsp ground black pepper

2 bay leaves

2 tbsp tomato paste (purée)

14oz/400g can chopped tomatoes

2 whole green chilies

2 thick carrots, quartered, and cut into finger lengths

2 thick parsnips, quartered, and cut into finger lengths

1lb/450g potatoes, peeled and cut into 2in/5cm chunks

2 thick zucchini (courgettes), quartered and cut into finger lengths

8oz/225g butternut squash or pumpkin, peeled, seeded, and cut into 2in/5cm chunks

2 tbsp harissa paste mixed with ½ cup/125ml hot water, to serve

SESAME AND MINT COUSCOUS:

2 cups/350g couscous

1 stick/115g butter, cut into pieces

¼ cup/15g chopped fresh mint

3 tbsp toasted sesame seeds

sea salt and ground black pepper

Food as Medicine

- **Lean protein** foods, such as chicken, turkey, or beef, can be added to this vegetarian dish if you like. They are a good source of L-carnosine; an important double amino acid with antioxidant properties that helps to increase the life of your cells. It has been found in far higher concentrations in long-lived people; however, levels naturally reduce with aging and in people with low levels of stomach acid—which in itself becomes lower as we age.

1 Melt the butter in a flameproof Dutch oven (casserole) dish, add the garlic, and cook for 1 minute over medium heat. Add the paprika, cumin, ginger, pepper, bay leaves, tomato paste, and canned tomatoes, then stir well. Bring to a boil and add the chilies, carrots, and parsnips.

2 Pour in enough water to cover (about 1¾ cups/425ml), bring to a boil, part-cover with a lid, then simmer gently for 20 minutes. Add the potatoes, zucchini, and butternut squash, pushing them under the liquid, and cook for a further 20 minutes or until the potatoes are tender. Do not overcook or the vegetables will disintegrate.

3 Meanwhile, put the couscous in a bowl. Put 2 cups/500ml boiling water in a heatproof measuring cup, stir in the butter and mint, then pour evenly over the couscous. Cover tightly with plastic wrap (clingfilm) and let stand for 5 minutes.

4 Uncover the couscous and fluff up the grains with a fork. Stir in the sesame seeds, taste, and season well with salt and pepper. Pile the couscous onto a large serving platter, make a hollow in the center, and heap the spicy vegetable stew into the middle. Serve immediately with the harissa sauce mixture in a small bowl.

cashew burgers with tomato chili relish

serves 4

1½ cups/150g cashew nuts

1 tbsp olive oil, plus extra for brushing

1 onion, finely chopped

2 tsp cumin seeds

1 tsp ground turmeric

2 tsp ground coriander

2 large garlic cloves, finely chopped

2 carrots, grated

1 cup/50g whole-wheat spelt bread crumbs

1 egg, lightly beaten

1 heaping tbsp plain (natural) sheep's yogurt

plain spelt flour, for dusting

sea salt and ground black pepper

TOMATO CHILI RELISH:

6 vine-ripened tomatoes, seeded and diced

1 long red chili, seeded and finely chopped

3 tbsp chopped fresh cilantro (coriander)

2 tbsp chopped fresh flat-leaf parsley

1 small red onion, diced

2 tbsp lime juice

Food as Medicine

- **Turmeric** has potent anti-inflammatory properties. Inflammation is linked to almost every major disease of aging, so it is well worth including more turmeric in your diet. There is a lower incidence of Alzheimer's and heart disease in countries where it is regularly eaten.

- **Cilantro** (coriander) is a great anti-aging herb that helps the liver to detoxify more easily.

- **Cashew nuts** contain iron for energy and to make red blood cells, also magnesium for healthy bones and teeth, and zinc for nourished skin and to boost immune function.

1 Preheat the oven to 350°F/180°C/Gas 4. Put the cashew nuts on a baking sheet and roast for 6–8 minutes until light golden all over. Leave to cool.

2 Heat the oil in a frying pan and fry the onion for 6 minutes or until softened. Add the cumin seeds and fry for another minute, then stir in the turmeric and ground coriander. Blend the onion mixture in a food processor until it is a coarse paste, then spoon into a large bowl.

3 Grind the cashew nuts in the food processor until very finely chopped, then tip into the bowl with the onion paste. Add the garlic, carrots, bread crumbs, egg, and yogurt; season well and mix together.

4 Cover a plate with flour and, with floured hands, divide the mixture into four, and then shape into burgers, dusting them in flour until lightly coated. Put on a plate, and chill the burgers for 30 minutes to firm up.

5 Meanwhile, make the relish. Put the tomatoes, chili, chopped herbs, red onion, and lime juice in a bowl.

6 Preheat the broiler (grill) to high and line the broiler rack with foil. Brush the tops of the burgers with oil and grill (broil) for 8–10 minutes, turning halfway and brushing with more oil, until golden. To serve, spoon a generous amount of the relish on the top of each burger.

almond milk

serves 1

¾ cup/75g almonds, preferably blanched

1 tbsp good quality honey, such as cold extracted or manuka

1 cup/250ml ice cubes or crushed ice

Put the almonds and honey into a blender, add the ice cubes, and 1 cup/250ml ice water. Blend to a paste. Gradually add extra ice water until the mixture is smooth. Strain and serve over ice.

Note: The process can be repeated several times, producing thinner and thinner "milk" each time. Eventually, the strained almond meal can be used to thicken sauces or flavor breads, cakes, or cookies.

Food as Medicine

• **Almonds** are an alkaline food, rich in magnesium, potassium, and calcium. They are also a good source of manganese and vitamin E, plus monunosaturated fatty acids. These high-protein nuts, when eaten in conjunction with high glycemic index (GI) foods, have been shown to dramatically lower the GI of the meal. This makes them an all-around superfood.

• **Walnuts** make good snacks, and walnut oil can be used in salad dressings. They are both rich in vitamin E—a major antioxidant—which helps to protect the B vitamins and vitamin C against oxidation. Vitamin E prevents oxidation of fats, such as LDL cholesterol, slowing the progression of arterial damage, and keeping our blood vessels younger for longer.

almond and banana shake

health TIP

• **In general,** people who are more positive, and who laugh a lot and are adaptable, tend to live longer, healthier lives. People who are negative, resentful, angry, and rigid in their beliefs, on the other hand, often live for fewer years. Never underestimate how your emotions, thoughts, and beliefs can affect your health and your wellbeing.

serves 2

½ cup/50g whole blanched almonds

1⅔ cups/400ml almond or other dairy-free milk

2 ripe bananas, thickly sliced

1 tsp pure vanilla extract

freshly grated nutmeg, to serve

1 Put the almonds in a food processor or blender and process until finely ground.

2 Add the milk, bananas, and vanilla, then blend until smooth and creamy. Pour into two glasses and sprinkle a little nutmeg over the top.

star anise poached pears

serves 4

4 slightly underripe pears, peeled

juice of ½ lemon

2 jasmine tea bags

1in/2.5cm piece fresh root ginger, peeled and sliced into rounds

1 cinnamon stick

1 heaping tbsp xylitol

2 star anise

1 Cut the pears in half and, using a melon baller or teaspoon, scoop out the cores. Squeeze the lemon juice into a bowl, add the pears and turn until coated—this will prevent them from browning.

2 Bring 1 quart/1 liter water to a boil in a large, deep pan. Reduce the heat to a simmer and add the jasmine tea bags. Stir, then add the pears, ginger, cinnamon stick, xylitol, and star anise.

3 Simmer the pears for 5 minutes, then remove the jasmine tea bags. Part-cover the pan with a lid and continue to poach the pears for 10–15 minutes until tender. Using a slotted spoon, remove the pears from the pan. Increase the heat and boil gently for 2–3 minutes, until the poaching liquor has reduced and thickened.

4 Serve 2 pear halves per person, with the syrup spooned over the top.

Food as Medicine

• **Raw chocolate** has antioxidant qualities, and these are probably the single most important food group when it comes to eating to stay youthful. Antioxidants take many different forms, and may have specific roles, but the one thing they all have in common is the ability to protect the body's cells from oxidative damage by free radicals. This protective action slows down the cells' natural decline, and so antioxidants are particularly important today in our over-polluted world.

raw choc 'n' nut bar

makes 12–16

7 tbsp/100g cocoa butter

6 tbsp raw cacao powder

3 tbsp organic agave syrup

1 tsp vanilla extract

½ cup/50g pecan nuts, roughly chopped

½ cup/50g unsalted shelled pistachio nuts, halved

¼ cup/60g unsulfured ready-to-eat dried apricots, roughly chopped

finely grated zest of 1 orange

1 Melt the cocoa butter in a heatproof bowl placed over a pan of gently simmering water, making sure the base of the bowl doesn't touch the water.

2 When the cocoa butter has melted, remove the bowl from the heat. Stir in the cacao powder, agave syrup, and vanilla until combined. Next, stir in the pecan nuts, pistachio nuts, apricots, and orange zest.

3 Line a 7 x 5½in/18 x 14cm baking dish with plastic wrap (clingfilm). Pour the chocolate mixture into the dish and level the top, then chill for 2 hours or until set. To serve, break into pieces. Store in an airtight container in the refrigerator for up to two weeks.

spiced berry compote

serves 4

2⅔ cups/300g frozen mixed berries

1 tbsp organic agave syrup

a pinch of ground cinnamon or 1 cinnamon stick

1 tbsp cornstarch (cornflour) or 2 tsp arrowroot

2½ cups/550ml plain (natural) sheep's yogurt, to serve

1 Put the frozen berries into a pan with the agave syrup, cinnamon, and 2 tbsp water. Cover and simmer for 5 minutes or until the berries have thawed and are juicy.

2 Blend the cornstarch with a little cold water, then stir it into the pan. Heat, stirring, until the compote has thickened. Pour into a bowl and let cool.

3 Serve the berry compote lightly swirled into the yogurt. If you like your compotes sweet, drizzle a good-quality honey, such as cold extracted or manuka, over this dish and sprinkle with a few raisins.

health TIPS

○ **Aging and virtually all disease** result from free-radical damage to cells. Free radicals, also known as oxidants, are produced by the billions daily, when oxygen is used to create energy. Certain free radicals have a beneficial function in the body, helping to neutralize viruses and bacteria, and kill cancer cells. However, as our bodies accumulate more free radicals from eating burnt foods, and from stress, pollution, pesticides, excess sunbathing, and the use of cell phones (mobile phones), the excess can damage DNA and trigger a host of health problems. To help maintain a balance, we need to ingest plenty of antioxidants, such as vitamins A, C, E, selenium, and zinc—found in most of the foods in this book—so that aging is slower.

pink grapefruit, blueberry, and pomegranate salad

serves 4

2 pink grapefruits

a large handful of blueberries

seeds from 1 ripe pomegranate

a handful of fresh mint leaves, roughly chopped

1 Hold a grapefruit with its base on the chopping board. Position a small, sharp knife at the top, and cut off a strip of peel and pith. Remove the remaining peel in the same way. Hold the fruit over a small bowl to catch the juice and cut between the segments on both sides of the membranes separating them. Squeeze the remaining juice from the membranes into the bowl. Put the grapefruit segments in a serving dish with the juices. Repeat with the other grapefruit.

2 Scatter over the blueberries and pomegranate seeds, then sprinkle with mint just before serving.

Food as **Medicine**

• **Pomegranate** is highly anti-aging and has been used in Ayurvedic medicine for thousands of years. High in vitamins C and B$_5$ (pantothenic acid), it is a rich source of antioxidants, particularly the anthocyanins (which give the plant its color). These have been shown to protect against genetic damage, as well as safeguarding heart and blood vessels, and having an anti-cancer action.

• **Sheep's and goat's yogurt** are important anti-aging foods because, along with other cultured or fermented foods, they provide the beneficial "soil", or environmental pH, in the gut that encourages friendly intestinal bacteria to populate. Other foods in this category include kefir, sauerkraut, tempeh, tamari, natto, miso, tofuyo (fermented tofu), and umeboshi plums.

chapter 16

healthy skin, hair, and nails

Your skin is your largest organ, and a visible barometer of your internal health. If you eat too many fatty, refined foods, your liver and bowel can become overloaded, in which case toxins are dumped into the skin, triggering symptoms such as spots, boils, acne, and rashes. A good naturopath, such as my co-author Stephen Langley, can tell a great deal about a patient's state of health by looking at their skin tone, structure and pigmentation, as well as the condition of their nails and hair.

The main component of the skin, collagen, requires vitamin C, whereas the antioxidant properties of vitamins E and A nourish and support the skin from the inside out. A skin-healthy diet should include plenty of fresh fruit, vegetables, whole grains, nuts, and seeds.

Vitamin A also protects the mucous membranes (such as the soft tissues in the throat and lungs) and provides strength to cell walls. Foods rich in natural-source carotenes convert to vitamin A in the body. These include the orange-colored foods—pumpkin, mangoes, carrots, sweet potatoes—plus leafy greens.

Vitamin E improves blood circulation and is found in avocados, wheat germ, olive oil, walnuts, peanuts, sunflower seeds and their oil.

Hyaluronic acid (HA) is the naturally occurring protein found in connective tissue and cartilage that keeps your joints, ligaments and tendons flexible. It also helps to repair the tissues in the skin. When we are young, the body makes plenty of HA, but as we age, levels fall. Chicken and turkey broth made from the bones, skin, and tendons is a good source of HA. Other foods are root vegetables and butter beans.

The bad and the good

One of your skin's biggest enemies is refined sugar. It triggers cross-linking of collagen fibers through a process called glycation, which stiffens collagen over time. The more refined sugars you eat, the faster your skin will age—and it is linked to fungal nail problems too. Other bad guys are fried foods, excessive animal fats, hydrogenated and trans-fats, alcohol, caffeine, and smoking.

Carnosine, however, has anti-glycating properties and helps to prevent the cross-linking of sugars and proteins. If you sunbathe too often over many years, cross linking occurs in your skin and you age faster. Carnosine is a powerful antioxidant, protecting skin, hair, and nails from this type of free-radical damage. It also blocks amyloid production—the substance found in the brain of Alzheimer's sufferers. Good sources of carnosine are lean organic beef and chicken.

Silica is an essential mineral for repairing damaged skin and for hair growth. It is especially needed by anyone with brittle, splitting hair and nails. Zinc also repairs skin, as well as reducing external skin bacteria, and a deficiency has been linked to acne and dermatitis. Hair and nails also need zinc, so make sure you include sunflower, pumpkin, sesame, and flax seeds, Brazil nuts, walnuts, hazelnuts, cashew nuts, barley, and rye in your diet. Copper works synergistically with zinc, so eat Brazil nuts, almonds, walnuts, and hazelnuts for copper, as well as sprinkling lecithin over your morning cereal

Silica is another essential mineral and is found in lettuce, bell peppers, cucumbers, brown rice, oats, strawberries, bean sprouts, alfalfa, cherries, and sea vegetables, with the highest concentration found close to, and in, the skins.

Selenium "mops up" free radicals from ultraviolet light and the chemicals in cigarette smoke, protecting the skin and hair against damage. Good sources are found in pheasant, partridge, scallops, squid, and lentils.

The B vitamins work synergistically to maintain good skin, hair, and nails. Together, vitamins B_1, B_2, B_3, and B_5 encourage good blood circulation and building protein, cellular growth, nourishment of the skin, and conditioning of the skin, hair, nerves, and eyes. Vitamin B_5 also helps to slow down the progression of baldness, and premature aging of the skin. Good sources of the B vitamins are lentils, peas, hazelnuts, cashew nuts, mung beans, and whole grains (millet, buckwheat, quinoa, brown rice, and spelt).

Hair loss can have multiple causes from hormonal changes at menopause or after childbirth to thyroid problems and iron deficiency, but stress is a major culprit, as it robs the body of important nutrients essential for healthy hair growth. Absorption problems in the gut can also be a factor in hair health—see Chapter 5.

Vitamins C and B_5 are both utilized in large amounts by the adrenal glands during periods of stress, so it is no wonder that hair can fall out or go gray and skin can wrinkle prematurely after prolonged stressful periods. Stress also impedes the blood flow necessary to carry these vital nutrients to the scalp, because we tend to tighten the surrounding muscles and tissues.

Choosing the best protein

Hair follicles consist predominantly of protein, and hair loss can be due to eating an inadequate vegetarian diet that has poor protein sources; and iron and zinc—two fundamental minerals for hair health—may be low in such diets. Conversely, hair loss can also be caused by eating too much red meat and cheese with insufficient fruit and vegetables. This produces an overly acidic environment in the tissues, and can deplete the body's reserves of alkaline minerals, such as magnesium, needed for blood flow to the head.

Good sources of protein include fermented soy products (tempeh), chicken, turkey, venison, quinoa, barley, organic non-farmed fish, lecithin granules, yogurt, goat's cheese, ricotta, and cottage cheese.

Hair and nails also need iron. Eat blackstrap molasses, spinach, almonds, venison, partridge, pheasant, dried fruit, dates, and dried plums (prunes). Brittle, transparent nails denote a lack of iron.

As we have seen, the best way to eat for a healthy head of hair is a mixture of good-quality meat and/or vegetarian protein sources. If you are vegan, eat a wide variety of beans, pulses, and grains such as quinoa, amaranth, spelt, kamut, or millet. If you are vegetarian, also eat organic eggs, goat's cheese and sheep's yogurt, nuts, seeds, avocados, and other fruit and vegetables.

Ideally your diet for beautiful skin, hair, and nails should include fish three times a week. Oily fish is especially good, because it's rich in omega-3 fats, which are crucial for keeping your skin looking young, and they encourage soft, shiny hair. Vegetarians or vegans should include hemp and flax seeds for their omega-3 and 6 content. Foods that are rich sources of zinc and essential fatty acids include sunflower, pumpkin, sesame, and flax seeds, Brazil nuts, walnuts, hazelnuts, sardines, mackerel, and salmon.

Finally, for great skin, hair and nails, don't forget to keep your stress—and your reaction to it—at sensible levels.

polenta bruschetta with roasted vegetables

serves 4

1 ½ cups/175g instant polenta or yellow cornmeal

3 tbsp/40g unsalted butter, diced

⅔ cup/50g finely grated Parmesan, plus shavings to serve

1 tsp dried chili flakes

sea salt and ground black pepper

extra-virgin olive oil, for brushing

fresh basil leaves, to garnish

ROASTED VEGETABLES:

3 tbsp olive oil for brushing

2 red onions, cut into wedges

2 red bell peppers, seeded and sliced lengthways

1 fennel bulb, fronds trimmed and sliced lengthways

2 long fresh rosemary sprigs, halved

16 cherry tomatoes

Food as Medicine

• **Bell peppers** are one of the best sources of vitamin C, which is necessary for the manufacture of collagen —essential for healthy skin. We cannot manufacture this vitamin in our bodies, so it must come from the food we eat. It needs to be continually replenished, because it is water-soluble and not retained in the body for long. Caffeine, alcohol, smoking, and stress also remove it from the body.

1 Preheat the oven to 400°F/200°C/Gas 6. To make the roasted vegetables, divide the olive oil between two roasting pans and add the red onions, red bell peppers, and fennel, and top with the rosemary. Turn to coat the vegetables in the oil, tuck in the rosemary, and roast for 30 minutes, turning once, until almost tender.

2 Remove from the oven, discard the rosemary and scatter over the tomatoes, then turn until combined. Swap the pans around in the oven and roast for another 10–15 minutes until deep golden in places.

3 Meanwhile, make the polenta. Put 3½ cups/875ml water in a pan, gradually stir in the polenta, and bring to a boil. Turn down the heat and simmer, stirring, for 8–10 minutes until thickened. Remove from the heat and stir in the butter, Parmesan, and chili flakes; season.

4 Lightly grease a baking pan (tin) and spread the polenta in an even layer about ¾in/2cm thick into it. Smooth the top, and leave the polenta to cool and set in the refrigerator.

5 Heat a large griddle pan over high heat. Cut the polenta into four squares, then cut each one diagonally in half. Brush the polenta with oil, then griddle for 4–5 minutes each side until golden; you will probably need to griddle the polenta in two batches.

6 Serve two wedges of polenta per person, topped with the roasted vegetables. Shave extra Parmesan over the top and scatter with basil leaves before serving. (You may also like to add an extra drizzle of olive oil.)

seared scallops with minted pea purée

serves 4

juice of ½ orange

2 tbsp tamari

1 tbsp good-quality honey, such as cold extracted or manuka

1 tbsp rice vinegar

1 tbsp olive oil

12 large scallops, without the coral, prepared, rinsed, and dried

1 long red chili, seeded and finely chopped

2 tbsp chopped fresh cilantro (coriander)

sea salt and ground black pepper

4 thin lime wedges, to serve

PEA AND MINT PUREE:

2 cups/225g frozen petit pois

vegetable stock, to cover

1 tbsp extra-virgin olive oil

3 tbsp chopped fresh mint

Food as Medicine

• **Scallops** are rich in selenium, an important antioxidant mineral that helps to mop up free radicals from ultraviolet light, and the chemicals in cigarette smoke. Selenium also protects the skin and hair against damage. It slows down the rate of oxidation of polyunsaturated fatty acids in the body, preserving the elasticity of the skin.

1 Mix together the orange juice, tamari, honey, rice vinegar, and olive oil in a large, shallow dish. Season, then add the scallops and turn to coat them in the marinade. Cover, and marinate in the refrigerator for up to 1 hour (no longer or the scallops will start to "cook" in the orange juice.)

2 To make the pea purée, cover the peas in vegetable stock. Bring to a boil and cook for 2–3 minutes until tender. Drain the peas, reserving 6 tbsp of the stock.

3 Return the peas and the reserved stock to the pan. Warm through then mash the peas with a potato masher, or the back of a fork, to make a coarse purée. Stir in the olive oil and mint, then season with pepper.

4 Heat a large griddle pan over high heat. Griddle the scallops for a minute each side until seared and golden in places. Divide the minted pea purée among four plates and top with the scallops. Scatter over the chili and cilantro, and serve with lime wedges on the side for squeezing over.

health TIP

○ **A baby's body** is made up of approximately 75 percent water; breast milk is 87 percent water—this is why babies have smooth, hydrated skin! As we age, we accumulate toxins, which clog our cells, reducing their ability to absorb water and to eliminate toxins. By the time we reach 65, our body is about 55 percent water. The message is clear—stay hydrated!

spinach and mozzarella polenta with roasted vegetables

serves 4

5 tbsp unsalted butter

1 tbsp olive oil

1 garlic clove, crushed

1 quart/1 liter vegetable stock

1 cup/115g polenta or yellow cornmeal

8 scallions (spring onions), thinly sliced

4oz/115g spinach, thinly sliced

sea salt and ground black pepper

2 x 4½oz/125g balls buffalo mozzarella cheese, sliced

ROASTED VEGETABLES:

1½lb/675g butternut squash, peeled, halved, and seeds removed

1 red Cubanelle pepper or bell pepper, halved and seeded

1 yellow Cubanelle pepper or bell pepper, halved and seeded

2 red onions, cut into wedges

1 whole head of garlic, cloves separated but skins left on

4 baby fennel bulbs, quartered, or 2 medium fennel bulbs, thickly sliced

a handful of fresh thyme sprigs

a handful of fresh oregano sprigs

2 fresh rosemary sprigs

¼ cup/60ml olive oil

8oz/225g cherry tomatoes

15 asparagus spears, trimmed

¼ cup/60ml balsamic vinegar

sea salt and ground black pepper

fresh herb sprigs, to garnish

Food as Medicine

• **Spinach** is a superfood for the skin. All foods rich in vitamin A and natural carotenes will nourish your skin from the inside out. These foods, which naturally convert to vitamin A in the body, also help to protect your mucous membranes (such as the soft tissues in your throat and lungs); and they encourage melanin production, which can reduce the chances for developing certain cancers. Superfoods for your skin include, tomatoes, pomegranates, carrots, sweet potatoes, cantaloupe melon, and leafy greens.

1 To make the polenta, put the butter, oil, and garlic into a medium pan. Cook lightly, then add the stock and bring to a boil. Pour in the polenta, beating constantly, then add the scallions and spinach. Add salt and pepper to taste, then continue stirring. Cook according to the pack instructions—the time will vary depending on the type of polenta used. Spoon into a 14 x 9in/35 x 23cm baking pan and set side for 2 hours or until firm to the touch. Preheat the oven to 400°F/200°C/Gas 6.

2 To cook the vegetables, put all the vegetables, except the tomatoes and asparagus, into a roasting pan. Sprinkle with the herb sprigs, olive oil, salt and pepper, and mix well. Roast for 30 minutes, then stir in the tomatoes and asparagus. Continue cooking for a further 20 minutes or until all the vegetables are tender.

3 Invert the polenta onto a work surface and cut out eight rounds using a 3in/7.5cm cookie cutter. Brush the baking pan with olive oil and put the rounds on the pan. Top each round with a slice of mozzarella, and bake for 10–15 minutes until the mozzarella is melted and lightly golden.

4 Put two rounds of polenta onto each plate, add the roasted vegetables, then sprinkle with 1 tbsp balsamic vinegar. Serve immediately garnished with herb sprigs.

health TIPS

- **If your liver and bowel** are overworked, thanks to a diet of processed, refined, fatty foods, fizzy drinks, and alcohol, toxins will be "dumped" into the skin for elimination, triggering symptoms such as spots, acne, rashes, and boils. To encourage clearer skin, eat more fresh fruits and vegetables.

Grapes, artichokes, black cherries, broccoli, onions, asparagus, beets (beetroot), pears, and celeriac are great liver foods. Flax seeds, eaten daily, plus ready-to-eat dried plums (prunes) and fresh figs (when in season), will help to keep you regular, and this, in turn, aids clearer skin.

griddled chicken and roasted bell pepper salad

serves 4

1 red and 1 yellow bell pepper

5oz/150g sugar snap peas, halved diagonally

14oz/400g can Great Northern (cannellini) beans, rinsed and drained

3 plum tomatoes, cut into wedges

2 boneless, skinless chicken breasts

½ tsp olive oil

DRESSING:

½ tsp ground cumin

a pinch of smoked paprika

1 tbsp lemon juice

2 tbsp extra-virgin olive oil

sea salt and ground black pepper

1 Preheat the oven to 400°F/200°C/Gas 6. Put the peppers directly on the rack in the oven, with a piece of foil on the shelf below to catch any cooking juices. Roast for 20 minutes or until the skins are blackened and blistered, then transfer to a bowl, cover, and let stand until cool enough to handle. Peel off the skins, discard the seeds, and cut the flesh into wide ribbons.

2 Meanwhile, blanch the sugar snap peas in a pan of lightly salted boiling water for 2 minutes, then drain and refresh under cold water. Beat the dressing ingredients together in a large bowl, then stir in the sugar snap peas, beans, tomatoes, and roasted peppers.

3 Cut the chicken breasts in half horizontally to make 4 escalops. Season, then brush with the olive oil. Cook on a preheated griddle pan for 2–3 minutes on each side until cooked through. Serve the chicken on a bed of the salad vegetables.

Food as Medicine

• **Chicken**, and any muscle meat, is a good source of carnosine, which helps to keep your skin looking younger. Carnosine's anti-glycating properties help to prevent sugars and proteins from forming tough, inflexible tissues, which adversely affect their ability to retain water.

sesame chicken and vegetable noodle salad

serves 4

2 boneless, skinless chicken breasts

6oz/175g dried thin egg noodles

2 tbsp vegetable oil

2 handfuls of fresh garlic chives, snipped into 1½ in/4cm lengths

1 leek, thinly sliced

1 small red bell pepper, seeded and thinly sliced

1 cup/50g bean sprouts

1 small bunch of watercress leaves or arugula (rocket)

1 tbsp lightly toasted sesame seeds

SESAME DRESSING:

2 tbsp sesame oil

2 tbsp reduced-salt light soy sauce

1 tbsp balsamic vinegar

1 tsp good-quality honey, such as cold extracted or manuka

1 Preheat the oven to 350°F/180°C/Gas 4. To make the dressing, put the sesame oil, soy sauce, vinegar, and honey into a small bowl and stir for a few seconds until the sugar has dissolved. Set aside until needed.

2 Put the chicken into a small roasting pan with ¼ cup/60ml water, cover firmly with foil and cook in the oven for 30 minutes. Remove from the oven and let cool. When cool enough to handle, shred the chicken and set aside.

3 Cook the noodles in boiling water for 3 minutes, or according to the pack instructions. Rinse them under cold water to cool, and drain well.

4 Heat the vegetable oil in a frying pan over high heat. Add the chives, leek, and red bell pepper and stir-fry for 1 minute or until the vegetables have just softened. Remove the pan from the heat and stir in the bean sprouts and watercress or arugula.

5 To serve, put the chicken, noodles, and vegetables in a large bowl. Add the dressing and sesame seeds, and toss well.

Food as Medicine

- **Sesame seeds** are a good source of zinc—an important nutrient for repairing the skin as well as maintaining the correct balance of external skin bacteria. A deficiency of zinc has been linked to a number of skin conditions, including acne and dermatitis. The condition of your hair will also be poor if you have inadequate zinc. Sunflower, pumpkin, and flax seeds, Brazil nuts, walnuts, hazelnuts, and cashew nuts all contain zinc.

steamed chicken over rice

serves 1

1 boneless, skinless chicken breast

3 scallions (spring onions)

1 garlic clove, crushed

1in/2.5cm fresh root ginger, peeled and grated

2 tbsp oyster sauce

2 tbsp tamari, plus extra to serve

1 red or yellow bell pepper, peeled, seeded, and sliced

a handful of asparagus tips, chopped into 1in/2.5cm lengths

1 cup/200g fragrant Thai or jasmine rice

health TIP

○ **Try the** Summer Rice Salad on page 241 as an alternative to serve warm with this dish. Brown rice is rich in B vitamins, which are vital for healthy skin, hair, nerves, and eyes. Deficiencies in B vitamins can lead to hair loss, or trigger premature graying. Foods to enjoy are lentils, peas, hazelnuts, cashew nuts, mung beans, spelt, buckwheat, and quinoa.

1 Cut the chicken into ½in/1cm slices lengthways. Put into a small bowl just large enough to fit into a pan, leaving about 1in/2.5cm all around.

2 Chop the scallions into ½in/1cm pieces and add to the chicken. Add the garlic and grated ginger, the oyster sauce, tamari, bell pepper, and asparagus, and turn to coat with the mixture. Set aside for 30 minutes to develop the flavors, if time allows.

3 Put the rice into the pan and add enough water to come one-and-a-half finger joints above the rice. Push the rice aside, leaving a bare circle in the middle. Put the bowl of chicken into the pan, with the base in the hole. Put the lid on the pan, bring to a boil, reduce the heat, and simmer for 12 minutes. Turn off the heat and set aside for 10 minutes without lifting the lid. By this time, the rice should be fluffy and dry, and the chicken tender. Serve with extra tamari.

Food as Medicine

• **Asparagus** is a good source of silicon (silica), which is essential for the health of skin, hair, nails, and teeth. Collagen and elastin are predominantly made up of silica, and without adequate amounts your skin's ability to hold water will be diminished, meaning a loss of integrity, and more wrinkles.

warm potato and tuna salad

health TIP

○ **Essential fats** are crucial for keeping skin looking younger for longer. Your skin will burn less and tan better, and it will appear smoother and more hydrated. Eat oily fish, such as salmon, sardines, and mackerel, for omega-3 essential fats. Hemp and flax seeds also contain omega-3s. Pumpkin, sesame, and sunflower seeds, walnuts, almonds, and their unrefined oils contain omega-6s, and olive oil is rich in healthy omega-9 essential fats.

Food as Medicine

• **Tuna** is a good source of protein as well as essential fatty acids and selenium, making it an excellent food for hair and skin. Hair follicles consist predominantly of protein, and some cases of hair loss can be caused by inadequate intakes of protein. Because of tuna's place at the top of the food chain, however, it is vulnerable to mercury pollution. Tuna's high selenium content offers some protection against mercury, but if you eat a lot of tuna, it would be wise to take extra selenium.

serves 4

4 fresh tuna steaks, about 6oz/175g each

3 tbsp olive oil

juice of ½ lemon

1½ lbs/675g new potatoes, scrubbed, halved lengthways if large

8oz/225g green beans, halved

2 handfuls of pea shoots

10 cherry tomatoes

1 small red onion, finely chopped

3 tbsp pesto

4 boiled eggs (cooked for 5 minutes), chopped

small bunch flat-leaf parsley, leaves chopped

sea salt and ground black pepper

fresh basil leaves, to garnish

lemon wedges, to serve

1 Put the tuna into a shallow dish and drizzle over 1 tbsp olive oil and the lemon juice. Season with a little salt and pepper.

2 Cook the potatoes in boiling salted water for 15 minutes or until just tender.

3 Just before the potatoes are ready, add the beans and continue to cook for a further 3–5 minutes until tender but still bright green.

4 Drain the potatoes and beans, and tip into a salad bowl. Stir in the pea shoots. Season with salt and pepper, then scatter the tomatoes and chopped onion on the top.

5 Mix the pesto with the remaining oil, and drizzle over the warm salad. Gently toss everything together.

6 Meanwhile, heat a griddle pan until very hot. Cook the tuna over a medium-high heat for 2–3 minutes on each side—don't overcook or it will be dry.

7 Divide the salad among four plates and put the tuna and chopped eggs on top. Sprinkle with a little chopped parsley and garnish with a few basil leaves. Serve with the lemon wedges.

health TIPS

○ **One of your** greatest enemies is refined sugar. Glucose, the simplest form of sugar, binds to proteins in a process called glycosylation, which then triggers "cross-linking," causing collagen proteins in your skin to appear as wrinkles. Cross-linking also occurs in your arteries, tendons, and lungs. Refined white sugar has a glycemic index (GI) of 59, and commercial honey (also a sugar) around 85, whereas xylitol, a plant sugar, rates at just 8, and 2 tbsp of organic agave syrup would rate at about 10. So these last two are much better choices for sweetening.

summer orange jellies

serves 4

2½ cups/600ml orange juice (freshly squeezed or organic juice from a carton)

5 sheets leaf gelatin or 1oz/25g powdered gelatin

1 tbsp xylitol

4 strawberries, quartered if large

8 raspberries

8 seedless grapes, halved

fresh mint leaves and extra fruit, to decorate

1 Pour ¼ cup/60ml orange juice into a small pan. Warm over a low heat for 5 minutes, then add the gelatin. Stir until completely dissolved—do not allow to boil. Remove from the heat.

2 Let cool for 5 minutes, then stir in the xylitol and the remaining orange juice.

3 Arrange the fruit equally among 4 x ¾ cup/185ml molds or glass dishes, then pour in the liquid jelly, pushing the fruit down into the liquid.

4 Cover with plastic wrap (clingfilm) and put in the refrigerator to set for about 3 hours.

5 Turn the jellies out of the molds onto serving plates and decorate with a sprig of mint and some fruit.

Food as Medicine

• **Flavored gelatin** (jelly) made with fresh fruit and orange juice is a great food for the skin. Gelatin, which is derived from collagen, has a long history as a food for the skin, hair, and nails, and studies have also shown its effectiveness in relieving joint pain. The vitamin C, and other antioxidants, in the fresh fruit add further benefits to the dessert. Carrageen (Irish moss) could be substituted for gelatin to provide a wider nutrient profile.

glossary

Acid and alkaline The environment in the body is mostly alkaline. The food we eat, once metabolized, breaks down into an alkaline or acid mineral-based "ash" or residue. Ill health and the effects of aging are more evident if the pH of the body's tissues tips into a more acid state, called body acidification.

Allergy An inflammation caused by the interaction of a foreign substance with the body's defense system. The body over-reacts to the substance and produces too many histamine-like chemicals, causing a violent reaction.

Amino acids The building blocks of proteins essential for most bodily functions. They include glutamine, glycine, phenylalanine, tryptophan, and methionine, which perform different critical functions in the body.

Anthocyanins A group of foods—including berries and pomegranates—that have a high antioxidant status.

Anti-inflammatory Foods that can help to reverse inflammation.

Antioxidants Foods that contain vitamins A, C, and E, as well as minerals such as zinc and selenium, can help the body to fight the effects of oxidation.

B-group vitamins The B vitamins have many functions in the body but are especially important in lowering the toxin homocysteine.

Cold extracted honey Also known as raw honey, this is honey that is straight from the hive and hasn't been heated or filtered. It's a very alkaline food, full of vitamins and minerals. UMF manuka is a good substitute.

Cultured foods Yogurt and fermented foods, such as kefir and sauerkraut, that encourage friendly intestinal bacteria to populate.

Curcumin The yellow pigment found in turmeric that has been found to be effective against breast and colon cancer, Alzheimer's disease, and other diseases caused by inflammation.

ELISA (enzyme-linked immunosolvent assay) A blood allergy test that is an accurate way of identifying an allergen and the strength of the reaction.

Essential fats (EFAs) Fats that the body cannot produce itself and so needs to obtain from foods. There are two main types, omega-3 and omega-6, which need to be in balance, but the modern Western diet usually has an excess of omega-6s, which can trigger conditions such as depression.

Fermented foods Traditional methods of preserving foods through fermentation—sauerkraut is an example—are good for the digestion because they encourage friendly intestinal bacteria to populate. They include kefir, tempeh, tamari, natto, miso, tofuyo (fermented tofu), and umeboshi plums.

Fiber A healthy diet includes fiber and there are two types. Soluble fiber (which absorbs water) is fiber from bran derived from rice, soya, or oats. Insoluble fiber (which does not absorb water) is from the skins of fruits and vegetables. Both are essential for a healthy digestive system as well as helping to control cholesterol.

Food diary A notebook where you write down exactly what you eat and the time you ate it to try to establish if you are intolerant to any foods.

Glycemic index (GI) A measure of the effect that foods have on your blood-sugar levels. Carbohydrate foods that release their sugar content in the body more slowly have a low GI. Carbohydrate foods with a low GI (such as oats) are healthier than those whose GI is high (such as cakes and biscuits).

Glycosylation Damage to proteins in the body caused by too high levels of sugar. The immune system may react if there are high levels of damaged proteins.

Homocysteine A toxic compound produced in the body. High levels can damage blood vessels throughout the body especially in the arteries, heart, brain, and kidneys. B vitamins are required to lower homocysteine levels.

IBS (irritable bowel syndrome) A condition that can include frequent and unexplained abdominal pain, diarrhea, or constipation.

Inflammation Pain and swelling in different parts of the body that can cause major health problems. Inflammation is inked to degenerative conditions of the brain, heart, and arteries. Caused by weight gain and blood sugar problems.

Intolerance The body's inability to properly process or assimilate a particular food, which can trigger symptoms such as diarrhea and bloating.

Leaky gut syndrome When the walls of the intestines become inflamed because food has not been digested properly. Holes appear, allowing undigested food to enter the bloodstream.

Medium-chain fatty acids (or medium-chain triglycerides) These fats are easily digested and absorbed by the body because the molecules are smaller, so they require less energy and fewer enzymes to break them down. Organic, unrefined coconut oil/butter is an example.

Neurotransmitters Chemicals that are released at the junctions between brain cells to allow communication between the cells.

ORAC (oxygen radical absorbance capacity) A score that is given to foodstuffs as a measure of their antioxidant capacity. The higher the score the better they are for combating oxidation.

Oxidation The damaging effects to cells by free radicals either through aging or through eating burnt foods or foods that are acid-forming, or though being exposed to pollution and stress. When we eat fresh fruit and vegetables the antioxidants contained therein help to "mop up" the free radicals.

Probiotics and prebiotics Probiotics are the good bacteria that live in the guts and can also be taken in live yogurt or supplements. Probiotics feed on particular types of food, called prebiotics, such as whole grains, fruits, vegetables, and fermented foods.

Salt Natural sodium found in celery, for example, is good for the body, but common inorganic sodium, or salt, is not. Sodium (in the form of salt) from processed foods is eaten to excess in Western diets and encourages the loss of calcium via the kidneys. Levels below 2g daily are recommended.

Soil degradation Modern commercial farming practices use chemicals as pesticides and fertilizers, but this weakens the soil composition, removing minerals. Food grown or produced from such soil will generally be low in minerals such as selenium and magnesium.

Xylitol A plant extract that looks and tastes like sugar but is low in calories and has a very low glycemic index (GI). This means that it releases glucose more slowly.

index

credits

Recipes

Vatcharin Bhumichitr
Chicken rice soup
Chicken salad with mint and
    toasted sesame seeds
Fish and spicy sauce
Papaya salad with squid
Shrimp with chili and basil
Sweet and sour fish
Thai fruit salad

Maxine Clark
Falafel with avocado, tomato,
    and red onion salsa
Overnight oatmeal
Sesame and mint couscous
    with vegetables
Spaghetti with lemon and
    green olives

Lyndel Costain and Nicola Graimes
Almond and banana shake
Baked trout with ginger and
    orange dressing
Beef and broccolini stir-fry
Blueberry and apple bircher
    muesli
Chicken and papaya noodle
    box
Citrus and melon fruit salad
    with mint
Griddled vegetable salad with
    parmesan
Herbed crab wrap
Honey glazed salmon with
    asparagus
Mackerel with citrus salsa
Peaches with pistachios and
    dates
Porridge with cinnamon plums
Seared duck and
    pomegranate salad
Sesame-ginger fish
Soba with chicken and
    vegetables
Strawberry and banana
    smoothie
Summer gazpacho with crisp
    croutons
Tagliatelle with half-dried
    tomatoes and toasted pine
    nuts
Thai salmon fishcakes with
    dipping sauce
Turkey and bay skewers with
    potato, olive, and tomato
    salad
Yogurt and summer fruit
    swirl

Ross Dobson
Asparagus and goat's cheese
    tart
Carrot and lentil soup
Figs with pecan nuts and blue
    cheese
Fish with walnut pesto and
    balsamic tomatoes
Mozzarella, peach, and
    chicory salad
Sesame chicken and
    vegetable noodle salad
Spicy red vegetable soup
Tabbouleh with chickpeas
    and spring salad

Rachael Anne Hill
Asian salmon with rice
    noodles
Baked garlic and tomato
    mushrooms
Full of beans soup
Kick-start kabobs
Pan-fried salmon with white
    bean purée
Salmon, spinach, and tomato
    stack
Shrimp and bean rice
Shrimp and mango salad
Summer pudding
Tuscan salad

**Rachael Anne Hill and
Tamsin Burnett-Hall**
Chermoula chicken with
    tomato pilaff
Chickpea, lemon, and mint
    soup
Figs with goat's cheese, pecan
    nuts, and honey-balsamic
    dressing
Flash-fried garlic and shrimp
Goa shrimp curry
Griddled chicken and roasted
    bell pepper salad
Hot-and-sour chicken noodle
    bowl
Italian bean and vegetable
    soup
Moroccan seven-vegetable
    tagine with quinoa
Mustardy mushroom
    stroganoff
Ribbon vegetable and
    hummus wraps
Spiced berry compote
Spiced pear, apricot, and fig
    compote
Spiced salmon and chickpea
    dhal
Tarragon chicken with beans
Tonno e fagioli

Jane Noraika
Buckwheat noodles in miso
    ginger broth
Roasted butternut squash
    risotto
Roasted sweet potatoes with
    beet and carrot salad
Spinach and mozzarella
    polenta with roasted
    vegetables
Tofu and shiitake mushrooms
    on crispy black rice patties

Elsa Petersen–Schepelern
Almond milk
Apricot, berry, and orange
    juice
Beet and orange juice
Beet soup with lemon zest
Big greek salad
Carrot and ginger soup with
    lime and clementines
Celery and grape juice
Char-grilled scallop salad
Chicken noodle soup
Fennel and mint salad
Fresh virgin mary
Green vegetable salad with
    hazelnut dressing
Herbed tomato and
    artichoke couscous
Indian yellow lentil soup with
    spicy mustard seeds
Insalata gonzaga
Italian lentil salad
Japanese steamed fish
Papaya and banana smoothie
Paprika chicken wraps
Pineapple crush
Pomegranate squeeze
Pumpkin soup
Quick chickpea salad
Red salad with beets, red
    cabbage, and harissa
    dressing
Roasted red bell pepper soup
Steamed chicken over rice
Thai eggplant salad with
    seafood
Thai marinated chicken
    stir-fried in chili oil
Waldorf salad
Watermelon and lime slush
Yellow gazpacho

**All other recipes by
Hazel Courteney and
Nicola Graimes.**

Photography

Key: a=above, b=below,
    r=right, l=left, c=center

Caroline Arber
Page 14

Jean Cazals
Page 3

Peter Cassidy
Pages 16–17 top; 18 top,a; 19;
    20c; 21c; 25; 44l,r; 53; 54; 64;
    80l; 87; 90; 116c; 122; 131;
    138c; 148; 158c; 166; 195;
    222c; 224l; 226; 248; 268c;
    272; 282l; 293

Nicky Dowey
Pages 39; 158r; 174; 178l; 183;
    191; 233; 247; 257; 285; 291

Tara Fisher
Page 16b

Jeremy Hopley
Pages 66c; 69; 104; 108; 222l;
    268l; 274

Richard Jung
Pages 11a; 12bl; 80r; 95; 282c;
    297; 326r; 336

Lisa Linder
Pages 10cl; 11bl

William Lingwood
Pages 170; 307r; 333; 338

David Merewether
Pages 4–7; 10–11 top; 12 top;
    15 top

David Montgomery
Page 17b

Noel Murphy
Pages 254; 271; 308c; 317

William Reavell
Pages 8; 13; 17a; 20c; 211,r; 34;
    66l; 70; 79; 96; 98r; 101; 110;
    116l; 120; 128; 133; 147;
    158l; 160; 163; 185; 202l,r;
    207; 217; 218; 222r; 223l,c,r;
    224r; 228; 234; 237; 244l,r;
    251; 261; 264; 294; 298;
    306l; 307l,r; 308l,r; 311; 325;
    334

Tim Ruddock
Pages 341, 342

**All other photography by
Stuart West.**